AMERICAN
INTELLECTUAL
HISTORIES AND
HISTORIANS

AMERICAN
INTELLECTUAL
HISTORIES AND
HISTORIANS

ROBERT ALLEN SKOTHEIM

PRINCETON, NEW JERSEY

PRINCETON UNIVERSITY PRESS

1966

150602

TO NADINE

WHAT follows is not intended to be a definitive investigation of all the problems and achievements of Americans who have dealt with their country's intellectual past. Such a definitive work would treat all those American historical works which have been concerned with thought; it would discuss them with respect to the methods and uses of evidence by a developing craft of writing specialized histories of ideas, and it would assess their strengths and weaknesses from a standpoint of present day knowledge; finally, it would relate the histories to the "climates of opinion" in which they were written, viewing the histories themselves as documents of the history of ideas. A book done in this complete fashion might need no prefatory statement of limitations.

This slender volume, however, does not do the things indicated above definitively, but only selectively. I have attempted to sketch the nature of American historians' interest in ideas in America, insofar as this interest has been expressed in their published writings. Most attention is directed to scholars of this century, and in particular, to academic historians, since it is they who have most often written intellectual histories or, what I generally refer to for the sake of clarity as histories of ideas. The writings of the last 100 years which have been selected for treatment are viewed partly from the perspective of an emerging specialty—the writing of histories of ideas. Certain recurrent problems of method and characteristic themes of interpretation are selected for discussion, but no attempt is made to assess the accuracy or inaccuracy of the histories. There is no intention to construct the "Compleat Guide to Writing Histories of Ideas." Such a purpose is beyond the book's scope and exceeds the author's knowledge.

There is, however, analysis of certain problems in the writing of histories of ideas as a separate specialty, and there is considerable treatment of the ideological positions, or the social thought, of the various historians of ideas discussed. Carl Becker's conception of written histories as themselves documents in the history of ideas, because of their expression of the climates of opinion in which they were composed, is to this extent accepted.

Because a good deal is said in the book concerning the climates of opinion in which modern histories have been written, it may be worthwhile suggesting the perspective from which this study was made. I am a young (born in 1933) member of a university history department, holding attitudes toward ideological questions and problems of historical method which are not greatly different from those of most of the younger and middle-aged academic historians discussed in the concluding chapter. This means that the ideological and methodological disputes of the first half of the twentieth century were those of my elders rather than of my own generation. I therefore take it for granted, as do most members of younger generations, that it is more important to make a viable synthesis of formerly opposing intellectual views than to perpetuate the differences intact. The most basic problem of method for historians of ideas today seems to me, as it seems to most historians who came of age after the pioneering classics from Beard to Curti, to be that of taking ideas seriously and describing them precisely without losing sight of their environmental relationships. The most elementary ideological or public policy problem, and again I think

I am quite typical in saying this, appears to be the articulation of ethical standards in a world increasingly governed by cold war considerations. Like most younger and middle-aged professional historians in the United States, my conception of the public good is derived in large part from American reform traditions, and to that extent I am a child of progressivism. But, like most who matured in the era of totalitarianism, my progressivism has been modified by reactions to totalitarianism which have ramifications for our views of human nature and of social progress through planning. All this, of course, is only to indicate that, like any other historian young or old, I have a relationship to the subject investigated in the book.

Throughout, the perspective is that of a member of the history guild, even if a young one, rather than the perspective of, say, a philosopher or sociologist. For better or worse, therefore, the book perpetuates many of the characteristics of the writings which are discussed. A philosopher, for instance, might insist upon greater analysis of definitions and ideas, and a sociologist might show more impatience with the failure of historians to quantify and to provide evidence for statements concerning the holding of opinions. This book about historians, then, is written by an insider rather than by an outsider. Nevertheless, I do conclude, as can be seen in the book's final paragraphs, by questioning whether the characteristic approach of American historians of ideas might not result in their disappearance and their replacement by topic specialists. These specialists will write about ideas as one part of their field, be it the ante-bellum South, patterns of urbanization, or political reform movements. In other words, American historians today seem to attach more importance to ideas in history than to histories of ideas. But, despite some present questioning of the history of ideas as a separate scholarly entity, there was in the past and there remains today the belief that histories of ideas can justifiably be written. That belief is the subject of this book.

I gratefully acknowledge the intellectual guidance and personal encouragement of several teachers, colleagues, and friends, including especially: W. Stull Holt, who suggested and supervised the study in its original form as a doctoral dissertation; Thomas J. Pressly, whose *Americans Interpret Their Civil War* was a model for my study; John Higham, who graciously extended help to a novice in a field Higham knew so well; Lee Benson, who stimulated my historiographical interest through conversations; and Kermit Vanderbilt, who generously contributed to my analysis of Vernon Louis Parrington. I also wish to thank Alfred H. Kelly, chairman of the History Department, Wayne State University, for providing me sufficient freedom from teaching duties to facilitate completion of the manuscript. Finally, I would like to thank Eve Hanle and Marjorie Putney of the Princeton University Press.

The first section of Chapter Three appeared in a somewhat different form as "Vernon Louis Parrington: The Mind and Art of a Historian of Ideas," in the *Pacific Northwest Quarterly*, LIII (July 1962), 100-113. I thank the editor of that journal for permission to incorporate the article.

Detroit, Michigan
June 1965

R.A.S.

Contents

Contents

AMERICAN
INTELLECTUAL
HISTORIES AND
HISTORIANS

TREATMENT OF IDEAS IN
THE EARLY WRITINGS

THERE is probably no aspect of historical writing which concerns such vague and elusive subject matter as histories of men's thoughts. "Writing intellectual history," the political historian William Hesseltine once grumbled, "is like trying to nail jelly to the wall." There is more than a little truth to the charge. For how exactly is the historian to approach the gelatinous part of man's past which we call his ideas? There is no agreement in historians' answers to the difficult question. Intellectual histories, or what this study will often call histories of ideas, have investigated all kinds of intellectual activities, from formal philosophies to works of art, to short-lived opinions on transitory public issues. Some ideas described by historians therefore are the rarefied creations of isolated genius, working apart from the surrounding society. But other ideas, devoid of intellectual abstraction, are so obviously part of the everyday pressures of life that they almost merge into general behavior. Is the historian then to be a chronicler of the abstract thought of great men? Or is he to be a George Gallup of past opinion on public issues?

As this already suggests, it is not only a question of the historian's source material, but also of his methods of analysis. Does he study his chosen ideas intensively as if they had intrinsic importance and interest? If so, the historian might analyze the internal structure, the tensions, the intellectual progenitors, and the legacies of the thought. Or does the significance of the ideas stem only from their relation to other and less cerebral aspects of man's behavior? In this case, perhaps the historian will be most interested in the extent to which ideas "mirror" society.

To mention different relationships between ideas and the societies in which they exist is to suggest the most serious question facing the intellectual historian. Do ideas play a causal role in human affairs? Are they mere reflections of a more "real" economic, political, and social world? Or does thought itself create that world? Our common sense may say that in this case, as in the others, truth lies somewhere in between the extremes—but where? And is the blend of environmental influence and the independent power of thought always the same, or does that blend vary? As the questions mount, one hears in the background Hesseltine's reply that the jelly will not survive our attempts to nail it to the wall.

Despite the criticisms expressed, or, more frequently left unsaid, by American historians who are not altogether convinced of the worth of histories of ideas, students of thought have made their specialty an increasingly popular one. The popularity is not to be found in essays giving theoretical answers to the problems and criticisms raised by the new specialty. Such essays until recently hardly existed. This increasing popularity is evidenced by the countless books, articles, and university courses which in general ignore the theoretical problems and proceed to recount the history of ideas in the United States.[1] To write and teach history, rather than to discourse upon the difficulties of doing so, has been the

[1] For evidence pertaining to the increased popularity of the history of ideas, see Appendix A.

American historian's motto. Americans have not been
completely oblivious to the problems of studying ideas in
their country's past, but neither in this area nor in other
areas of their historical writings have they expressed
particular interest in what they have regarded as "theoretical" or "analytical" matters.

From the time of the earliest American chronicles, an
active desire to tell what happened has prevailed over a
more philosophical perusal of the theoretical problems of
historical analysis. The traditional conception of the
meaning of history has not been significantly different
from the common sense of the community at large, or at
least that part of the community which writers have
represented. This has been true from the beginning. The
voice of everyday judgment never spoke more loudly
than in Puritan New England chronicles. Writers of
these seventeenth century accounts were usually leading
citizens of their colonies, acting as record keepers and
defenders of the faith. They reflected the concerns of
their colonies and dealt primarily with the hazards of
hunger, Indians, religious heresy, and political disor-
ganization.

The conception of the role of ideas in human affairs
which was expressed in Puritan histories mirrored what
the colonists took to be the common sense of the matter.
New England was developed in accordance with right-
eous ideas, and in opposition to ideas born in evil. God
directed the entire drama between the holy and the un-
holy, to be sure, but nonetheless the players were attempting to adhere to good and to shun evil. It was in
this sense that New Englanders, as Richard Dunn has
said, saw their history "as an idea in action."[2] Thus,
regardless of the fact that Puritan writers were more

[2] "Seventeenth Century Historians of America," in James Morton Smith, ed., *Seventeenth Century America: Essays in Colonial
History*, Chapel Hill, 1959, p. 196.

like local annalists than later specialists in the history of thought, it should be noted that these seventeenth century writers paid special attention to certain ideas.

To these religious ideas which they singled out, the chroniclers attributed great causal power. The beliefs comprising Puritanism were assumed to affect human behavior decisively. Original emigration from Europe to New England, for example, was interpreted by seventeenth century chroniclers at Plymouth and Massachusetts Bay as a direct result of conflicts over religious views. The Pilgrims, who went eventually to Plymouth colony, left England, William Bradford (1590-1657) wrote, because of a "bitter warr of contention and persecution about the ceremonies, and servise-book, and other popish and antichristian stuffe."[3] Future Massachusetts Bay colony Puritans too, according to Edward Johnson (1598-1672), were opposed to the doctrines of the "irreligious, lascivious and popish affected persons" in England who participated "in vaine Idolatrous Ceremonies," and who thought heaven could be reached by good works alone.[4] The assumption in these two statements explaining why emigration occurred is that certain religious beliefs in the minds of men caused historical events to occur. The same assumption is reflected in histories written later in the 1600's. William Hubbard (1621-1703), giving the reasons for emigration to Massachusetts Bay, asserted that "the chiefest intentions and aims of those that managed the business were to promote religion, and if it might be, to propagate the Gospel, in this dark corner of the world."[5] At the end

[3] William T. Davis, ed., *Bradford's History of Plymouth Plantation 1606-1646*, New York, 1952, p. 25.

[4] J. Franklin Jameson, ed., *Edward Johnson's Wonder-working Providence of Sions Saviour in New England, 1628-1651*, New York, 1959, p. 23.

[5] William Hubbard, *A General History of New England from the Discovery to MDCLXXX*, Massachusetts Historical Society

of the century, Cotton Mather (1663-1728) repeated the declaration that "the sole end" of settling the Plymouth and Bay colonies was to "plant the gospel in these dark regions of America."[6] The attitude which these quotations express is a familiar one, as most later historians have followed the chroniclers in emphasizing the influence of religious opinions in early New England settlement. What needs to be stressed is that the familiar attitude implies a crucial temporal role for at least some ideas in history, irrespective of the role of ultimate responsibility accorded God.

Original emigration from the Old World to the New was not the only result of beliefs associated with Puritanism, according to seventeenth century chronicles of New England. The development of the colonial communities after initial settlement also was interpreted as being largely dependent upon religious ideas. The reason that heresy in the Bay colony had to be located and expelled, the chroniclers said, was that bad religious beliefs would lead to a colony which behaved badly. It was assumed that actions followed thoughts. Therefore, John Winthrop (1588-1649) characterized Anne Hutchinson's religious opinions as dangerous not merely because they were theologically unorthodox, but because he took for granted that unorthodox theology threatened the social order of the Bay colony in the early 1600's. As Winthrop told it, Anne Hutchinson unleashed an anarchy of emotional individualism by holding that "the person of the Holy Ghost dwells in a justified person," and she encouraged social upheaval against the ruling saints by holding that "no sanctifica-

---

Collections, Second Series, Vols. 5, 6, Boston, 1848, Vol. 5, pp. 115-116.

[6] Cotton Mather, *Magnalia Christi Americana*, 2 vols., Hartford, 1855, Vol. 1, p. 45.

tion can help to evidence to us our justification."⁷ Winthrop detected a threat to the community's stability in her minimization of the importance of worldly status, hierarchy, and government. Because he assumed that ideas had consequences, he was convinced that heresy had to be uprooted.

The same assumption appeared in the other chroniclers' accounts of Hutchinsonian doctrines. Edward Johnson declared that they threatened the social order by denigrating good works so far as to deny "the Morral Law to be the Rule of Christ."⁸ William Hubbard echoed Johnson and Winthrop, asserting that the assault on earthly status and works challenged communal authority and stability:

> These erroneous notions [Hubbard wrote of Anne Hutchinson's ideas] inspired many of the place also with a strange kind of seditious and turbulent spirit, and that upon every occasion they were ready to challenge all, that did not run with them, to be legal Christians, and under a covenant of works. Under the veil of this pretence men of corrupt minds and haughty spirits secretly sowed seeds of division and schism in the country, and were ready to mutiny against the civil authority.⁹

Cotton Mather too assumed that heretical ideas such as those propagated by Anne Hutchinson seriously threatened the texture of the Bay colony. Hutchinsonians argued, according to Mather, that the most important evidence of an individual's justification was " 'the spirit of God by a powerful application of a promise,' begetting in us, and revealing to us a powerful *assurance* of

⁷ James Kendall Hosmer, ed., *Winthrop's Journal 1630-1649*, 2 vols., New York, 1908, Vol. 1, p. 195.
⁸ *Edward Johnson's Wonder-working Providence*, p. 31.
⁹ Hubbard, *General History of New England*, pp. 281-282.

our being *justified.*"[10] Mather agreed with the Orthodox that this heresy opened the door "for new *enthu-
siastical revelations*," for the "neglect" of worldly vir-
tues, and for "subversion to all the peaceable order in
the colonies."[11]

Musty theological quarrels such as this may seem
to the modern reader to offer the choice of Tweedle-
dum and Tweedledee, but the importance of the disputes
to seventeenth century writers reflected the chroniclers'
assumption that certain ideas made history. It is this
assumption which makes their writings relevant to the
later appearance of intellectual histories in the United
States. Mather, like Hubbard, Johnson, and Winthrop,
viewed religious beliefs as crucial factors in determining the development of colonial society after original
settlement, just as all seventeenth century chroniclers
interpreted emigration from England as a direct result
of religious ideas. And though Providence was held ultimately responsible even for the ideas men held, the
ideas themselves were crucial determinants on earth.
Ordinarily God did not appear in the pages of the chronicles as an immediate, temporal causal force. Instead,
as a rule, men acted independently upon their beliefs.

The attention paid Puritanism in seventeenth century
writings was repeated in the following century's histories. Puritan ideas continued to be held responsible
for original European emigration to New England, and
for the early development of society there. But a new
idea, or group of ideas, which appeared in the colonies
during and after the 1600's began to receive joint emphasis along with Puritanism in eighteenth century historical writings—religious toleration. The growing belief
in toleration was added to Puritanism as another idea
which influenced American history. The eighteenth cen-

[10] Mather, *Magnalia*, Vol. 1, p. 508.
[11] *Ibid.*, pp. 508-509.

tury writers who first described the development of tolerance did not deny the earlier causal significance of Puritan doctrines, but rather moved chronologically from the original importance of Puritanism to the later rise of toleration.

Religious toleration provided the foundation for Rhode Island, according to John Callender (1706-1748), just as religious Puritanism was the basis for first New England settlement. "Liberty of conscience was the basis of this Colony," wrote Callender of Rhode Island: "Our fathers thought it just and necessary to allow each other mutually to worship God as their consciences were respectively persuaded. They thought no man had power over the spirit of God, and that the duty of the magistrate was to leave every one to follow the light of his conscience."[12] Rhode Island's dedication to the principle of toleration was also emphasized by Isaac Backus (1724-1806), in his account of New England and the Baptists, whose growth he equated with the success of tolerance.[13] These eighteenth century allegations of the influence of belief in toleration extended to a new idea the same assumption customarily made earlier concerning belief in Puritanism. Certain ideas made history. Writers during the 1700's, however, went no further than did their predecessors in making general statements concerning the influence of thought. They did not indicate, for example, whether they thought that the power of religious ideas in the 1600's was indicative of the pervasive significance of human

[12] John Callender, *An Historical Discourse on the Civil and Religious Affairs of the Colony of Rhode-Island*, Collections of the Rhode Island Historical Society, Vol. 4, Providence, 1838, p. 159.

[13] Isaac Backus, *A History of New England with Particular References to the . . . Baptists*, Backus Historical Society, 2 vols., Newton, Mass., 1871, originally published in three volumes in 1777, 1784, 1796.

opinions in history. Nor did they indicate whether special circumstances were responsible for the successes
of Puritanism and toleration, circumstances which controlled the power of the ideas. Nor, again, did the
eighteenth century writers any more than the seventeenth
century writers, analyze in detail the components of
the ideas to which they ascribed such strength. American colonists simply made the common-sense assumption that certain ideas had had important consequences
in the history of the colonies.

The two triumphs of human thought—New England's Zion in the Wilderness and the rise of toleration
—were brought together by Benjamin Trumbull (1735-
1820) in his history of New England which featured
Connecticut. "The settlement of New-England, purely
for the purposes of Religion, and the propagation of
civil and religious liberty," he wrote, "is an event which
has no parallel in the history of modern ages." He continued: "The happy and extensive consequences of the
settlements which they made, and of the sentiments
which they were careful to propagate, to their poster-
ity, to the church and to the world, admit of no description." Enthusiastically, he concluded that "they are still
increasing, spreading wider and wider, and appear more
and more important."[14]

Few chronicles were written outside of New England during the seventeenth century. During the eighteenth century, however, other authors on occasion contributed to the celebration of the power of ideas. Robert
Proud (1728-1813), writing of Pennsylvania and the
Quakers, told of the "oppression, persecution and big-

[14] Benjamin Trumbull, *A Complete History of Connecticut:
Civil and Ecclesiastical from the Emigration of its First Plant-
ers, from England in the Year 1630, to the Year 1764: and to
the Close of the Indian Wars*, 2 vols., New London, Conn.,
1898, Vol. 1, p. 1. Vol. 1 was originally published in 1797,
Vols. 1 and 2, in 1818.

otry," which the Quaker views provoked in England and in the original colonies. It was for the "restoration and enjoyment of those natural and civil rights and privileges," Proud explained, that "the predecessors of the present inhabitants of *Pennsylvania*, at first, peaceably withdrew into this retirement."[15] Proud, the Quaker, Callender and Backus, the Baptists, and Trumbull, the Congregationalist, were all in agreement that religious ideas caused the settlement of the New World, and that the idea of religious diversity was crucial to the development of the colonies in the late 1600's and 1700's.

As soon as the American Revolution worked its way into historical narratives, the great causal influence attributed to ideas associated with Puritanism and with the rise of freedom of conscience came to be attributed to a third allegedly powerful idea, or group of ideas, namely, those beliefs declared to be responsible for American independence.

Isaac Backus, who had not finished his last volume on New England and the Baptists until the Revolution was over, added the newly powerful idea of American political liberty to the older idea of religious liberty which he had discussed earlier in his narrative. Just as New World immigrants originally sought freedom from English tyranny in the seventeenth century, just as the principles of tolerance rose to combat intolerance in the colonies after settlement, so the idea of independence grew to throw off English secular control.[16]

The merging of the allegations concerning the power of human ideas in the three events—colonial settlement, rise of toleration, and Revolution—was also expressed

[15] Robert Proud, *The History of Pennsylvania in North America*, 2 vols., Philadelphia, 1797, 1798, Vol. 1, pp. 15, 5.
[16] Isaac Backus, *A History of New England with Particular Reference to the . . . Baptists*, Chapters 23-24.

by Jeremy Belknap (1744-1789), in his history of New Hampshire. Belknap, like all previous commentators on the founding of New England, accepted the immigrants' profession that "their principal design was to erect churches on the primitive model."[17] His assumption as to the power of ideas was implicit as he traced the rise of toleration:

> It is melancholy to observe what mischiefs were caused by the want of a just distinction between civil and ecclesiastical powers, and by that absurd zeal for uniformity, which kept the nation in a long ferment, and at length burst out into a blaze, the fury of which was never thoroughly quelled till the happy genius of the revolution gave birth to a free and equitable toleration, whereby every man was restored to the natural right of judging and acting for himself in matters of religion.[18]

To understand the Revolution, Belknap insisted upon the necessity of understanding "the ideas" the colonists had of "their political connexion with the parent state."[19] It was these ideas, which included the belief that "no part of the empire could be taxed, but by its own Representatives in Assembly," which caused the colonists to revolt.[20]

Belknap was a patriot, but loyalist affiliation during the Revolution did not prevent Thomas Hutchinson (1711-1780), when he wrote his history of Massachusetts, from making similar implications concerning the influential role of thought in the conflict with England, as well as in colonial settlement and in the growth of toleration. Massachusetts assumed its original political, legal, and ecclesiastical form because of "one great de-

---

[17] Jeremy Belknap, *History of New Hampshire*, 3 vols., Philadelphia, 1784, 1791, 1792, Vol. 1, p. 61.
[18] *Ibid.*, p. 58.   [19] *Ibid.*, p. 95.
[20] *Ibid.*, Vol. 2, p. 256.

sign" of the founders to have a society "as appeared to them to be most agreeable to the sacred scriptures."[21] Hutchinson also took for granted the power of ideas in his discussion of the Salem witchcraft episode, although he regretted the bigotry which preceded the rise of toleration. "In all ages of the world," he wrote, "superstitious credulity has produced greater cruelty than is practised among the Hottentots, or other nations, whose belief of a deity is called in question."[22] Behind Hutchinson's detailed political narrative of the coming of the Revolution, was the assumption that opposing principles, rival conceptions of empire, were at issue. He asserted that by 1767 "the colonies, in general" had "acquired a new set of ideas of the relation they stood in to the parliament of Great Britain. The constitutional authority of parliament to impose taxes on America was admitted in none." Hutchinson concluded, "From admitting a principle of partial independency, gradual advances were made until a total independency was asserted."[23] Thus a Tory, while differing in his evaluation of the rebellion, joined with patriots in viewing it as originating in a conflict between rival ideas.

Even this brief glance into seventeenth and eighteenth century writing reveals that these histories attributed causal significance to certain ideas. Twentieth century historians of ideas in the United States are to this extent only carrying on an old native tradition when they take ideas seriously. But these early writers of the seventeenth and eighteenth centuries did not analyze at length the ideas which they stressed—nor did they ex-

[21] Lawrence Mayo, ed., Thomas Hutchinson's *The History of the Colony and Province of Massachusetts Bay*, 3 vols., Cambridge, 1936, Vol. 1, p. 352. Vol. 1 was originally published in 1764, Vol. 2 in 1767, Vol. 3 in 1828.

[22] *Ibid.*, Vol. 2, pp. 44-45. Discussion of witchcraft appears on pp. 12-47.

[23] *Ibid.*, Vol. 3, p. 119.

plore the environmental contexts from which the ideas emerged. Further, they left unsaid what conception, if any, they held concerning the role of thought generally in history. Finally, they did not expand their interest in certain ideas into a suggestion that historians might write histories focused exclusively upon ideas.

To sketch these characteristics of the treatments of ideas by colonial historians is not to ridicule the primitive state of their scholarship. On the contrary, the characteristics of colonial histories have been re- markably enduring. There is probably no field of learn- ing in the United States in which there are so many similarities between the colonial and the modern as in written histories. Modern historians can and, compared with their fellow scholars in other disciplines, do read their predecessors with relative understanding and sym- pathy. The traditional goal of a well-told story on a subject important to the community, interpreted with manly good sense, has largely survived the centuries.

An approach to ideas similar to that of the colonial historians was expressed in the works of the nineteenth century scholar whose books are customarily said to mark the coming-of-age of the writing of American history. George Bancroft (1800-1891) was the first American historian who had been exposed to the new seminars in German universities, and his research for his multi- volume *History of the United States* was unprecedented. But his treatment of ideas was almost identical with that of his colonial predecessors. Like them, he attrib- uted great causal significance to Puritanism, to re- ligious toleration, and to Revolutionary thought. And like them too, he did not depict the ideas in detail nor investigate the environments from which they emerged. Further like his predecessors, Bancroft's attribution of grandiose power to human thought was only one part of his history which was largely concerned with other matters. Bancroft's volumes, composed and revised during the half century after 1830, focused almost exclusively upon military and political events, but behind the events and decisively influencing them were ideas.[24]

He synthesized the traditionally emphasized ideas of Puritanism, toleration, and national independence into a progressive development toward democracy. "From Protestantism," according to Bancroft, "there came forth a principle of all-pervading energy," which was "the right of private judgment."[25] European emigration to New England was consequently an attempt to realize freedom of conscience for the colonists. "The enfranchisement of the mind from religious despotism," he wrote,

> led directly to inquiries into the nature of civil government; and the doctrines of popular liberty, which sheltered their infancy in the wildernesses of the newly-discovered continent, within the short space of two centuries, have infused themselves into the life-blood of every rising state from Labrador to Chili, have erected outposts on the Oregon [*sic*] and in Liberia, and, making a proselyte of enlightened France, have disturbed all the ancient governments of Europe, by awakening the public mind to resistless

[24] One of Bancroft's contemporaries, Richard Hildreth, devoted even less space to ideas in his history than had his predecessors. Hildreth's indifference to thought in *The History of the United States of America* was particularly striking in view of his exceedingly great involvement with the social and philosophical ideas of his time. He wrote two works of social philosophy, *Theory of Morals* and *Theory of Politics*, and the abolitionist novel, *Archy Moore*. For Hildreth's biography, see Donald Emerson, *Richard Hildreth*, The Johns Hopkins University Studies in Historical and Political Science, Series LXIV, No. 2, Baltimore, 1946.

[25] Bancroft, *History of the United States*, 10 vols., 1834-1874 (25 edns.), 15th edn., 1852, Vol. 5, p. 4. All quotations will be from this edition.

action, from the shores of Portugal to the palaces of the czars.[26]

Following successful settlement and later toleration in the colonies, the eventual political effect of the idea of liberty was the movement for independence from Great Britain. "Principles grow into life by informing the public mind," he said, "and in their maturity gain the mastery over events." In the mid-eighteenth century, "the hour of revolution was at hand," according to Bancroft, and it promised "dominion to intelligence" as well as "freedom of conscience."[27] American democracy during Bancroft's day, which had enthroned the opinions of the people, was thus the culmination of the earlier ideas of individual freedom. As liberty for individuals had formerly been achieved in certain areas, American democracy had extended liberty more widely throughout all areas of life. The result was, in Bancroft's view, that the beliefs of the people ruled. "Public opinion," he declared, "knows itself to be the spirit of the world, in its movement on the tide of thought from generation to generation."[28] It was in this sense that Bancroft was a "democratic historian," as von Ranke called him, glorifying the ideas of the common man, though he devoted

[26] *Ibid.*, Vol. 1, pp. 266, 267. Bancroft treated Puritan ideas approximately as had his predecessors. He devoted eight pages to the "character of Puritanism," and adopted a similar tone. He avowed the desire to refrain from defense of Puritan "excesses," but argued vigorously that the Puritans were only trying "to protect themselves" from Roger Williams, Wheelright, the Quakers, and the Anabaptists, who were threats to the civil state and so had to be expelled. See *ibid.*, pp. 461-468.

[27] *Ibid.*, Vol. 4, p. 4.

[28] *Ibid.*, p. 11. The quotation suggests Bancroft's transcendentalism, which I have not discussed in the text. It is not clear in such cases to what extent Bancroft's attribution of causal power to ideas is an attribution to a Hegelian world-spirit. Insofar as Bancroft expressed a transcendental interpretation of the power of ideas over and through worldly events, he had no followers among later American historians of ideas.

few pages either to ideas or to the common man.[29] Despite Bancroft's celebration of the democratic mind, his approach to ideas was essentially that of his colonial predecessors.

During the later years of George Bancroft's long lifetime, after the Civil War, there were two developments in American historical scholarship which contributed to a new interest in the history of ideas. These late nineteenth century developments do not in themselves fully explain why the first consciously conceived histories of ideas were written. But the new scholarly tendencies in the writing of history did suggest a definition of subject matter which prominently featured ideas.

One of these developments, anticipated by Bancroft himself, was a democraticizing of the subject matter of written histories. There was increased talk of studying "the life of the people" rather than solely the public acts of the leaders.[30] Because of the breadth of activities in the lives of the people, intellectual activity had at least a chance to be included. John Bach McMaster (1852-1932) opened *A History of the People of the United States from the Revolution to the Civil War* (1883-1913) by declaring:

it shall be my purpose to describe the dress, the occupations, the amusements, the literary canons of the times; to note the changes of manners *and morals*:

[29] David Levin, in *History as Romantic Art*, Palo Alto, 1959, in a chapter entitled "Representative Men," discusses the manner in which Bancroft kept the traditional focus upon the "leaders" while glorifying the "followers." Heroic leaders were assumed to be representative of common men.

[30] It is a curious fact that despite the many pleas during the last century for allegedly unprecedented "histories of the people" rather than "political and military histories," there is an old American tradition of "social histories." Virtually all the colonial chroniclers, for instance, were concerned with what most scholars would today call social history.

to trace the growth of *that humane spirit which abol-*
ished punishment for debt, which reformed the dis-
cipline of prisons and of jails, and which has, in our
own time, destroyed slavery and lessened the miseries
of dumb brutes. Nor shall it be less my aim to recount the manifold improvements which, in a thousand ways, have multiplied the conveniences of life
and ministered to the happiness of our race; to describe the rise and progress of that long series of
mechanical inventions and discoveries which is now
the admiration of the world, and our just pride and
boast; to tell how, under the benign influence of liberty and peace, there sprang up, in the course of a
single century, a prosperity unparalleled in the an-
nals of human affairs; how, from a state of great poverty and feebleness, our country grew rapidly to one
of opulence and power; how her agriculture and her
manufactures flourished together; how, by *a wise*
system of free education and a free press, knowledge
was disseminated, and the arts and sciences ad-
vanced.[31]

As the added italics indicate, McMaster's statement
of intention included ideas, or opinion, within the com-
prehensive scope. But even as announced, the interest in
beliefs was merely part of a wide-ranging interest in
social history. In McMaster's history, as it was actually
written, thought received much less attention than the
prefatory announcement suggested. (McMaster's volumes were not even social histories except for occa-

[31] McMaster, *A History of the People of the United States*
from the Revolution to the Civil War, 7 vols., New York, 1907,
Vol. 1, pp. 2-3. McMaster first vowed to write a history of the
people of the United States, according to his biographer, when
he read Thomas Macaulay's famous third chapter "The State
of England in 1685," in *History of England from the Accession*
of James II. See Eric Goldman, *John Bach McMaster*, Philadelphia, 1943, p. 13.

sional sections.) From the standpoint of the development of the writing of histories of ideas, John Bach McMaster was a publicist for writing about thought by the accident of his plea for a proposed history of the people. But, finally, as in the case of Bancroft, thought was celebrated, rather than described, in the course of writing conventional political history.

McMaster admitted Thomas Macaulay's influence in originally directing him to social history, but apparently McMaster was not influenced by the other Englishman who wrote an early history of the English people, John Richard Green.[32] It was, however, Green's history which led John Fiske (1842-1901) to consider writing a parallel history of the American people, according to Fiske. He invidiously compared "old-fashioned history, still retaining the marks of its barbaric origin," which "dealt with little save kings and battles and court intrigues," with the newly broadened histories best exemplified by Green's, which paid attention, among other things, "to changes in beliefs."[33] But Fiske, while as willing as McMaster to speak favorably of a "new history," was no more successful in writing one, and his historical writings and public lectures of the 1880's and 1890's were narrowly political and military in context.[34]

Despite the fact that early supporters of a broadened social history which would include ideas, such as McMaster and Fiske, did not themselves write histories

[32] William Hutchinson, "John Bach McMaster," in *The Marcus W. Jernegan Essays in American Historiography*, Chicago, 1937, p. 125; Goldman, *McMaster*, p. 15.

[33] On Fiske, see Milton Berman, *John Fiske*, Cambridge, 1961, pp. 145-146. Quotation is from John Fiske, *Essays Historical and Literary*, 2 vols., New York, 1902, Vol. 2, p. 23.

[34] Fiske's choice not to write the history of thought is particularly striking in view of his intense involvement in philosophical questions of his own day. See his *Outlines of Cosmic Philosophy*, 2 vols., Boston, 1874.

according to these new precepts, nevertheless the variety and breadth of social history did presumably encourage the growth of the history of ideas. One cannot read, for instance, the following plea from Frederick Jackson Turner in 1891 for broadened studies of history which would investigate "all the spheres of man's activity," without thinking that it explains how a teacher of the westward movement could produce a student of the history of ideas such as Carl Becker:

> The economic life and the political life touch, modify, and condition one another. Even the religious life needs to be studied in conjunction with the political and economic life, and vice versa. Therefore all kinds of history are essential—history as politics, history as art, history as economics, history as religion—all are truly parts of society's endeavor to understand itself by understanding its past.[35]

Turner's enthusiasm for broadly conceived histories happened to be one part of his conscious desire to investigate the past more "scientifically" than was usual. Turner's implicit admiration for science was common; this constituted the second development in American historical scholarship in the late nineteenth century which contributed to the new interest in the study of the history of ideas.[36] The apotheosis of science yielded

[35] "The Significance of History," in Fulmer Mood, ed., *The Early Writings of Frederick Jackson Turner*, Madison, 1938, pp. 53-54. The article was originally published in the *Wisconsin Journal of Education*, October and November, 1891.

[36] There were of course other developments important to historical scholarship, such as the emergence of the professional historian through graduate training, the growth of universities, the founding of the American Historical Association in 1884, and the publication of the *American Historical Review*. Such developments, however, did not affect the study of the history of ideas differently than it affected historical scholarship generally.

both a "scientific history" and an interest in "scientific" ideas in history.

The concept of "scientific history" which contributed to the history of ideas was, to employ W. Stull Holt's distinction, grandly interpretative rather than fact-finding.[37] The grand-interpreters valued exact knowledge but they cherished imaginative hypotheses even more, and their writings encouraged the study of the history of ideas. Specifically, these scientific historians raised the question of the causal relationship between thought and its environment. They sought an answer which could be expressed in scientific terms.

Henry Adams (1838-1918), for example, raised the possibility of ascertaining the causal influence of ideas while he sketched the intellectual life of early nine-teenth century Americans. More than eight volumes of the nine comprising Adams' *History of the United States During the Administrations of Thomas Jefferson and James Madison* were political narrative, but he appended introductory and concluding sections which discussed ideas.

He opened with a 150-page survey of the "intellect" of various sections of the United States in 1800, and he concluded with a shorter assessment of ideas in politics, religion, and the arts in 1815. These first and last sections were utterly disconnected from the body of his history, yet he avowed great interest in them. "The movement of thought," Adams wrote, was "more inter-esting than the movement of population or of wealth."[38]

[37] W. Stull Holt, "The Idea of Scientific History," *Journal of the History of Ideas*, I (June 1940), 352-362. Fact-finding scientific history, which emulated science by its careful, de-tailed, seemingly objective investigation of evidence, probably diminished interest in the history of ideas by preferring the more concrete source material of political history.

[38] Adams, *History of the United States During the Administrations of Thomas Jefferson and James Madison*, 9 vols.,

He suggested that there was genuine significance to be found in pursuing the popular mind: "A few customs, more or less local; a few prejudices, more or less popular; a few traits of thought, suggesting habits of mind, —must form the entire material for a study more important than that of politics or economics."[39] Adams went on to indicate the popular mind which he thought would be discovered if such a study were made: progressive, democratic, secular, libertarian. "European travellers who passed through America noticed," according to Adams, "that everywhere, except for a few Federalists, every American, from Jefferson and Gallatin down to the poorest squatter, seemed to nourish an idea that he was doing what he could to overthrow the tyranny which the past had fastened on the human mind."[40]

To the popular mind Adams gave the name "national character," and he explicitly raised the question of the impact of national character, by which he meant opinion and belief, upon other human behavior. "Of all historical problems," he wrote, "the nature of a national character is the most difficult and the most important." He posed the problem with specific reference to his own political narrative: "Readers will be troubled, at almost every chapter of the coming narrative, by the want of some formula to explain what share the popular imagination bore in the system pursued by government."[41] Whether or not troubled, the reader in fact received no suggested answers throughout the following eight volumes to the question of the relationship between beliefs and actions.

New York, 1889-1891, Vol. 9, p. 175. The political narrative which comprised the bulk of Adams' *History* exemplified W. Stull Holt's fact-finding scientific history, in contrast to the exceptional pages concerning the history of thought.

[39] *Ibid.*, Vol. 1, p. 42. [40] *Ibid.*, p. 175.
[41] *Ibid.*, p. 176.

But Adams was himself troubled, at least troubled enough to return in his last chapter to the subject of the emergent democratic national character of the early 1800's. As if to admit the hopelessness of finding a "formula" by which to determine the impact of opinion, or national character, upon political events, but as if to hold out still the hope of some kind of scientific history, Adams suggested that perhaps the focus of American historical researches should be the national character itself. In a democratic society, he argued, individuals were more important as types than as unique heroes, and the concept of national character would allow a direct avenue to types of individuals.[42] Thus, even though he turned to European history when he chose to write at length about man's "inner life," in *Mont Saint Michel and Chartres*, Adams expressed interest in the history of the American mind which he characterized as remarkably democratic, and which he suggested could be approached scientifically.

Another American who urged scientific histories of thought, but who preferred to deal with the ideas of Europe and the politics and wars of the United States, was John William Draper (1811-1882). Draper was born and raised in England, and wrote his *Intellectual Development of Europe* (1862) after he made a reputation as an American scientist. Draper conceived of the science of history as an exploration into the laws of human development. "The equilibrium and movement of humanity are altogether physiological phenomena," he wrote.[43] When Draper spoke in this vein, he minimized the causal power of thought and emphasized the determining influence of the material environment:

If from its original seats a whole nation were trans-

[42] *Ibid.*, Vol. 9, p. 222.
[43] Draper, *History of Intellectual Development of Europe*, 2 vols., 1862, rev. edn., 1876, Vol. 1, p. 2.

posed to some new abode, in which the climate, the seasons, the aspect of nature were altogether different, it would appear spontaneously in all its parts to commence a movement to come into harmony with the new conditions—a movement of a secular nature, and implying the consumption of many generations for its accomplishment.[44]

But Draper was a reforming man of science whose belief in human progress included a celebration of certain ideas which he did not relate to their physical environment. "I come to the conclusion," he said, "that in the unanimous consent of the entire human race lies the human criterion of truth—a criterion, in its turn, capable of increased precision with the diffusion of enlightenment and knowledge":

> In the intellectual collisions that must ensue, in the melting down of opinions, in the examinations and analyses of nations, truth will come forth. Whatever can not stand that ordeal must submit to its fate. Lies and imposture, no matter how powerfully sustained, must prepare to depart. In that supreme tribunal man may place implicit confidence.[45]

The truth which Draper had in mind was above all scientific knowledge as opposed to historic religious superstition. Thus the *History of the Intellectual Development of Europe* traced mainly the conflict between science and religion, and it was the story of emergent truth. In this way the scientific historian's zeal to locate the environmental or physiological influences upon ideas gave way to enthusiasm for the ideas of modern science.

But whether European thought was a cause or a result of its environment, American thought was left

[44] *Ibid.*, p. 14.   [45] *Ibid.*, p. 236.

unexplored by Draper. For when he chose to write American history, rather than European, a three-volume military and political narrative was the product.[46] The same relative lack of interest in American thought was revealed by others who, like Draper and Adams, wrote of European thought.

Andrew Dickson White (1832-1918) attempted to show, as did John William Draper, the importance of scientific thought through his argument that science had liberated the modern mind from the ignorance of traditional theology. This interest in modern scientific thought joined with the interest in scientific history to stimulate the study of the history of ideas. For White studied the past to expose the evils of religious ideas and the glories of science. Although White's *A History of the Warfare of Science with Theology in Christendom* (1896) was not a "scientific history" in Draper's and Adams' sense of exploring the relation between ideas and their environments, or in their sense of establishing laws, it did argue for the importance of the history of ideas.[47]

White's and Draper's interest in showing the superiority of modern science over medieval religion, as well as Draper's and Adams' interest in finding the relationship between ideas and their environments, were American expressions of currents in European historical scholarship during the last half of the nineteenth century. The history of European ideas, rather than American thought was, of course, the focus of these European studies.

Draper's mid-century and Adams' late-century pleas

[46] *History of the American Civil War*, 3 vols., New York, 1867, 1868, 1870.

[47] See also Henry Charles Lea, *An Historical Sketch of Sacerdotal Celibacy in the Christian Church*, Boston, 1867, and *A History of the Inquisition of the Middle Ages*, 3 vols., New York, 1887-1888.

for scientific investigation of the relationship between ideas and their environments were paralleled by the Englishman Henry Thomas Buckle's (1822-1862) *History of Civilization in England*, published in two volumes in 1857 and 1861. "I hope to accomplish for the history of man," Buckle wrote, "something equivalent, or at all events analogous, to what has been effected by other inquirers for the different branches of natural science."[48]

His plea for scientific history featured the role of thought, because man's history was "the fruit of a double action; an action of external phenomena upon the mind, and another action of the mind upon the phenomena." According to Buckle, "we have man modifying nature, and nature modifying man," and "out of this reciprocal modification all events must necessarily spring." Buckle's dream was to make written history a science which would discover "the laws of this double modification," and so find out "whether the thoughts and desires of men are more influenced by physical phenomena, or whether the physical phenomena are more influenced by them."[49]

Buckle's own conclusion, like John William Draper's, was one which suggested his faith in progress and education: that ideas have been increasingly more influential than the physical environment as man has moved away from barbarism toward civilization. The enlightened modern man of science and democracy could control the environment, even though the environment controlled early man. Buckle's enthusiasm for making a

[48] Buckle, *History of Civilization in England*, 3 vols., New York, 1913, Vol. 1, p. 5. Draper's biographer concludes that "it seems fairly certain that Draper had arrived at his conclusions independently" of Buckle. Draper announced his projected history of European thought in 1856, prior to publication of Buckle's first volume. See Donald Fleming, *John William Draper*, Philadelphia, 1950, p. 74.

[49] *Ibid.*, p. 15.

science of history extended to both situations. Thus, he wrote, "the advance of European civilization is characterized by a diminishing influence of physical laws, and an increasing influence of mental laws."[50] Buckle made it clear that physical laws would define the impact of the environment upon human thought. It was not so clear what mental laws would define, for he was mainly occupied in indicating the grandeur of ideas which governed their environments instead of being governed by them. Human progress was due to the triumph of those ideas which were not conditioned by the physical environment. "I pledge myself to show," wrote Buckle, "that the progress Europe has made from barbarism to civilization is entirely due to its intellectual activity; that the leading countries have now, for some centuries, advanced sufficiently far to shake off the influence of those physical agencies by which in an earlier state their career might have been troubled." When he discussed these ideas to which man owed his progress, Buckle did not relate them to environmental factors but instead celebrated them for their autonomy:

> it is to them we owe all that we now have, they are for all ages and all times; never young, and never old, they bear the seeds of their own life; they flow on in a perennial and undying stream; they are essentially cumulative, and giving birth to the additions which they subsequently receive, they thus influence the most distant posterity, and after the lapse of centuries produce more effect than they were able to do even at the moment of their promulgation.[51]

Buckle thus placed stress upon the autonomous quality of thought even as he argued for a science of the environmental influences upon ideas. He was as enthusiastic about the unchallenged power of ideas in the

[50] *Ibid.*, p. 112.　　　　　[51] *Ibid.*, pp. 162-163.

modern age as he was concerning the possibility of showing the environment's power over ideas in ages past. In its entirety then, Buckle's theoretical outline for scientific history proposed a system which would study the relative power of the physical environment and of thought. And if determinism received support in his conclusion that "lower" civilizations were largely controlled by nature, free will seemed to be endorsed by the celebration of human thought in "higher" societies.

Buckle's plea for a scientific history of thought, like the Frenchman Hippolyte Taine's (1828-1893) argument for scientific literary history (*History of English Literature*),[52] was rooted in his confidence concerning the superiority of modern scientific ideas. Traditional theological wisdom was relegated to an ignorant past. This championing of skeptical scientific thought was the foundation for other pioneer European historians of ideas too, even if they did not join in Buckle's and Taine's search for hidden laws of history.

William Edward Hartpole Lecky (1838-1908), whose first notable work, *History of the Rise and Influence of the Spirit of Rationalism in Europe*, was published in 1865, shared his contemporaries' faith in human progress. Like Buckle and Taine, Lecky spoke of "the great laws of eternal development which preside over and direct the progress of belief."[53] And, like them too, Lecky mentioned the nonintellectual environment as one of the factors influencing the course of thought. "It is impossible to lay down a railway without creating intellectual influences," he wrote, just as to create a commercial society "is to encourage the opinions that

[52] Taine's *History of English Literature* was published in three volumes in the late 1860's in French, and translated into English by the next decade.

[53] *History of the Rise and Influence of the Spirit of Rationalism in Europe*, 2 vols., rev. edn., New York, 1890, Vol. 1, p. 113.

are most congenial to it."[54] Unlike Buckle and Taine, however, Lecky spent almost all his time describing the beliefs with which he was concerned, and he devoted only slight space to their environmental relationships.

Leslie Stephen's (1832-1904) *History of English Thought in the Eighteenth Century* (1876) analyzed ideas at even greater length and in more depth than did Lecky's writings. Stephen's plan of approach to the history of ideas was "to deal chiefly with the logical condition," that is, to analyze thought without regard to influences other than ideas.[55] He articulated the concept of an intellectual "spirit of the age," which he attempted to describe, indicating how this "spirit" was transformed into a new intellectual temper. But Stephen, as well as Lecky, shared Buckle's and Taine's evolutionary viewpoint and belief in human progress through modern knowledge. "The history of thought is in great part a history of the gradual emancipation of the mind from the errors spontaneously generated by its first childlike attempts at speculation," Stephen wrote. "Doctrines which once appeared to be simply expressions of immediate observation have contained a hypothetical element, gradually dissolved by contact with facts."[56]

Thus Leslie Stephen and W. E. H. Lecky, who were more interested in ideas than in their environmental relationships, shared the progressive faith of rationalism expressed by the scientific historians Henry Thomas Buckle and Hippolyte Taine. It was in this

[54] *Ibid.*, p. 8.

[55] Stephen, *History of English Thought in the Eighteenth Century*, 2 vols., 3rd edn., New York, 1902, reprinted 1949, Vol. 1, p. 19.

[56] *Ibid.*, Vol. 1, p. 5. See also Vol. 2, p. 91: "A scheme of morality deduced from self-evident and necessary truths must produce a code as rigid as its fundamental axioms, and, therefore, incapable of varying with the development of the race."

sense that most of the pioneer writings on the history of thought, whether by Europeans or Americans, were rooted in an admiration for secular knowledge and the rational, scientific outlook of the modern western mind. The idea of modern science joined with the idea of modern scientific history to argue for the importance of the study of the history of ideas.

The history of European ideas received the most benefit from these new currents in scholarship during the late 1800's, but the currents were present in the United States and they comprised part of the background from which the first conscious American histories of ideas emerged. Much of the scholarly background, of course, was not new and scientific, but was old and originally Puritan.

MOSES COIT TYLER

From Bradford to Bancroft, American chroniclers and historians expressed the conviction that ideas were important in history. Early writers, however, did not single out ideas for exclusive treatment in their histories, nor did they analyze the relationship between ideas and their environments. After the Civil War, enthusiasm for social histories which would cover all of man's activities, including intellectual ones, gave indirect support at least to the study of the history of ideas. Enthusiasm for modern science, too, stimulated new interest, on the one hand through scholars who spoke of writing a "scientific" history of ideas and, on the other hand, through scholars who wrote histories of the "enlightened" scientific thought which they championed. But these currents of scholarship during the late nineteenth century were reflected primarily in histories of European ideas rather than in histories of American ideas. European historians of ideas did not turn to American thought, and even in the United States scholars preferred to study European ideas.

The two Americans who did pioneer significantly during the late 1800's in the treatment of their own country's past, Moses Coit Tyler and Edward Eggleston, had similar backgrounds in several respects. Both were raised in the Midwest among Calvinist protestants, after which they were pastors for a time, both turned to the writing of history only in middle-age, and both focused upon intellectual life in the colonies. In their writings, they both emphasized the causal importance of ideas in history. They differed, however, on the ideas and the periods in history which they found admirable: they did not agree in their estimates of the colonial period. And they agreed neither in their assessments of modern currents of thought nor on the theoretical desirability of scientific history that would investigate the influence of the environment upon ideas.

Moses Coit Tyler (1835-1900), who wrote in the 1870's the first history of American ideas, was born in Connecticut of long New England ancestry and was raised in the Midwest. He graduated from Yale and then attended schools of theology in Connecticut and Massachusetts. Throughout his life he retained the religious concern of his forebears. After theological school he became a Congregational pastor; he frequently gave guest sermons after he left the ministry and became a college professor. In middle life, a religious re-examination provoked Tyler to become an Episcopalian; he was ordained a priest and thereafter conducted regular Episcopal services.[57] Both his identification with

[57] All the facts concerning Tyler's life are taken from Howard Mumford Jones and Thomas Edgar Casady, *The Life of Moses Coit Tyler*, Ann Arbor, 1933. This study was based upon a dissertation by Casady, who died before he was able to prepare it for publication. The usefulness of this study is due partly to the fact that Jones was particularly interested in the

New England and his continuous religious sympathy were clearly expressed in his studies of colonial literature.

Tyler was a professor of English literature at the University of Michigan from the late 1860's until he went to Cornell in 1881 as the nation's first professor of American history. While originating courses in American literature for the Michigan curriculum, Tyler was asked by the publisher George Haven Putnam to compile a manual of American literature. As Tyler worked upon the proposed literary manual, it slowly became not only historical but also concerned with the ideas expressed in the literature. Because of the broadened scope of Tyler's topic, his first two volumes, *A History of American Literature, 1607-1765* (1878), dealt with only the colonial years.[58] He carried his subject forward two decades when he added his final two volumes, *The Literary History of the American Revolution, 1763-1785*, in 1897.[59]

"There is but one thing more interesting than the intellectual history of a man," Tyler wrote in his opening sentence of his first volume, "and that is the intellectual history of a nation."[60] Twenty years later, as he began his Revolutionary history, he declared that the "Revolution was pre-eminently a revolution caused by ideas, and pivoted on ideas."[61] Such an enthusiastic con-

---

development of the writing of history of ideas. See also Jessica Tyler Austen, ed., *Moses Coit Tyler, 1835-1900: Selections from His Letters and Diaries*, New York, 1911.

[58] Originally published by Putnam in two volumes. Quotations cited here refer to the revised two-volume edition, New York, 1897. There is also a one-volume edition published in 1949 by Cornell University Press.

[59] 2 vols., New York, 1897. Quotations cited here refer to the 1941 two-volume edition, Facsimile Library, New York.

[60] *A History of American Literature*, Vol. 1, p. 5.

[61] *The Literary History of the American Revolution*, Vol. 1, p. 8.

viction concerning the fascination and significance of thought in history marked all Tyler's writings. Symptomatically, when Tyler once praised Buckle, there was no reference to the latter's scientism, but instead to his "recognition of a spirit of the age as ruling the evolution of the events of the age, and using kings, presidents, statesmen, warriors, as the tide uses the chips that are carried upon its top."[62] Tyler was impressed, in other words, by that strain in Buckle's work which argued the power of ideas, rather than by the strain which placed emphasis upon environmental control over thought.

Tyler's attribution of great influence to ideas was perhaps less a theoretical statement about thought generally than an affirmation of the importance of the particular ideas which he described in his books. These ideas which Tyler treated, usually expressions of New England Puritanism or the making of an American nationality, comprised the center of his work—insofar as it was, as he announced it, an "intellectual history." In Tyler's colonial volumes, his focus was most clearly upon ideas in the sections discussing New England writings, which took up more than two-thirds of the pages. Chapters were devoted to "New England Traits in the Seventeenth Century," "Topics of Popular Discussion," and "The Dynasty of the Mathers."

Tyler's prose, always full-bodied and alive, became enthusiastic when he wrote of early New England Puritans. His chronicle of their intellectual achievement was a labor of admiration. He respected the intellectuality of the Puritans, and he interpreted their theological interests as basically intellectual. He attributed the considerable Puritan literary output to the fact that they were the only "thinkers" among the New World colonists:

[62] Jones and Casady, *Tyler*, p. 141.

Primarily, then, these first New-Englanders were thinkers in some fashion; they assumed the right to think, the utility of thinking, and the duty of standing by the fair conclusions of their thinking, even at very considerable cost . . . the one grand distinction between the English colonists in New England and nearly all other English colonists in America was this, that while the latter came here chiefly for some material benefit, the former came chiefly for an ideal benefit. In its inception New England was not an agricultural community, nor a manufacturing community, nor a trading community: it was a thinking community; an arena and mart for ideas; its characteristic organ being not the hand, nor the heart, nor the pocket, but the brain.[63]

Tyler noted with pride that "probably no other community ever so honored study. . . . Theirs was a social structure with its corner-stone resting on a book."[64]

The specific theological doctrines of the Puritans were not championed by Tyler, but he treated them with respect, emphasized their achievements, and stressed the intellectuality of the Puritan religious quest.

Above all, it was toward religion, as the one supreme thing in life and in this universe, that all this intellectuality of theirs and all this earnestness, were directed. The result was tremendous. Perhaps not since the time of the apostles had there been in the world a faith so literal, a zeal so passionate: not even in the time of the apostles was there connected with these an intelligence so keen and so robust. For the first time, it may be, in the history of the world, these people brought together the subtle brain of the metaphysician and the glowing heart of the fanatic;

[63] *A History of American Literature, 1607-1765*, Vol. 1, p. 98.
[64] *Ibid.*

and they flung both vehemently into the service of religion. Never were men more logical or self-consistent in theory and in practice. Religion, they said was the chief thing; they meant it; they acted upon it.[65]

Tyler's respect for the Puritan mind, and some of his lack of respect for his own late nineteenth century period—"a grinning and flabby age"—were indicated in his remarks on Puritan sermons.

Without doubt, the sermons produced in New England during the colonial times, and especially during the seventeenth century, are the most authentic and characteristic revelations of the mind of New England for all that wonderful epoch. They are commonly spoken of mirthfully by an age that lacks the faith of that period, its earnestness, its grip, its mental robustness; a grinning and flabby age, an age hating effort, and requiring to be amused. The theological and religious writings of early New England may not now be readable; but they are certainly not despicable. They represent an enormous amount of subtile, sustained, and sturdy brain-power.[66]

This Puritan mind—earnest and learned—Tyler depicted sympathetically as it appeared in Puritan writings.

Tyler's entrance to the Puritan mind was through biographical sketches, whether in chapters where the figures were grouped together because of ideas ("Topics of Popular Discussion"), or family and ideas ("The Dynasty of the Mathers"), or genre of writing and ideas ("Verse-Writers," "History"). Common Puritan ideas were indicated in many of these sketches, despite the fact that the sections were not organized principally according to ideas. For example, Tyler's description of William Bradford, "Historical Writer," emphasized the

[65] *Ibid.*, p. 10.   [66] *Ibid.*, p. 192.

Pilgrim's dedication to the Plymouth Zion as he composed his chronicles; John Cotton, "Theological and Religious Writer," was treated in relation to Puritan spirituality; and Anne Bradstreet, "Verse-Writer," was discussed in part, at least, with reference to the Puritan mind. "Literature, for her," according to Tyler, "was not a republic of letters, hospitable to all forms of human thought, but a strict Puritan commonwealth."[67]

Thus, to a considerable extent, Tyler fulfilled his declaration of writing a history of thought. Puritanism supplied a body of ideas which so permeated early New England writings that any study of the literature necessarily involved a study of the ideas. In addition to Puritanism, he also looked for literary manifestation of the idea of a separate American identity—"genuine American talk." He noted writings which expressed "that new note of hope and help for humanity in distress, and of a rugged personal independence":

> this single word America blossomed into a whole vocabulary of words, all testifying plainly to them of a better time coming, of a reasonable chance, somewhere, in this world, of getting a fresh start in life, and of winning the victory over poverty, nastiness, and fear; nourishing within them a manly might and pride, a resolute discontent with failure, a rightful ambition to get on in the race, a healthy disdain of doing in this life anything less than one's best.[68]

The delineation of the American dream, a combination of belief and hope, idea and faith, was one of Tyler's purposes. Perhaps the nationalism implicit in his desire to locate a peculiarly American dream was what provoked Tyler to study his own country's intellectual life, instead of Europe's, as was more commonly done.

This search for an American credo blurred the dis-

[67] *Ibid.*, p. 281.　　　　[68] *Ibid.*, pp. 56-57.

tinction beween "high" and "low" thought insofar as "American" characteristics were not restricted to any single stratum of ideas. Although Tyler's survey, which was confined to written works, necessarily constituted a study of an "elite" group in the population, early American writings offered few examples of intellectual works which were remote from the immediate "popular" concerns of the community. The attempt to locate an American identity also blurred to some extent the distinction between an environmental approach to ideas and one which analyzed thought irrespective of environmental factors. For Tyler assumed that the new wilderness environment, that is, the lack of an Old World environment, had contributed to the formulation of the American dream.

Despite Tyler's interest in depicting attitudes characteristically American, and in describing Puritanism, his first colonial volumes did not comprise an unalloyed history of ideas. Tyler was writing of literature as well as of ideas; his book, *A History of American Literature, 1607-1765*, pioneered equally in each area. As extraordinary as his dual achievement was, it necessitated a dual focus, which meant that Tyler's history of ideas was not consistently or exclusively a history of ideas. He faced the problem of writing the history of thought from sources which had esthetic, as well as intellectual, relevance to the historian. Literature, like painting or architecture, presents the historian with a question of esthetic judgment as well as the customary ones of historical description and explanation. Although it is theoretically possible to ask only historical questions of esthetic works, historians have seldom refrained from making esthetic evaluations when studying art. The failure stems not so much from weaknesses of historians (for historians have not really tried to refrain from making those judgments), as from the very nature of art itself. To discuss art is to imply standards of judgment. Works of art survive and are discussed by mankind on the basis of esthetic criteria, which is not the case with other historical source material. Thus as soon as a historian selects for historical treatment a work of "art," as contrasted with a work too esthetically deficient to be considered "art," he has allowed esthetic rather than purely historical criteria to enter.

Apart from the problem of evaluation, esthetic source material presents a second problem to the historian of ideas. Art forms have their own special histories, and these are not necessarily relevant to anything outside the art form. Literature has its internal development of genre and style, for example, and a historian of literature almost by definition is interested in those developments. But the relationship between the history of genre and style on the one hand, and the history of ideas on the other, may be nonexistent. Tyler's history exemplified the extent to which the history of literature and the history of ideas, though not mutually exclusive, are not really focused in the same direction.

That the volumes would be concerned with the history of literature as well as with the history of ideas was clearly indicated in Tyler's prefatory remarks. For at the same time that he said he was interested in the history of ideas, he also said that the history of literary form was of concern to him, and he noted that he would use a criterion of esthetic value for the inclusion of certain writings. Tyler wrote in the Preface that he had attempted to give a history of writings "which have some noteworthy value as literature," in addition to "some real significance in the literary unfolding of the American mind." He said that he had "aimed in these volumes to make an appropriate mention of every one of our early authors whose writings, whether many or few, have any appreciable literary merit, or throw any helpful light upon the evolution of thought and of style in America, during those flourishing and indispensable days."[69]

Tyler's volumes themselves reflected the dual focus of his prefatory comments. The organization, as noted above, was not ordinarily by ideas, but by writers—usually lumped together by time and region, and sometimes by subject matter and genre of their writings. With the exception of such a chapter as "New England Traits in the Seventeenth Century," ideas were discussed within a chapter organization which was basically literary.

Within this fundamentally literary organization, Tyler's individual sketches discussed both the literary and the intellectual characteristics of the figures treated. Sometimes, as in the chapters on "Verse-Writers," the sketches were predominantly or wholly literary; at other times, as in the chapters on theologians, the sketches were mainly concerned with ideas. This inconsistency was exemplified in Tyler's discussion of Puritan poet Michael Wigglesworth and his verse-writing son Samuel Wigglesworth. In his sketch of Michael Wigglesworth, Tyler placed stress upon the ideas embodied in Wigglesworth's verse and devoted several pages to the discussion. Tyler wrote, for example, that "Michael Wigglesworth stands for New England Puritanism confronting with steady gaze the sublime and hideous dogmas of its creed, and trying to use those dogmas for the admonition and the consolation of mankind by putting them into song. . . . He chants, with utter frankness, the chant of Christian fatalism, the moan of earthly vanity and sorrow, the physical bliss of the saved, the physical tortures of the damned."[70] Here Tyler was clearly using verse as a source for the history of ideas. Yet in his next sketch of Samuel Wigglesworth, Tyler

[69] *Ibid.*, p. v.　　　　[70] *Ibid.*, Vol. 2, pp. 24-25.

said nothing about the ideas expressed in his verse, but remarked that his poems showed esthetic potentiality. Similarly, the following sketch of the poet Nicholas Noyes was almost wholly occupied with Noyes' poetic techniques and included an evaluation of his verse. These three poets, the two Wigglesworths and Noyes, were treated in succession because they all wrote verse in colonial New England, not because their ideas were strikingly similar or significantly dissimilar. In fact, the ideas of the elder Wigglesworth only were discussed at any length. *A History of American Literature, 1607-1765* was indeed a history of literature as well as a history of ideas.

The role of ideas was made more consistently important in Tyler's second two-volume work, *The Literary History of the American Revolution, 1763-1785*, which was not published until almost two decades later in 1897.[71] Ideas played a somewhat different part in the Revolutionary volumes than they had in *A History of American Literature, 1607-1765*, because in the earlier volumes Tyler had attempted to discuss large numbers of different types of writings and writers. In the Revolutionary volumes, the somewhat heterogeneous minds of all the colonials, North and South, were crystallized into two opposing minds poised for intellectual combat; similarly, almost all literature was drawn into the same combat. The result was that there was much more in common between Tyler's history of ideas and his history of literature in the Revolutionary volumes than there had been earlier in his work on the colonies. The two channels, intellectual and literary, flowed into one and he had an opportunity to investigate both currents at the same time.

Tyler in his second work focused quite consistently

[71] Quotations cited refer to a 1941 two-volume edition, New York.

on the intellectual conflicts of the Revolutionary era as expressed in literature, which he defined to include almost all writings. He wrote that whereas the earlier colonial period had no single issue around which ideas were magnetically drawn, the Revolutionary period, by contrast, witnessed a virtually complete attraction to the issue culminating in independence. Imaginative literature and all other writings were drawn into intellectual combat and therefore became best understood in terms of ideas. American writing of all types, wrote Tyler, was characterized during the years 1763-1785 by

> its concern with the problems of American society, and of American society in a peculiar condition— aroused, inflammable, in a state of alarm for its own existence, but also in a state of resolute combat for it. The literature which we are thus to inspect is not, then, a literature of tranquillity, but chiefly a literature of strife, or, as the Greeks would have said, of agony; and, of course, it must take those forms in which intellectual and impassioned debate can be most effectually carried on. The literature of our Revolution has almost everywhere the combative note; its habitual method is argumentive, persuasive, appealing, rasping, retaliatory; the very brain of man seems to be in armor; his wit is in the gladiator's attitude of offense and defense. It is a literature indulging itself in grimaces, in mockery, in scowls: a literature accented by earnest gestures meant to convince people, or by fierce blows meant to smite them down.[72]

In these Revolutionary volumes, consequently, Tyler's concern for significant literature was little different from his concern for significant ideas.

[72] *Ibid.*, Vol. 1, p. 6.

In this literature we must not expect to find art used for art's sake. Nay, art itself, so far as it is here at all, is swept into the universal conscription, and enrolled for the service of the one party or of the other in the imperilled young Republic. No man is likely to be in the mood for aesthetics who has an assassin's pistol at his head. Even the passion for the beautiful has been known to yield to the instinct for self-preservation.[73]

Not only did the Revolutionary conflict shake disparate intellects and poets into a single battle, in Tyler's view, but it was a battle of ideas and determined by ideas. He stated that the "Revolution was pre-eminently a revolution caused by ideas, and pivoted on ideas."[74] He argued that this was true of all revolutions, but it was especially true that

an epoch like this, therefore,—an epoch in which nearly all that is great and dear in man's life on earth has to be argued for, as well as to be fought for, and in which ideas have a work to do quite as pertinent and quite as effective as that of bullets,—can hardly fail to be an epoch teeming with literature, with literature, of course, in the particular forms suited to the purposes of political co-operation and conflict.[75]

Tyler here expressed a view of the Revolutionary period totally involved in ideological combat, similar to the in-

[73] *Ibid.* Only rarely did Tyler, in these volumes, discuss literature without reference to revolutionary intellectual conflicts. For these exceptions, see Vol. 1, Chapter 7, "Descriptions of Nature and Man in the American Wilderness: 1763-1775"; Chapter 8, "Beginnings of New Life in Verse and Prose: Philadelphia, Princeton, and New York, 1763-1775"; Chapter 9, "Beginnings of New Life in Verse and Prose: New England, 1763-1775."

[74] *Ibid.*, p. 8. [75] *Ibid.*, p. 9.

volvement of many Americans in battle with totalitarianism during and after the 1940's. As many interpreted the contemporary conflict with totalitarianism, so Tyler saw the Revolutionary turmoil: ideas were not only viewed as interesting expressions of differences of opinion, but also as causally important historical forces.

Tyler's conviction that ideas were crucial led him, in the Preface to *The Literary History of the American Revolution*, to discuss the originality of his written history of the American Revolution, focused as it was on ideas:

> There would, perhaps, be no injustice in describing this book as the product of a new method, at least of a method never before so fully applied, in the critical treatment of the American Revolution. . . . In the present work, for the first time in a systematic and a fairly complete way, is set forth the inward history of our Revolution—the history of its ideas, its spiritual moods, its motives, its passions, even of its sportive caprices and its whims, as these uttered themselves at the time, whether consciously or not, in the various writings of the two parties of Americans who promoted or resisted that great movement.[76]

Since there was little literature except that drawn into the Revolutionary conflict and therefore dominated by the ideas of that conflict, literature in an esthetic sense as well as all other writings were equally well studied by a historian of ideas.

Tyler went on to say, in words which were reminiscent of his enthusiasm over Buckle nearly thirty years before, that his interest in ideas required a history different from that of the narrowly political historians.

The proceedings of legislative bodies, the doings of

[76] *Ibid.*, p. vii.

cabinet ministers and of colonial politicians, the movements of armies, are not altogether disregarded, but
they are here subordinated: they are mentioned, when
mentioned at all, as mere external incidents in connection with the ideas and the emotions which lay
back of them or in front of them, which caused them
or were caused by them. . . . Instead of fixing our
eyes almost exclusively, as is commonly done, upon
statesmen and generals, upon party leaders, upon
armies and navies, upon Congress, upon parliament,
upon the ministerial agents of a brain-sick king, or
even upon that brain-sick king himself, and instead of
viewing all these people as the sole or the principal
movers and doers of the things that made the American Revolution, we here for the most part turn our
eyes toward certain persons hitherto much neglected,
in many cases wholly forgotten—toward persons who,
as mere writers, and whether otherwise prominent
or not, nourished the springs of great historic events
by creating and shaping and directing public opinion
during all that robust time; who, so far as we here
regard them, wielded only spiritual weapons; who
still illustrate, for us and for all who choose to see,
the majestic operation of ideas, the creative and decisive play of spiritual forces, in the development of
history, in the rise and fall of nations, in the aggre-
gation and the division of races.[77]

Tyler's view that ideas were important causal agents
in influencing attitudes and behavior found expression
in his sketches of individuals. In his description of
James Otis' speech protesting writs of assistance, before
the Massachusetts superior court in 1761, Tyler concluded with John Adams' contemporary remark that
"American Independence was then and there born; the

[77] *Ibid.*, p. viii.

seeds of patriots and heroes were then and there sown.
. . . Every man of a crowded audience appeared to me
to go away, as I did, ready to take up arms against
writs of assistance."[78]

Another example of attributing significant causal
power to ideas occurred in Tyler's discussion of Stephen
Hopkins. After discussing Hopkins' pamphlet arguing
that American colonists deserved the full rights of Brit-
ish subjects, Tyler noted that "the impression made by
this strong and sober-minded pamphlet was very great
throughout the colonies," and that it "carried conviction
to many minds."[79] A Loyalist letter written against Hopkins' pamphlet was also thought by Tyler to have "genuine power" among colonists, evidenced by "the instant
and angry" opposition it engendered.[80] Similarly, after
an analysis of Daniel Dulany's pamphlet in 1765 denying the propriety of parliamentary taxation, Tyler
concluded that Dulany's thought not only "made a deep
impression upon a vast number of his fellow colonists,"
but that it also had "no small effect upon the leaders
of liberal politics in England."[81] John Dickinson's "letters" were second only to Tom Paine's writings "in direct power upon events,"[82] and Tyler discussed both
Dickinson's and Paine's ideas at length. Paine's writings, according to Tyler, had "astonishing effects" and
"precipitated the popular debate" upon the question of
independence.[83] Thus, Tyler's volumes were infused
with the conviction that ideas played a crucial part in
determining men's actions.

Because of the nature of the Revolutionary era, as
he interpreted it, Tyler the literary historian went un-
obtrusively along with Tyler the historian of ideas. In
other words there was little literary history during the

[78] *Ibid.*, p. 36. [79] *Ibid.*, p. 69.
[80] *Ibid.*, p. 74. [81] *Ibid.*, p. 110.
[82] *Ibid.*, p. 236. [83] *Ibid.*, pp. 475, 476.

period distinct from the history of ideas, in Tyler's view, and so he was free to write two volumes of history fairly consistently focused on ideas. This may have been an accident of Tyler's subject matter, however, as much as any conscious decision on Tyler's part to separate the history of literature from the history of ideas and to concentrate on the latter. In 1897, as in 1878, Tyler was pioneering in literary history at the same time that he was pioneering in the history of ideas.

Tyler's pioneering was recognized at the time. His inclusion and discussion of so many colonial writings of theology, history and other narratives, verse, and public affairs surprised and pleased commentators. One reviewer expressed astonishment that Tyler had made such apparently dead source material live for the late nineteenth century reader. Political historians praised the contribution Tyler made to the study of the American Revolution by telling the history of the ideas of that revolt. All reviewers were impressed by the original way Tyler used colonial writings—many of them not used previously by any historians—to get at ideas.[84]

Tyler was recognized after 1878 as one of the outstanding students both of literature and of history in the United States. He was asked to fill the first chair of American history in 1881; he was one of the founders of the American Historical Association in 1884; he was vice-president of the Association and would nor-

[84] See the following reviews and comments upon Tyler's work: *Atlantic Monthly* review of the colonial volumes (March 1879), p. 405; Paul Leicester Ford's review of the Revolutionary history in *American Historical Review* (July 1897), pp. 738-740 and (January 1898), pp. 375-377; Herbert Osgood's review of the last work in *Political Science Quarterly* (March 1898), pp. 41-59; William Peterfield Trent, "Moses Coit Tyler," *Forum* (August 1901), pp. 750-758; George Lincoln Burr, "Moses Coit Tyler," *Annual Report of the American Historical Association*, 1901, Vol. 1, pp. 189-195.

mally have been elected president had he not died in 1900.

Moses Coit Tyler's reputation as a distinguished pioneer was deserved (and, it may be added, his failure to attract followers immediately was not). He was the first to announce his work as a history of American thought, he presented a vast body of previously un-digested seventeenth and eighteenth century writings, and he expressed an attitude toward America's intel-lectual past which would be repeated by several his-torians long after his death. Tyler's celebration of Puri-tan and Revolutionary thought, his sympathy for Amer-ican religious traditions, and his view of the virtual autonomy of ideas over events were all characteristic of one approach to the writing of American histories of ideas which was followed later.

EDWARD EGGLESTON

Tyler's only scholarly contemporary to join in an in-vestigation of the history of American ideas, Edward Eggleston (1837-1902), made an approach to their common subject which was in several respects different from Tyler's. Eggleston's ideological position contrasted with Tyler's, as did his conception of the role of ideas in history, and the interpretations of history made by the two men were dissimilar.[85]

Eggleston, who wrote novels before he turned to histories, spoke of his fiction in a way which echoed the scientific histories of Draper, Buckle, and Taine. Eggleston remarked that the characters in his novels

[85] For Eggleston's life, see William Peirce Randel's published dissertation, *Edward Eggleston*, New York, 1946, or virtually the identical volume in the Twayne series on American authors, New York, 1963. See also George Cary Eggleston, *The First of the Hoosiers: Reminiscences of Edward Eggleston*, Phila-delphia, 1903.

"were all treated in their relations to social conditions."[86] The people in his stories, he wrote on another occasion, were "the logical results of the environment."[87] Because of this perspective, he concluded that his novels had been, however unintentionally, "forerunners of my historic studies."[88] In the preface to one of his early novels, Eggleston wrote that "I have wished to make my stories of value as a contribution to the history of civilization in America":

> A novel should be the truest of books. It partakes in a certain sense of the nature of both history and art. It needs to be true to human nature in its permanent and essential qualities, and it should truthfully represent some specific and temporary manifestation of human nature: that is, some form of society.[89]

He again sounded like Draper, Buckle, and Taine when he said of himself, that as novelist and as historian, "I am mainly interested in the evolution of society; that in either sort of writing this interest in the history of life, this tendency to what the Germans call 'culture-history,' is the one distinguishing trait of almost all that I have attempted."[90]

Eggleston came to a Darwinian interpretation, and to a serious study of society, hesitantly and only in middle-age. Born and raised in Indiana, he was a Methodist preacher throughout his twenties, a writer for Christian denominational publications as well as other periodicals during his thirties, and as late as his forties

[86] "Edward Eggleston: An Interview," *Outlook*, LV (1897), 433.

[87] Eggleston, "Formative Influences," *Forum*, X (November 1890), 286.

[88] "Edward Eggleston: An Interview," p. 433.

[89] Eggleston, *The Mystery of Metropolisville*, New York, 1873, p. 7.

[90] Eggleston, "Formative Influences," p. 287.

he returned to a pastorate. In these respects, his background was like Tyler's. But, unlike Tyler, Eggleston wrote of himself that the "long and painful struggle for emancipation from theological dogma" started when, as a young man, he could not reconcile evolutionary geology with dogmatic Methodism. Finally, "there came a time, later in life than crises usually come," Eggleston recollected in 1887, "when my intellectual conscience insisted that sentiment of every sort ought to be put aside in the search for truth." He had read Thomas à Kempis while riding circuit as a youth, Eggleston recalled, but no more:

> the true way is to "look upward and not downward, outward and not inward, forward and not backward." À Kempis may rest where he is; I would rather walk in wide fields with Charles Darwin; and, above all, I would rather, if it were possible, get one peep into the epoch-making book of the next century, whatever it may be, than to go back to the best of the crypt-worshippers. Perhaps it is but a reaction from the subjective training of my youth, but the objective life seems the better. I doubt whether one can be greatly benefited by a too constant dia-monologue with his own soul such as à Kempis is given to.[91]

By 1880, Eggleston called himself an unbeliever, but the passage quoted above suggests that as one belief was lost another was gained.[92]

[91] Eggleston, "Books That Have Helped Me," *Forum*, III (1887), 584, 586.

[92] In a letter to his daughter, Mrs. Elizabeth Eggleston Seelye, July 5, 1880. The letter, now among the Eggleston papers in the Collection of Regional History at Cornell University Library, is cited by Charles Hirschfeld, "Edward Eggleston: Pioneer in Social History," *Historiography and Urbanization*, Eric Goldman, ed., Baltimore, 1941, p. 199. Eggleston's faith in the progressive accumulation of knowledge allowed him to minimize the significance of changing answers to spe-

Belief in progress through modern science provoked Eggleston to speak of history in scientific terms. History could be made "a reasonable science" by studying "the action of cause and effect and the continuity of institutions and usages."[93] Prefacing the first of two colonial studies in what was intended to be a multivolume series on American life, he wrote that it was "a history in which the succession of cause and effect is the main topic—a history of the dynamics of colony-planting in the first half of the seventeenth century."[94]

At this point, as Eggleston was preparing to begin his first colonial volume, he might easily have been likened by a contemporary observer to Draper, Buckle, and Taine. Faith in progress through science, hostility toward man's religious past, and criticism of traditional histories were positions shared by all four writers. Further, Eggleston's two future books on the 1600's were to be histories of ideas. But despite these important similarities, Eggleston's colonial histories of American thought turned out to be significantly different from Draper's, Buckle's, and Taine's writings. Eggleston's histories were less theoretical, less grandiose, less daring. They kept close to the more limited piece of

---

cific questions: "What conclusions the detached mind reaches on grave questions is a matter of secondary importance. Such conclusions may well be inconstant quantities, for the sphere of the universe is large and that of a human brain very small." ("Books That Have Helped Me," p. 586.)

[93] Eggleston, *A History of the United States and Its People for the Use of Schools*, New York, 1888, p. iv; "A Full Length Portrait of the United States," *Century Magazine*, XXXVII (1889), 791. I am indebted to Charles Hirschfeld for these citations and for first making me aware of Eggleston's scientism. See Charles Hirschfeld, "Edward Eggleston: Pioneer in Social History," in Eric Goldman, ed., *Historiography and Urbanization*, pp. 189-210.

[94] Eggleston, *The Beginners of a Nation*, New York, 1896. Quotations cited refer to fourth edition, 1899, p. viii.

ground they attempted to cover, and they were based upon new research in the primary source materials rather than upon philosophic interpretations of history. Finally, Eggleston in his histories expressed only a common sense approach to the role of ideas despite the frequent statements he had made previously concerning the desirability of ascertaining the influence of the environment in human affairs. What was left in Eggleston's histories to link him with the more ambitious attempts of the more thoroughgoing scientific historians was an ideological predisposition in favor of progress, democracy, skepticism, rationality, and science.

The lack of theory in Eggleston's approach to ideas in his colonial volumes was revealed in part by the fact that he was not altogether conscious of the extent to which he was writing a history of ideas. *The Beginners of a Nation* was in fact ostensibly a pioneering work in the field of social history—hence, "A History of Life in the United States"—even though it actually pioneered in the history of ideas as well. Subtitled *A History of the Source and Rise of the Earliest English Settlements in America with Special Reference to the Life and Character of the People*, there was perhaps a hint of concern with ideas in the word "Character," and the hint was elaborated in the Preface:

> It has been my aim to make these pages reflect the character of the age in which the English colonies were begun, and the traits of the colonists, and to bring into relief the social, political, intellectual, and religious forces that promoted emigration. This does not pretend to be the usual account of all the events attending early colonization. . . . Who were the beginners of English life in America? What propulsions sent them for refuge to a wilderness? What visions

beckoned them to undertake the founding of new
states? What manner of men were their leaders?[95]

These comments seemed to announce a history which
was to be both social and intellectual in its emphases,
at a time when to execute either emphasis successfully
would have been unusual.

Eggleston's *The Beginners of a Nation* described in
part "the life of the people," and it also narrated the
history of ideas associated with early seventeenth century colonization. In most chapters the ideas were
treated together with the social history, as many of the
chapter titles suggest: "The Procession of Motives";
"Rise and Development of Puritanism"; "Separation
and the Scrooby Church"; "The Pilgrim Migrations";
"The Great Puritan Exodus"; and "The Catholic Mi-
gration." The ideas Eggleston described were mainly
religious in character, and he related them to seventeenth century behavior, that is, emigration and re-
settlement in the New World. For example, Eggleston's
opening chapter on Renaissance explorations was titled
in terms of ideas, "English Knowledge and Notion of
America at the Period of Settlement," and he implied
that he included the chapter because

> these erratic notions regarding America give one an
> insight into the character of the English people at
> the period of discovery and colony-planting. Credulity
> and the romantic spirit dwell together. . . . Like
> every other romantic age the period of Elizabeth and
> James was prodigal of daring adventure; every nota-
> ble man aspired to be the hero of a tale.

If one knew this, one better understood that "English
beginnings in America were thus made in a time
abounding in bold enterprises—enterprises brilliant in

[95] *Ibid.*, p. vii.

conception, but in the execution of which there was often a lack of foresight and practical wisdom."[96] Eggleston had turned a discussion on Renaissance exploration into an example of the mentality of the age. Under Eggleston's scrutiny past ages usually revealed a lack of mentality. The insight which "erratic notions" of the 1600's revealed was just how unenlightened the early colonists were.

Commentators on Eggleston's *Beginners*, at the time and since, have differed as to whether the volume seemed orthodox or unorthodox in content. Those who have failed to see the unorthodox implications of Eggleston's search for ideas as a part of the "life of the people" have probably been deceived by the fact that *The Beginners* was restricted to that early colonization which American historians have always depicted with unusual regard for ideas and for the "life of the people."[97] No previous account had ever denied, for instance, that seventeenth century religious ideas were crucial to the story of New England settlement. Similarly traditional were the source materials Eggleston cited: chronicles, letters, official colony records, diaries, and other familiar writings of the settlers. Because Eggleston was repeating what historians of early colonization had in part already emphasized—its social and intellectual aspects—it was easy to overlook the fact that Eggleston had left out everything else.

If it was difficult to perceive how original were the

[96] *Ibid.*, p. 20.

[97] Commentators who have stressed the orthodox nature of Eggleston's *Beginners*: review in *Outlook*, LV (February 6, 1897), 462-463; Herbert Osgood's review in *American Historical Review*, II (April 1897), 528-530; Arthur M. Schlesinger, introduction to *The Transit of Civilization*, Beacon paperbound edition, 1959, p. xvi. Commentators who have emphasized the unorthodoxy: W. P. Trent's review in *Forum*, XXII (November 1897), 590-599; Charles Hirschfeld, "Edward Eggleston: Pioneer in Social History," pp. 201-204.

innovations of Eggleston in *The Beginners*, it was not
hard to see his personal point of view. Reviewers noted
Eggleston's unsympathetic account of the Puritans;[98]
Eggleston had even warned readers of his intention to
debunk, stating in the Preface that he "had not been
able to treat" the founding fathers "otherwise than un-
reverently." He warned that he had "disregarded that
convention which makes it obligatory for a writer of
American history to explain that intolerance in the first
settlers was not just like other intolerance, and that
their cruelty and injustice were justifiable under the
circumstances."[99] The intolerance of the first settlers
was identified with Puritanism in Eggleston's pages,
and Puritanism was vigorously criticized: "When, however, it comes to judging the age itself, and especially
to judging the Puritanism of the age, these false and
harsh ideals are its sufficient condemnation. Its government and its very religion were barbarous."[100]

Complementing Eggleston's condemnation of the
Puritan establishment was praise for such individuals
as Roger Williams or John Robinson, whom Eggleston
pictured as forerunners of modern thought. He praised
Roger Williams as a forward-looking man of the future
who believed in free thought rather than tyranny, and
who believed in uncertainty rather than adherence to
doctrine:

> Here at the very outset of his American life we find
> that Williams had already embraced the broad prin-
> ciple that involved the separation of church and state
> and the most complete religious freedom, and had
> characteristically pushed this principle to its logical

[98] See *Outlook* (February 6, 1897), pp. 462-463; W. P.
Trent's review in *Forum* (November 1897), pp. 590-599.
[99] *The Beginners*, pp. vii-viii.
[100] *Ibid.*, pp. 300-301.

result some centuries in advance of the practice of his age.[101]

And again, he wrote:

It is interesting to know that Williams, the most romantic figure of the whole Puritan movement, at last found a sort of relief from the austere externalism and ceaseless dogmatism of his age by traveling the road of literalism until he had passed out on the other side into the region of devout and contented uncertainty.[102]

Eggleston's criticism of Puritanism contrasted dramatically with the traditional accounts, but in particular it differed strikingly from Moses Coit Tyler's admiring treatment of the early New Englanders. Even what Eggleston did find to praise suggested his different intellectual outlook. Eggleston complimented the Pilgrim leader John Robinson for his "modern" ideas which contrasted with those of his contemporaries, just as Eggleston had praised Williams. "Robinson understood the progressive nature of truth as apprehended by the human mind in a way that makes him seem singularly modern . . . he declared it 'not possible that . . . full perfection of knowledge should break forth at once.' "[103] Eggleston thought he saw in this seventeenth century divine the same attitude toward truth which Eggleston himself had avowed. It was a conception of truth as both relativistic and progressive; truth was apprehended differently in different periods, but became progressively more true. This conception of truth seemed compatible with the contemporary evolutionary and pragmatic thought of Eggleston's day. Eggleston's own concern with scientific ideas, and his belief in the progress of science and skepticism in making a pro-

[101] *Ibid.*, p. 272.   [102] *Ibid.*, p. 304.   [103] *Ibid.*, p. 176.

gressively better world, were distinctive characteristics of his second volume, *The Transit of Civilization.*

Although there was considerable concern for ideas in *The Beginners of a Nation,* it was Eggleston's second and last volume, published in 1900, which was a startlingly original contribution to the history of ideas in America: *The Transit of Civilization: From England to America in the Seventeenth Century.*[104] Eggleston pioneered to such an extent, in fact, that some commentators, in 1900 and afterwards, felt that the book deviated so far from conventional written history as to be pointless and without any comprehensible organization.[105]

The Transit of Civilization was published as the second volume in what was expected to be Eggleston's multivolumed "History of American Life." *The Transit* was not announced as a history of ideas, any more than *The Beginners* had been so announced, but the Preface to the 1900 volume clearly implied that ideas would be featured, and that the ideas would be drawn from previously unexplored areas of colonial intellectual activity. "The complex states of knowing and thinking, of feeling and passion, must be explained," announced Eggleston. "The little world as seen by the man of the seventeenth century must be understood." When Eggleston

[104] Originally published in New York by Appleton and Co. Quotations cited here refer to the 1959 Beacon edition, Boston.

[105] For examples of those who did not know quite what to make of *The Transit,* at the time of publication and since, see Charles Andrews' review in *Political Science Quarterly,* XVII (March 1902), 162-166; Charles Hirschfeld, "Edward Eggleston: Pioneer in Social History," 207-208. Defenders of the volume, on the other hand, have praised its nonpolitical focus, but they have not pointed out explicitly that it was mainly a history of ideas—featuring previously unstudied areas of ideas. An exception is Bernard Bailyn, *Education in the Forming of American Society,* Chapel Hill, 1960, pp. 5-6, who praises it highly.

illustrated briefly what this seventeenth century world was, it turned out to be a world of ideas.

> Its sun, moon, and planets were flames of fire without gravity, revolved about the earth by countless angels; its God governed this one little world with mock majesty. Its heaven, its horrible hell of material fire blown by the mouth of God, its chained demons whose fetters might be loosed, its damnation of infants were to be appreciated and expounded. The inhumanity of punishments and of sport in that day, the mixture made of religion and revenge—these and a hundred other things went to make up the traits of the century.[106]

As Eggleston continued his prefatory remarks, he implied a specific interest in seventeenth century sources of knowledge.

> Eclipses, parhelia, comets, were danger signals hung out in the heavens as warnings. Logic was the only implement for the discovery of truth. Observation was in its birth throes. . . . Right and wrong were thought of only as the result of direct revelation; they had not yet found standing room in the great theater of natural knowledge. Until we understand these things we write the history of the seventeenth century in vain. It is the last age which sought knowledge of physical things by deduction.[107]

Unlike Moses Coit Tyler, Eggleston nowhere actually said he was writing "intellectual history" or a "history of ideas," but he made it clear that he was in effect doing exactly that. Further, Eggleston's prefatory comments implied an interest in a wide variety of areas which had heretofore been untouched.

The variety of the areas is quickly revealed by a sur-

[106] *Ibid.*, p. xxi. [107] *Ibid.*, p. xxii.

vey of the chapters. The first chapter, "Mental Outfit of the Early Colonists," discussed scientific ideas, particularly astronomical ones. Chapter Two, "Digression Concerning Medical Notions at the Period of Settlement," treated early colonial medical thought. Chapter Three, "Mother English, Folk-Speech, Folk-Lore, and Literature," covered these areas of intellectual activity. Chapter Four, "Weights and Measures of Conduct," treated religious ideas in relation to conduct. Chapter Five, "The Tradition of Education," discussed educational ideas and practices. The concluding section, "Land and Labor in the Early Colonies," described laws and customs of real estate and enforced labor in the colonies. In sum, early seventeenth century ideas of astronomy or astrology, medicine, language, subliterature, religion, education, and property were for the first time in American historical writing discussed in relation to each other and in relation to colonial life generally.

The first chapter exemplified the breadth of Eggleston's scope and yet at the same time his focus on the history of ideas. Entitled "Mental Outfit of the Early Colonists," he argued the importance of understanding colonial ideas:

> Seminal ideas received in childhood, standards of feeling and thinking and living handed down from one overlapping generation to another, make the man English or French or German in the rudimentary outfit of his mind. A gradual change in fundamental notions produces the difference between the character of a nation at an early epoch and that of the same people at a later age.[108]

In the first two pages of this opening chapter, Eggleston mentioned in addition to all the synonyms for ideas

[108] *Ibid.*, p. 1.

already quoted, "controlling traditions," "mental furniture," "opinions," "prejudices," "modes of thinking," "intellectual life," "folk-lore," "superstitions," "beliefs," "binding traditions," and "mental outfit." Specifically Eggleston thought ideas about the astronomical world crucial to "the popular imagination in the seventeenth century."[109] Views on astronomy revealed, for example, the relation of scientific to religious thought:

> When modern light began to dawn and science tried to observe, it was not mainly the ordinary and the regular that were noted; members of the new Royal Society and others thought to learn from the monstrosities and marvels; New England ministers acted as soothsayers and expounded the hidden meaning of monstrous births, and even played showmen to exhibit these ghastly messages from the Almighty.

Scientific and religious ideas were related as well to everyday life.

> The world invisible as conceived in every age is a reflection of the familiar material world; the image is often inverted: it may be exaggerated, glorified, distorted, but it is still their own old world mirrored in the clouds of heaven. Even the love of rank and ostentation in the seventeenth century—the snobbery of the age—projected itself into heavenly arrangements.[110]

Eggleston devoted attention to the effect of the New World environment on the imported ideas:

> The American settlers lived in a different world from that which they had left in England, and their conceptions of the invisible could not escape modification. Far removed from the ostentatious conventions of the

[109] *Ibid.*, p. 3.   [110] *Ibid.*, p. 16.

old civilization, the minds of the colonists could no
longer form vivid pictures of heavenly retinues.[111]

Eggleston's opening chapter illustrated also his personal ideology. He repeatedly denigrated the minds of
the seventeenth century and earlier, contrasting them
unfavorably with later minds. References to "that procession of philosophers who with pedantic learning
copied incredibilities from one Latin book to another
down the ages,"[112] to the "never-to-be-questioned authority" of earlier periods, and repeated references to
witchcraft in New England set the tone of Eggleston's
volume. Even the organization of *The Transit* may have
been an expression of Eggleston's unsympathetic attitude toward the past he was describing. The sections
dealing with the scientific ideas of the colonists—those
sections which seemed most absurd to a twentieth century reader—comprised the first one-third of the book
and set the stage for the appearance of the perhaps less
odious remainder of the book. It was a stage set for
unenlightened ideas.

Eggleston's attitude toward the ideas he chronicled
was strikingly different from that of Tyler. Tyler leaned
toward celebrating the ideas he depicted, whereas
Eggleston inclined toward deprecation. In a real sense,
while both focused on the colonial period, Eggleston
wrote a history of "foolish ideas," and Tyler, a history
of "splendid ideas."

The Transit of Civilization, published in 1900, was
Eggleston's last historical writing, and his presidential
address to the American Historical Association, presented in December of 1900, was his last statement
concerning historical scholarship. Eggleston's address,
prepared when he was extremely ill and read for him
because he was unable to attend the meeting, is signifi-

[111] *Ibid.*, p. 18.   [112] *Ibid.*, pp. 12-13.

cant both for the subject matter which he sought to include in written history and for the ideological position which the address revealed.

Eggleston's paper was entitled, "The New History," and this New History was to be largely the "history of culture." When Eggleston spoke for a broadened history which would tell the life of the people, "the real history of men and women," he spoke for historians who, irrespective of their particular social outlooks, objected to history which was primarily political and military in scope. In this vein, Eggleston asked for "the history of culture," history which was "literary," "religious," "cultur-geschichte" [sic]:

> Never was a falser thing said than that history is dead politics and politics living history. Some things are false and some things are perniciously false. This is one of the latter kind. In this saying Freeman expressed his whole theory of history writing, and one understands the point of Green's remark to him: "Freeman, you are neither social, literary, nor religious." A worse condemnation of a historian could hardly be made.[113]

This was not a plea for a separate discipline of intellectual history, but for any broadened history in which the history of ideas would play a large part.

Eggleston predicted that this New History would capture future scholarship, for "when the American Historical Association shall assemble in the closing week a hundred years hence, there will be, do not doubt

[113] *Annual Report of the American Historical Association, 1900*, published in 1901, pp. 39-40. Edward Augustus Freeman (1823-1892) wrote a maxim to the effect that politics constituted the only proper subject matter of history. His friend and fellow English historian, John Richard Green (1837-1883) wrote the pioneering social history, *Short History of the English People* (1874).

it, gifted writers of the history of the people . . . the
history of culture, the real history of men and women."[114]
The New History ought to replace the old-fashioned,
narrow political and military history which, he argued,
was as old as Thucydides. Scientists had constantly
changed their approach with good results, whereas history was unfortunately always written in the same way.
After all, "it would be strange if we had not learned
anything of the art of writing history in a cycle of nearly
twenty-four hundred years. Let us brush aside once for
all the domination of the classic tradition."[115]

The classical histories, which featured politics and
wars, were criticized by Eggleston because of the view
of man and of the human condition which these histories implied. A particular ideology was intimately
associated with this "methodological" plea for different
subject matter. Historians had in effect sanctioned political and military conflict in human affairs, according to
Eggleston, by spotlighting these conflicts. Scholars
should instead help man realize that other aspects of
life were both morally superior and more important.

> Politics is the superficial struggle of human ambi-
> tions crossed occasionally, but rarely, by a sincere
> desire to do good. . . . It often sails under false col-
> ors, and it will deceive the historian unless he is ex-
> ceedingly vigilant. It likes to call itself patriotism.
> . . . But what is patriotism? It is a virtue of the half-
> developed. Higher than tribal instinct and lower than
> that great world benevolence that is to be the mark
> of coming ages.[116]

[114] *Ibid.*, p. 47.   [115] *Ibid.*, p. 38.

[116] *Ibid.*, p. 40. Eggleston expressed his blend of dislike for
scholarship in the service of patriotism, and of disinterest in
politics in a letter to Herbert Baxter Adams, April 14, 1898:
"I dont [*sic*] care for historical study for the sake of American
citizenship. Living right at the door of Congress in this tire-

Mankind should be taught to progress beyond the igno-
bility of politics and to try especially to escape beyond
war, which was the extreme example of human dis-
agreement and conflict. "We can not always cover our
pages with gore. It is the object of history to cultivate
this out of man; to teach him the wisdom of diplomacy,
the wisdom of avoidance—in short, the fine wisdom of
arbitration, that last fruit of human experience."[117] This
plea for minimizing the attention paid to war in written
histories was apparently part of a general desire to write
the history of the past in terms of what Eggleston
hoped would be the future—a future which would bring
greater rationality and increased resolution of conflict
by peaceful means to the human situation.

In 1900 Eggleston not only coined the phrase the
"New History" (under which the history of ideas would
first be publicized after the turn of the century), but
he also expressed many facets of the ideological position shared by these "New Historians." In his colonial
histories, Eggleston pioneered in the writing of the history of ideas and intellectual life in America. Just as
his views contrasted with those of Tyler concerning religion, war, science, human progress and Puritanism,
so did Eggleston's discussion of ideas differ in his histories of ideas from Tyler's. Whereas Tyler celebrated
the grandeur and decisiveness of thought in human affairs, Eggleston saw ideas mainly as an index of how
"progressive" and "modern" life was in the past. The

---

some time I don't seem to care much for American citizenship;
it is a brand that covers a discouraging lot of clap-trap. . . .
I am constitutionally not interested in politics living or dead."
For entire letter see W. Stull Holt, ed., *Historical Scholarship
in the United States, 1876-1901: As Revealed in the Corre-
spondence of Herbert B. Adams*, Baltimore, 1938, pp. 253-254.
  [117] *Ibid.*, p. 41.

study of the history of ideas in the United States in the twentieth century was to be undertaken first by the intellectual followers of Edward Eggleston (even though the followers never referred to their predecessor) rather than by the followers of Moses Coit Tyler.

JAMES HARVEY ROBINSON

PURITAN chroniclers and their eighteenth century successors represented with reasonable accuracy, as far as we know, the dominant attitudes and problems of their local communities. These writers, who were usually leading citizens, interpreted intelligently but in a common-sense way the apparent importance which ideas had in determining men's lives. It seemed obvious to the chroniclers that religious opinions had caused emigrations to the New World, and had influenced the character of society after settlement. Ideas were in this sense assumed to be important by early historians, but that assumption was not joined by analysis as to the precise nature of the role of ideas. And from Bradford through Bancroft, ideas were not focused upon for special treatment.

When American ideas were first featured in late nineteenth century histories by Moses Coit Tyler and Edward Eggleston, legacies from earlier American chroniclers remained. The colonial period, particularly in New England, was studied at length and religious beliefs were assumed to be causally powerful. In these pioneer American histories of ideas, as in earlier writings, common sense rather than intensive analysis, concern with the origin and development of the community or nation rather than detached theory, were characteristic.

In the most important American histories of ideas after 1900, theory and specialization of scholarship became increasingly evident, but even more obvious was the intimate relationship between the New Histories of ideas and the major currents of American social thought. The most influential American ideas concerning man and society, in the years between roughly the turn of the century and World War II, comprised a climate of opinion which can be called intellectually "progressive." Despite complexities, ambiguities, and outright disagreements in the intellectual climate of the period, it is possible to perceive a comparatively unified and coherent predisposition for progressive reform.

The philosophical fountain for this overflowing progressivism was William James' pragmatism and, perhaps even more, John Dewey's variant of pragmatism, instrumentalism. Dewey, whose mature intellectual years spanned the entire first half of this century, drew upon the method of modern science in an attempt to reform the quality of life. At the same time, archaic traditions were subjected by reformers to the stringent test of meeting present needs in areas such as education, law, social work, and government. To experiment freely with hypothetical solutions to current problems until solutions were found, was only to apply the scientific approach to everyday life, said Dewey. It has often been pointed out that ultimate goals were not emphasized by Dewey and other reformers as much as immediate techniques, probably because the ultimate goals were assumed to be agreed upon by the community. Pragmatism's, or instrumentalism's, accent upon "means," and its assumption that men would not disagree seriously as to "ends," marked progressive thought in almost all areas. In its analyses of the various "means" which individuals and societies use, pragmatic thought was empirically hardheaded; in its confident assumption of the ease by which agreements as to "ends" could be achieved, pragmatic thought was somewhat less hardheaded. A blend of slashing analysis and softer dream ran throughout pragmatism, pervaded progressivism generally, and permeated the heart of many of the most important histories of the period. It is easier today to see the leaps of faith of early intellectual progressivism than it is to recapture the excitement stemming from its early breadth of interest and its sense of the relevance of knowledge for everyday life. Out of intellectual progressivism's scholarly investigations and commitment to reform came most of the famous intellectual histories of the first half of the twentieth century.

A closer look at intellectual progressivism as the ideological source of many histories of ideas is possible through an examination of the writings of James Harvey Robinson (1863-1936). He was a historian of Europe rather than of the United States, he made his enormous reputation as a teacher and popularizer instead of as a researcher, but he became the best-known New Historian and publicist for the history of ideas in the United States. An examination of Robinson's writings, and a comparison with the earlier writings of Eggleston, also provokes the interesting question of why progressive histories of ideas were not written sooner.

Robinson was born a generation after the births in the 1830's of Tyler and Eggleston, and he received his first two degrees at Harvard. He followed the proper path for one of his period aspiring to be a professional political historian by going to Germany to complete his formal training. In 1890 he submitted to Hermann Eduard von Holst at Freiburg a revision of his earlier Harvard work entitled, "The Original and Derived Features of the Constitution of the United States."[1] Rob-

[1] For Robinson's biography, see Luther V. Hendricks, *James*

inson's first publications, while he was teaching during the 1890's at the University of Pennsylvania and later at Columbia, featured political-constitutional history and edited collections of documentary source materials —both characteristic of orthodox professional scholarship at the time. Robinson was preoccupied with medieval and early modern political history, and—for a few more years—he expressed little interest in expanding the scope of the subject matter of history, just as, in his academic work, he faced away from contemporary problems.

It might seem in one sense normal that Robinson should have devoted his scholarly energies along the same "fact-finding" and political lines which most professional historians were following at the time. He was a young man attempting to secure a place in his academic discipline. But, in another sense, Robinson's youthful orthodoxy which continued until his late thirties might be considered strange, for after 1900 he became increasingly reformist in his demands for a New History. Furthermore, there were several voices calling for a New History during the late 1800's which Robinson ignored, at least at the time.

Working in Robinson's own field of European history, Henry Thomas Buckle in his *Introduction to the History of Civilization in England* made a plea for present-minded histories which strikingly resembled Robinson's call for New Histories a half-century later. Hippolyte Taine, in his history of English literature, also anticipated a much later Robinsonian concern by

---

Harvey Robinson: Teacher of History, New York, 1946. For Robinson's ideas, see Harry Elmer Barnes, "James Harvey Robinson," *American Masters of Social Science*, Howard W. Odum, ed., New York, 1927, pp. 321-408; Morton White, *Social Thought in America: The Revolt Against Formalism*, New York, 1949, *passim*.

investigating the relationship between ideas and their environments. Among Robinson's own countrymen and fellow members of the American Historical Association, Henry Charles Lea, Andrew Dickson White, Moses Coit Tyler, and Edward Eggleston helped break down the narrow structure of political history which Robinson at the time supported. Tyler's wide sweep of source materials included all kinds of written records so that he announced his subject as the "intellectual history of a nation." Eggleston not only wrote a new kind of history, but entitled his presidential address to the guild "The New History."

Finally, there was an anticipation of Robinson's New History in certain social science scholarship of the late nineteenth century which attempted to contribute to the reform of society through an understanding of past and present historical processes. In the field of economics, for example, leaders in the formation of the American Economic Association in 1885, such as Richard Ely, argued that "this younger political economy no longer permits the science to be used as a tool in the hands of the greedy and avaricious for keeping down and oppressing the laboring classes."[2] The new economics, moreover, was historical in approach, for man's experience rather than classical theory was announced as the proper subject matter. It was indicative of the close relationship existent between historians and economists that the first meeting of the economists in 1885 was held jointly with the historians. Close too was the relationship between the sociologists and the economists during the late 1880's and 1890's. The leaders of the young discipline of sociology were members of the American Economic Association, and they expressed

[2] Richard Ely, "The Past and Present of Political Economy," *Johns Hopkins University Studies*, Second Series, III, March 1884, p. 64.

the same blend of enthusiasm for both science and reform. Sociology had to become empirically oriented and therefore aware of changing historical conditions, said Lester Frank Ward, the founder of American sociology, but at the same time the ultimate goal was to improve society.[3]

James Harvey Robinson was aware of the various late nineteenth century pleas for histories with broadened subject matter, and for scholarship geared to the improvement of contemporary society. But it was not until the turn of the century that he began to show a change of mind in this new direction. He then expressed increasing enthusiasm for a wider conception of the content of written history, for a new reliance on the emergent social sciences, and for histories relevant to the present. In his lectures at Columbia he created the first course in the United States entitled "intellectual history," and in *The New History* (1912), *The Mind in the Making* (1921), and *The Humanizing of Knowledge* (1924), Robinson repeated, systematized, and significantly extended Eggleston's plea for a New History.[4] Robinson protested against the "bias for political history" which resulted in "a great many trifling details of dynasties and military history which merely confound the reader and take up precious space." Vigorously Robinson publicized the need for a written history which would be of greater usefulness to the present day: "The present has hitherto been the willing victim of the past; the time has now come when it should turn on the past and exploit it in the interests of advance."

[3] For a convenient survey of the interrelationships of ideas and individuals in the emergent social sciences during the late nineteenth century, see Sidney Fine, *Laissez-Faire and the General Welfare State*, Ann Arbor, 1956, Chapters 7-8.

[4] *The New History*, New York, 1912; *The Mind in the Making*, New York, 1921; *The Humanizing of Knowledge*, New York, 1924, published for Workers Education Bureau of America.

Robinson's ideal histories were to be important to mankind, rather than being the scribblings of antiquarians.

When Robinson talked of his desired New History, he emphasized its usefulness to progressive social betterment.

> Society is to-day engaged in a tremendous and unprecedented effort to better itself in manifold ways. Never has our knowledge of the world and of man been so great as it now is; never before has there been so much general good will and so much intelligent social activity as now prevails. The part that each of us can play in forwarding some phase of this reform will depend upon our understanding of existing conditions and opinion, and these can only be explained, as has been shown, by following more or less carefully the processes that produced them.[5]

This exploitation of the past for the use of the present would come by virtue of the historian asking questions of contemporary significance, he said. The emphasis on explaining what will happen in the present and future through a study of the past implies laws or uniformities which have validity both in the past and in the future. Thus the social sciences were destined to contribute mightily to the New History. Robinson consciously apotheosized science's methods and achievements, and he hoped to make history more scientific:

> The historian is coming to see that his task is essentially different from that of the man of letters, and that his place is rather among the scientists. He is at liberty to use only his scientific imagination, which is quite different from a literary imagination. . . . He esteems the events he finds recorded, not for their dramatic interest, but for the light that they cast on the

[5] "The New History," *The New History*, pp. 8, 24, 23-24.

normal and generally prevalent conditions which gave rise to them. . . . In this respect history is only following the example set by the older natural sciences.[6]

In urging that history become more scientific, Robinson did not say that historical knowledge could ever become as precise or predictive as, say, knowledge of chemistry, but he pleaded for recognition of history's close relationship to all the sciences, and to the social sciences in particular. With characteristic open-mindedness, Robinson argued that

if history is to reach its highest development it must surrender all individualistic aspirations and recognize that it is but one of several ways of studying mankind. It must confess that, like geology, biology, and most other sciences, it is based on sister sciences, that it can only progress with them, must lean largely on them for support, and in return should repay its debt by the contribution which it makes to our general understanding of our species.[7]

A note of excitement ran throughout Robinson's frequent discussions of the social sciences, an excitement which stemmed from the conviction that the new knowledge derived from the social sciences had radically altered man's understanding of himself. Consequently, Robinson asserted that the New History "will avail itself of all those discoveries that are being made about mankind by anthropologists, economists, psychologists, and sociologists—discoveries which during the past fifty years have served to revolutionize our ideas of the origin, progress, and prospects of our race."[8]

Robinson's enthusiasm for the social sciences, his denigration of traditional history, his dream of model-

[6] "The History of History," *ibid.*, p. 52.
[7] "The New Allies of History," *ibid.*, p. 74.
[8] "The New History," *ibid.*, p. 24.

ing the study of history more closely upon the sciences, and his conception of the uses of the New History for reform were elaborations upon Eggleston and all harked back to Buckle. While there was no doubt diminished hope for scientific exactitude in Robinson's pleas for written histories, as compared with Buckle, there was increased hope for worldly reform. It is not far-fetched to observe that Robinson, by moving from traditional political history in the 1890's to his advocacy of the New History in the early 1900's, had paralleled in his intellectual life the move of many Americans in political allegiance from McKinley in 1896 to support of reform after 1900. Just as Robinson himself had changed his mind, so his interest in the history of thought became in part a study of how people changed their minds.

Robinson's specific interest in the history of ideas was related to his curiosity as to how humans "learned" and "re-learned," which, of course, includes changing their minds. Tyler gloried in the nobility of the early American ideas he described, and Eggleston excoriated the stupidity of the beliefs he depicted, but neither Tyler nor Eggleston pondered in print over theories of learning and intellectual change. Like Eggleston, Robinson looked to the present and to the future for an improvement over the past, but Robinson explained in considerable detail how the study of the history of ideas was going to contribute to man's improved state. Cultivation of the history of ideas was to show how certain ideas originated and developed historically in particular situations. By examining whether the present environment has changed, historians would then be able to show what function these and other ideas play in the present environment. For, asked Robinson,

> what more vital has the past to teach us than the manner in which our convictions on large questions

have arisen, developed and changed? We do not, assuredly, owe most of them to painful personal excogitation, but inherit them, along with the institutions and social habits of the land in which we live. The content of a well-stocked mind is the product of tens of thousands of years of accumulation. Many widespread notions could by no possibility have originated in modern times, but have arisen in conditions quite alien to those of the present. We have too often, in consequence, an outworn intellectual equipment for new and unheard-of tasks. Only a study of the vicissitudes of human opinion can make us fully aware of this and enable us to readjust our views so as to adapt them to our present environment.[9]

The total historical environment responsible for ideas (and for nonintellectual aspects of man's past as well) was, to Robinson, comprised of psychological and intellectual components as well as material ones. This overall environment demanded, in evolutionary fashion, certain responses to it, but the historian should know not only the history of the responses—be they ideas or institutions—but also the history of the causal conditions. Robinson explained, in 1912, that

> contemporaneous religious, educational, and legal ideals are not the immediate product of existing circumstances, but were developed in great part during periods when man knew far less than he now does. Curiously enough our habits of thought change much more slowly than our environment and are usually far in arrears.[10]

[9] *Ibid.*, pp. 102-103.
[10] *Ibid.*, p. 22. There is an Egglestonian tenor to Robinson's remark that these ideals grew up in the past "when man knew far less than he now does."

"Existing circumstances," including an understanding of the state of knowledge in the past, would thus be needed to understand the origin of religious, educational, and legal ideals. Robinson assumed that the existing historical environment prodded human thought to change, and he assumed that this was a good thing. He argued that a proper historical examination of the origin and development of ideas, in relation to their changing environments, would show whether or not present ideas were up-to-date and rightly adjusted to the contemporary environment. Robinson's discussion usually tended to emphasize the outmoded ideas which he hoped would be changed:

> Our respect for a given institution or social convention may be purely traditional and have little relation to its value, as judged by existing conditions. We are, therefore, in constant danger of viewing present problems with obsolete emotions and of attempting to settle them by obsolete reasoning. This is one of the chief reasons why we are never by any means perfectly adjusted to our environment.
>
> Our notions of a church and its proper function in society, of a capitalist, of a liberal education, of paying taxes, of Sunday observance, of poverty, of war, are determined only to a slight extent by what is happening today. The belief on which I was reared, that God ordained the observance of Sunday from the clouds of Sinai, is an anachronism which could not spontaneously have developed in the United States in the nineteenth century; nevertheless, it still continues to influence the conduct of many persons.[11]

Robinson's most emphatic utterances quoted here are to the effect that new, good ideas, which are well adjusted to present day conditions, need to be widely ac-

[11] *Ibid.*, pp. 22-23.

cepted for the cause of better, more efficient personal and social action. But beneath this hope that new ideas will be accepted that fit the environment, can be detected Robinson's belief that at some earlier time in history it was the environment itself which called these now out-dated ideas into being. In his pleas for changing certain old ideas, it is quite true that he stressed the current, temporary inapplicability of these ideas. But he viewed their persistence not as testimony to their independent strength, but rather to the fact that temporarily the new and different environmental conditions had not as yet compelled these old ideas to be altered. Robinson thought that time would finally see the demise of ideas hopelessly unrelated to their environment, and that the environment would be ultimately responsible for their demise as it was for their origin.[12] In this strain of Robinson's thought, ideas were ultimately creatures, rather than creators, of the environment. Human thought was a tool which was fashioned by an environmental crucible to help man adjust to his changing environment. Of all environmental components, and Robinson emphasized that both psychology and the state of knowledge were important components, he thought the one most crucial was the economic factor.[13]

[12] The same phenomenon—the existence of ideas not in harmony with their environment—could obviously also have been interpreted as evidence that ideas are strikingly independent of environmental conditions.

[13] Robinson called the economic interpretation of history the best "single explanation ever offered." See "The History of History," *The New History*, pp. 50-51:

Few, if any, historians would agree that everything can be explained economically, as many of the socialists and some economists of good standing would have us believe. But in the sobered and chastened form in which most economists now accept the doctrine, it serves to explain far more of the phenomena of the past than any other single explanation ever offered. In any case, it is the economist who has opened up the most fruitful new fields of research by emphasizing

It is striking that Robinson did not develop his assumption that historical environments significantly determine the character of human thought into a theory of the historical relativism of ideas. He did not because he, like Eggleston, was too much an evolutionist, too much a believer in the progressive improvement of human history. Robinson's conviction that society had evolved and was still evolving into a better society was the basic reason for the fact that he was an environmental interpreter but not a relativist. The same conviction was also related to the fact that Robinson did not emphasize an environmental interpretation as much when he referred to the origin and development of some ideas as when he discussed others.

The numerous quotations from Robinson already cited have revealed that when he emphasized the influence of some particular historic environment as an explanation for the origin and development of certain ideas, the ideas were most often those to which he was not sympathetic and whose replacement he was urging. "Outworn" ideas in the early 1900's concerning religion generally and Christianity specifically, ideas about education, capitalism, poverty, war, and the law were deprecated by Robinson as products of historic environments. In depicting various kinds of thinking, Robinson characterized, with obvious pejorative connotation, as "rationalizations" those ideas which people have unthinkingly absorbed from their environment:

> The "real" reasons for our beliefs are concealed from ourselves as well as from others. As we grow up we simply adopt the ideas presented to us in regard to such matters as religion, family relations, property,

---

the importance of those enduring but often inconspicuous factors which almost entirely escaped historians before the middle of the nineteenth century.

business, our country, and the state. We unconsciously absorb them from our environment.

Rationalizing ideas usually have their roots in self-interest: "*Rationalizing is the self-exculpation which occurs when we feel ourselves, or our group, accused of misapprehension or error.*" Or, again: "We are by nature stubbornly pledged to defend our own from attack, whether it be our person, our family, our property, or our opinion."[14] Throughout Robinson's comments emphasizing the decisive power of the environment in forming thought, a tenor of criticism of the resulting thought is evident.[15]

But Robinson did not always emphasize the power of the environment in originating and developing ideas. There was another strain in his remarks on the nature of ideas, a strain which stressed the creativity of ideas and their independence from any environmental influence. He expressed this view of human thought when referring to ideas he admired. Minimizing the influence of any environmental factors in influencing these ideas, Robinson labeled them "creative thought," in contrast to "rationalizations." Creative thought, he said,

is not the defense of our own cherished beliefs and prejudices just because they are our own—mere plausible excuses for remaining of the same mind. On the contrary, it is that peculiar species of thought which leads us to *change* our mind.

It is this kind of thought that has raised man from his pristine, subsavage ignorance and squalor to the

[14] *The Mind in the Making*, pp. 42-43, 44, 41.

[15] And, strangely enough, this critical tenor was present despite the fact that Robinson was virtually in the same breath urging that old ideas be brought into adjustment with new environments. The contradiction is explained only by the differing degrees of sympathy he felt for the ideas being discussed in each case.

degree of knowledge and comfort which he now possesses.

The most impressive examples of "creative intelligence" to Robinson were modern scientific ideas, "the most striking instances of the effects of scrupulous, objective thinking."[16] Whereas rationalizations were ideas as instruments in the sense that the environment molded them, creative ideas were instruments in a sense which defined their creative force as coming from thought itself. Creative thought was an instrument which could be used to change, to reform, the environment.

Robinson might be called an "environmental-relativist" when destructively criticizing ideas which he disliked, and a "progressive-absolutist" when praising ideas of which he approved. There were thus two sides to Robinson's conception of the influence of ideas in human affairs, but both sides were built on a common foundation: the faith or hope that man had improved and would continue to improve his situation significantly. Robinson's belief in progress was intertwined with his whole ideological position. He shared the progressivism of many later historians which was expressed by all of them in piecemeal fashion rather than in a philosophical system. Robinson viewed modern society in western Europe and in the United States as constituting the zenith in human achievement, and challengers of this alleged superiority—defenders of ancient Greece, for example—irritated Robinson considerably. He pointed out that "The Greeks had no telescopes, nor microscopes, nor thermometers, nor spectroscopes. Their knowledge was at best the result of what would seem to us crude and haphazard observation which tended to take the form of accepted authority." In addition to modern experimental science constituting evidence of

[16] *The Mind in the Making*, pp. 48-49, 55.

human progress, in Robinson's eyes, there was also strong evidence for progress in the fact that "the democratic spirit" continued to develop. Indeed, the newer social sciences were related to modern democratic thought, according to Robinson:

> It is this appreciation of the common man which is reflected in our development of social sciences, undreamed of by the Greeks, and in the socializing of older subjects, such as psychology and ethics. Political economy was born in the eighteenth century; in the nineteenth anthropology developed on a large scale, together with the comparative study of religions, sociology, and social psychology.[17]

Robinson was equally optimistic about industrialism, urbanization, and increased communication. The industrial revolution provoked "unsuspected possibilities of social readjustment and the promotion of human happiness." He wrote:

> Associated with these same economic changes is the development of world-commerce and of incredibly efficient means of communication, which have brought mankind together throughout the whole earth in a spirit of competition, emulation, and co-operation. It will not be many years before every one on the face of the globe can read and write and be in a position through our means of intercommunication to follow the course of events in every portion of the earth. This astonishing condition of affairs suggests boundless possibilities of human brotherhood.[18]

So deep was Robinson's optimistic belief in progress that he virtually equated "change" and "betterment." He stated that "history, *namely change*, has been mainly

---

[17] "Reflections on Intellectual History," *ibid.*, pp. 123-124.
[18] *Ibid.*, pp. 125, 126.

due to a small number of 'seers,'—really gropers and monkeyers—whose native curiosity outran that of their fellows and led them to escape here and there from the sanctified blindness of their time."[19]

Robinson thought that the progress achieved in the past had been largely unconscious, but it had become increasingly realized that man could consciously direct even more rapid progress: this realization was the birth of the idea of human progress.

> The nineteenth century proved conclusively that he [man] *had* been learning and *had* been bettering himself for hundreds of thousands of years. But all this earlier progress had been *unconscious*. For the first time, close upon our own day, progress became an ideal consciously proclaimed and sought. So, whatever the progress of man has been during the twelve hours which we assign to him since he became a man, it was only at about one minute to twelve *that he came to wish to progress, and still more recently that he came to see that he can voluntarily progress, and that he has progressed*. This appears to me to be the most impressive message that history has to give us, and the most vital in the light that it casts on the conduct of life.

The concept of progress thus seemed to Robinson "the greatest single idea in the whole history of mankind."[20] With the help of this idea, man could more efficiently bend history to his own ends. What these ends were, for Robinson, has perhaps already been suggested because Robinson's social thought permeated his historical writing.

Democratic social reform was of course important in

[19] *The Mind in the Making*, pp. 79-80.
[20] "The Spirit of Conservatism," *The New History*, pp. 251-252, 247.

Robinson's thought, and it was linked with pacifistic sentiment.[21] Robinson felt that "The abolition of poverty and disease and war, and the promotion of happy and rational lives" could be successful if people would simply look forward to the potential future rather than backward to what has always been. "The reformer who appeals to the future is a recent upstart," but "it is clear enough today that the conscious reformer who appeals to the future is the final product of a progressive order of things." Indeed, Robinson thought that "the long-disputed sin against the Holy Ghost has been found; it

[21] The precise extent of Robinson's pacifism is difficult to determine from his published writings. It is obvious that he thought World War I and American participation in it disappointingly irrational.

In *The Mind in the Making* (1921), while criticizing the great cost of the traditional, "muddling through" approach to social relations, Robinson brought up the First World War:

An arresting example of what this muddling may mean we have seen during these recent years in the slaying or maiming of fifteen million of our young men, resulting in incalculable loss, continued disorder, and bewilderment. Yet men seem blindly driven to defend and perpetuate the conditions which produced the last disaster. (p. 13)

It seems also, but this is a matter of tone rather than explicit statement, that Robinson afterwards regarded American participation in World War I as a disastrous mistake. See his 1929 presidential address to the American Historical Association:

Beginning with 1914 the old ways of historians were put to a fearful test. How did these old ways bear the test? Very badly, as I think we must all admit. Did such knowledge as historians have arduously accumulated of the past serve to make them wiser than their fellows? Hardly. In all countries they were unable to overcome their native susceptibility to the prejudices of their particular tribe. They applauded the old battle cries. They blew trumpets and grasped halberds. They gulped down propaganda which in a later mood they realized was nauseous. They were, in short, easily sold out, for their studies had not prepared them to assess the sudden emotional crisis much better than the man in the street. ("The Newer Ways of Historians," *American Historical Review*, xxxv [January 1930], 252.)

She felt her anger simmering just below the surface, and occasionally tiny sparks shot from her eyes or her fingers. It was past time to embrace the destruction inside her and let it out.

That night, after she nursed her aches, she practiced directing her magic. It came a little easier this time, and she managed not to knock herself out. She destroyed a small bone to pieces, missing it only twice before backing up a little and hitting it right where she intended to.

When she'd used up the last of her energy after the long day, she prepared to sleep. And that's when she heard the three sharp knocks on the back wall.

Her eyes flew open, and then she realized who it must be. Despite feeling exhausted, Thisbe climbed up the bone pile, all the way to the small space along the back wall, near the ceiling. She picked up a bone—a dragon toe, it must have been—about the size of her forearm. She pounded the wall with it three times, and was surprised at the loud sound it made. She hadn't expected that with solid rock.

A moment later came the response. Two knocks this time. A warm feeling came over Thisbe. Two knocks—it felt like Rohan was saying "good night" in a secret language. It reminded her of the secret language Lani and Samheed had made up when they'd been captives on Warbler, only they'd been together and had used their fingers to tap in each other's cupped hands.

Pound, pound, Thisbe replied, and whispered, "Good night." It might not be what Rohan had intended. It might be nothing but a way to feel human by communicating. But it was very comforting to Thisbe to think it, so she did.

Secret Training

By the next day in Artimé, Henry's magical medicines had done their job quite thoroughly, and he declared that Fifer was well enough to leave the hospital ward. No one but the falcon was around to celebrate it with her—Seth and Alex were in the middle of Magical Warrior Training on the lawn, and Crow had left to be with his mother and Scarlet on Warbler. Aaron had gone back to the Island of Shipwrecks by now so that Kaylee could be here to train.

Fifer took the bird outside in case it wanted to fly away, but it stayed on her shoulder most of the time, only fluttering to the ground now and then to catch bugs or sip from dew on the grass. It seemed to want to stay with Fifer. But she still wasn't sure it was a good idea to keep the poor bird trapped inside the mansion. So she set it down and urged it to fly away. Even as fond as she'd grown of it, she wanted it to be free to make the decision to stay with her or move along.

Eventually the colorful falcon flew to a tree. Fifer, growing tired, went back inside. Noting the time, she took the tube to her theater class and sat in the shadows of the auditorium. Onstage Samheed and Ms. Claire Morning, who lived in Quill now but still taught music in Artimé, directed some of the dancers for a new musical Lani and Samheed had written together. Thisbe was supposed to be in it, but her spot on the stage was glaringly empty.

Before class ended, Fifer slipped out and went unnoticed back to the mansion's entryway, then outside again to see if the bird was sitting there, but it wasn't. Fifer saw Carina with Seth's younger siblings, six-year-old Ava and five-year-old Lukas, starting to gather flower petals for the dragon wings. She sighed. If only she and Seth had had proper items to work with, Alex and the others wouldn't have to remake the wings.

It put Fifer in a foul mood. She felt like nobody really understood what she and Seth had gone through to make the new wings—all the pressure they'd faced with so little material. She went back inside and caught a glimpse of Alex and Florence through the west window, working outside on the private lawn again. Fifer pulled a stool from the kitchen so she could sit and watch the proceedings.

Just like he'd done the previous day, Alex was practicing his throwing technique. Sweat poured down his temples as he concentrated on an imaginary target. Ms. Octavia was out there today too, and Fifer watched, fascinated, as Alex graduated to using actual components. After some time doing that, Ms. Octavia bravely volunteered to play the part of the enemy, as many more-advanced mages of Artimé often did for the sake of the ones in training.

Alex wound up and flung a handful of scatterclips at Ms. Octavia. They veered wildly to one side and seemed unsure what their target was, then appeared to lose momentum. The thin pieces of metal sailed to the ground, doing nothing. "Buckets," muttered Alex. He tried again and again, working hours to develop his skills.

LISA McMANN

As Alex did so, Fifer paid vast attention and memorized everything. She took in the way Florence taught him to stand and wind up and flick his wrist and hook his elbow just so. Fifer soon slipped off her stool and imitated the movements.

Every now and then, Florence glanced through the window to see if Fifer was there. But Fifer stayed back in the shadows. At one point she lifted her fingers and waved them, and Florence nodded satisfactorily. Florence was teaching her, too. On purpose. At least Fifer would be able to defend herself . . . if she ever got any components. Which wouldn't happen until Alex said so, or until she turned thirteen. But she was using her time wisely now in preparation.

After a while, when Florence switched to working with Alex on building his strength, Fifer went up to her room, where she hadn't spent any time since before she and Thisbe had left. It felt empty without Thisbe there.

Fifer practiced her scatterclips throw a few times, mimicking what she'd seen Florence teach Alex. Then she found some loose buttons from a sweater that no longer fit her and ripped them off so she could pretend they were components. She threw them across the room at the wall, aiming for the center of her blackboard. They hit dead on.

Desdemona surfaced, pushing her face from the screen. "What was that?" she said, trying to look all around.

"Nothing," said Fifer, hoping the buttons had fallen out of sight. "Sorry I bumped you."

"I heard you were back. I'm glad you're okay. I'm sorry about Thisbe."

"Thanks."

Desdemona raised an eyebrow, warning Fifer not to throw things at her again, then melted into the blackboard. Fifer picked up the buttons and put them in her pocket. She'd have to practice somewhere else.

She went into her bedroom and looked out her window— the one that she and Thisbe had climbed out of—and watched as a small group of people and creatures gathered on the big lawn for what appeared to be a special session of Advanced Magical Warrior Training.

Fifer placed her hand on the window. "Release," she whispered, wanting to be able to hear what was happening. The glass pane melted away, and Fifer turned her ear toward the outside, hoping some of the verbal instructions

LISA McMANN

would be carried on the wind all the way up to her room.

Florence led the team in practicing their spells as they got ready to rescue Thisbe, and Fifer absorbed everything she could.

Seth was down there with the more advanced mages, and that made Fifer feel bad again about Alex not letting her go with them. He was trying out a small red heart-shaped component for what seemed like the first time. Fifer guessed it was a heart attack spell—Seth had told her and Thisbe that the heart attack spell wasn't something the beginning mages usually got to try, and he hadn't had any of those components before today. She was sure Florence and Carina and Alex had made an exception for Seth since he was going on the rescue. Fifer's expression flickered. No exceptions were to be made for her.

Just then Samheed sent off a handful of scatterclips with a wild throw, leaving him yelping in pain and holding his shoulder. The scatterclips struck Florence and sent her careering backward into the mansion wall, making the whole building shake. When Florence pulled herself out of the giant dent she'd made, she looked sternly at Samheed.

"Sorry," said Samheed meekly. "I think I pulled a muscle."

LISA McMANN

"You all need to do strength training too," Florence declared. "Everybody drop and give me twenty push-ups."

Seth groaned and flopped to the ground, and Fifer could see he was already tired and sweaty by the way his blond hair stood up. He hated exercise. Fifer took a tiny bit of satisfaction from it, but not too much.

Then Florence turned to Alex. "You see? This is why we have to take the time to train. There's only one person I can think of who needs less training than any of you, but you won't let her go. So. Get moving."

Fifer's lips parted. Florence was talking about her. Tears sprang to her eyes, and she strained to hear Alex's response.

"Okay, I get it," Alex said begrudgingly. "We're all really out of practice. We want to get this right." But he didn't say anything about changing his mind to let Fifer go with them. Instead he frowned and eased to the ground to attempt twenty one-armed push-ups, and was already faltering by the time he finished the third one.

After a moment Fifer stopped watching. She replaced the glass and sank onto her bed, her chin quivering. Across the room, Thisbe's bed was empty and unmade from when they'd

LISA McMANN

snuck out. Carina, Seth, Lani, Samheed, Alex, and Thatcher were all outside training. Even Talon and Kaylee were out there with their swords, all of them getting ready to rescue Thisbe. And Fifer would be stuck here alone, with only a little knowledge and a handful of useless shirt buttons. And a bird, maybe—unless it had decided to leave her too. It wasn't fair.

She fell into a restless sleep and was awakened by the sound of Desdemona calling to her. Bewildered, Fifer fought her way out of her sheets and rolled out of bed. She glanced out the window and saw that the training session was over, then staggered to the living area feeling woozy. "What is it?"

The blackboard personality wore a puzzled look. "Seth sent a message. He says you should go outside the main entrance—there's something on the front lawn you've got to see."

A Change of Heart

Feeling a bit better after her nap, Fifer made her way down the grand mansion staircase, past Carina and her little ones in the entryway, who were back to collecting and stacking items for the new dragon wings. Fifer opened the huge entry door and went outside to look for Seth. Instantly a small flock of large red-and-purple falcons squawked and fluttered about, then settled around her. The one that had stayed with her earlier was front and center, strutting a little, then going right up to Fifer's feet and flying up to land on her shoulder. She winced as its talons gripped her right where her wounds were healing. "Well, hello there. I see you've brought friends."

LISA McMANN

Seth came walking up behind the flock, an amused expression on his face. "I think your new bird wants to show you off."

"Weird, isn't it?" said Fifer, but she was pleased. She turned to look at the bird. "What's going on with you, Shimmer?" she murmured. The name seemed to fit. She petted it, making it shine brightly, then knelt in the grass, being careful not to startle the falcon on her shoulder. The other birds crowded around her, their necks darting out like pigeons going for seeds, trying to get Fifer to pet them, too. She did, and each of them shimmered extraordinarily brightly as well.

Just then Alex rounded the corner of the quiet west side of the mansion with Florence. Had they done a second session today? He was training hard. Alex waved but kept going—he seemed like he didn't want anyone to ask what he'd been doing. "It's great to see you up and around! I've got to help with the wings," he added apologetically, and slipped inside. But Florence stopped when she saw Fifer and Seth surrounded by birds, and went over to them. "How are you feeling, Fifer?"

"A lot better. Just a little tired."

"You've been watching the side yard, haven't you?" She

nodded in the direction of where she and Alex had been working.

Fifer nodded. "Yeah. Thanks," she said quietly. "It means a lot that you trust me."

"As the Magical Warrior trainer, I made an executive decision. I want you to be able to defend yourself. But let's not mention that to your brother just yet."

"Okay."

Florence took a closer look at the birds, who hadn't scattered when she approached, which seemed odd since she was such a large presence. "And . . . these birds? Why are they shining like that? Did you make them do that?"

"I didn't do anything but pet them, I promise," said Fifer a bit defensively, since she was used to people in Artimé accusing her and Thisbe of doing magic when they weren't supposed to.

Florence flashed a sympathetic smile. "It's okay. I think you did something to them, though. Nothing bad." She knelt and observed the birds. "Have you ever petted the birds before when they've come to you after one of your screams?"

"I—I don't know," said Fifer. "I don't think so. I've never really thought about it. I usually just shoo them away because

Thisbe is afraid of them. But since she's gone, I've let them stay . . . and now they don't seem to want to leave." She looked down at the birds. Thinking of Thisbe, Fifer was reminded of all the things she was worried about. She turned her face to Florence's concerned gaze. "Any chance you've been able to convince Alex to let me go on the rescue?"

Florence sighed. "Not yet." She didn't seem hopeful that she would succeed. "I'm trying."

"I know. I'm going to ask him myself," she said. "I'm feeling better every day."

"I'll go with you if you want," Seth offered.

Fifer shrugged. She was still feeling a bit jealous of him, but maybe he could help. "Okay." She lifted the bird off her shoulder and set it on the grass, then went inside with Seth right behind. They followed the noise to Ms. Octavia's classroom, where Carina and Alex and a few others were just starting to assemble the first of many gorgeous wings for the dragons, sculpted from thick jungle vines and the finest cloth and prettiest flower petals in Artimé.

Seth and Fifer looked at the beautiful creation, then glanced at each other, shook their heads, and laughed ruefully. "It's so beautiful," Fifer said, thinking of the horrid tree-branch-and-burlap-feed-bag wings *they'd* made back at the castle.

"I'm almost embarrassed about what we did to those poor dragons' wings," said Seth.

"I'm not," Fifer declared. "We freed them. Who cares what they looked like as long as they worked." She looked at her friend. "We did magic that only Alex had done before. You and me."

"That's true." Seth and Fifer made their way through the various workstations to where Alex was standing, looking over Ms. Octavia's sketches for each of the five young dragons.

"Hi, Alex," said Fifer.

Alex smiled and looked up. "Hi. Feeling better? It's nice to see you walking around."

"Yep. I'll be good enough to go with you to rescue Thisbe in a few weeks."

Alex squeezed his eyes shut and sighed deeply, ending it with a slight shake of the head. "Here we go," he muttered. "Don't you ever let up? The answer is no, Fife. You're staying home. No more discussion." He turned back to the sketches.

Fifer looked at him and suddenly felt exhausted. It wasn't

LISA McMANN

that she hadn't expected this response. And she'd planned to cajole and plead like she always did. She'd planned to list all the reasons why she was capable of going, why she'd be an asset to the team, why she of all people would be the absolute best person to have along because of her relationship with Thisbe and her experience in the land of the dragons and her magical strength. But for some reason, all those arguments became unbearably tiresome to repeat. Because this was Alex she was talking to. And the truth was that her reasoning wouldn't work anyway. It would only result in a fight.

Fifer couldn't explain why, but right now she couldn't stand the thought of another heated argument with Alex. She narrowed her eyes and muttered something unintelligible, almost like she was having an argument with herself. It wasn't worth it.

After a moment Alex glanced at her, surprised she wasn't saying anything.

Fifer remained silent as something inside her twisted and ached and groaned in its unsettledness. Her lips parted and closed. And all she could do was stare at him, her eyes growing shiny, but this time she willed the tears away. She was done with those—done with that way of trying to convince her brother to let her do things. Sick and tired of the arguments that never changed his mind. Her whole body seemed heavily weighed down by this mundane method that wasn't working, and she couldn't carry it anymore.

Maybe it was because she was still recovering and feeling weak and tired. Maybe it was because Thisbe wasn't there this time to help her. And maybe it was because Fifer finally found her own inner strength after what she'd gone through, and she'd realized that the harder she begged, the more Alex dug in his feet to oppose her. He didn't understand that she had changed in the short time she'd been away. And he wasn't trying to either—he'd hardly asked her any questions about what they'd accomplished, choosing to focus only on how they'd failed. And that wasn't fair. But Fifer was done waiting for Alex to catch up to figuring out her level of ability. She was done being shot down. Forever.

"Okay, Alex," said Fifer quietly. She looked away, not wanting to see his look of victory. "Okay. I'm finished trying to get you to see my way. I am so much stronger and more capable than you think I am, but I'm done trying to convince you to see what you don't want to see. And I'm tired of fighting you. You're wrong. And you're selfish and stubborn and you won't admit it. And I've had enough of that. So go do your thing with your team and leave me out of it, just like you planned. You'll realize once you get there that I could have helped you. But by then it'll be too late." She hesitated, then added, "And if you mess this up and it costs me my sister, I will never, ever forgive you. And I will focus on your failures just like you focus on mine."

Alex's eyes widened in shock and pain, and for a moment he was too taken aback to reply.

Seth poked Fifer's arm to show her that others had paused in their work and turned to listen to their discussion.

Alex set the sketches down and looked squarely at Fifer. "Of course I won't mess up," he said softly. "And Thisbe is my sister too," he said. "I know you don't think I can run things properly, but I can assure you we'll be going in extremely prepared. That's why we're taking all this time."

Fifer frowned. Is that what Alex thought? That Fifer didn't think he was capable? She didn't care to find out. Ignoring everyone, she whirled abruptly. Then she walked back the way she'd come, with Alex and the whole room staring after her in shock.

River of Tears

The next few days Thisbe threw herself into the task of dragging two bones a day. Her muscles ached, and she was sore where the harness cut into her skin, leaving her bruised and bloodied, but she didn't let up. She knew that the faster she went, the more time she'd have in the evenings to work on her magical abilities.

Every day she saw Rohan twice in passing—when he came up behind her on the way to the extraction laboratory and when he passed her again as he was coming back. He always offered a sympathetic smile, and at first he tried to help her, but she consistently refused. She didn't want him to get caught, for one. But there was something else driving her refusal as well. Thisbe didn't want help because she knew she could do it herself. Sure, it hurt. Sure, it took her longer. But she wasn't incapable. And she didn't want to feel like she owed anybody anything. And besides, she was growing stronger muscles all the time from it. That would help her when she took on the Revinir and the entire blue army once she was good and ready. It was like she was in training.

Every night, after hours of concentrating on directing her magic accurately, Thisbe heard Rohan's knocks on the back wall. He always began with three knocks and waited for Thisbe. She responded with three, or sometimes four. Then he with two, and she with two. Thisbe often made up words to match the initial three knocks. "How are you?" she imagined him saying, and she would respond with five knocks. "I am doing well." Sometimes she imagined him saying, "I am here." She'd respond with four knocks. "I am here too."

They'd always end the same way, though, with two knocks each. "Good night." "Good night."

Often, after the satisfying final knocks, Thisbe would close her eyes and fall asleep imagining asking Rohan about their ritual the next day in the passageways. But the next day, she wouldn't do it. For some reason it embarrassed her. What if he was just doing it out of boredom and thought she was making too much of it by imagining conversations to go with the knocks? What if he laughed at her? What if, out of the context of her lonely crypt, her imagining him saying "I am here" sounded as dumb as it did when she said it out loud in the passageway. It was enough to bring heat to her face. "Ridiculous," she muttered. "Of course you're here. Where else would you be?"

A few days later, as Thisbe passed the steep side hallway near the testing room, she realized no one was around. She hesitated, then took the risk and went up it toward the exit so she could have a closer look at the river—and have another glance at the sky she missed so much. She peered around the corner and saw a group of soldiers standing near the rushing river, guarding the path.

One of the soldiers saw her. "Hey!" the woman shouted, then said something else in a different language.

"I don't understand you," Thisbe said falteringly.

"I said come over here. Did you understand that?"

"Yes." Thisbe was surprised to be called over, and a bit suspicious, but she really wanted a closer look. She didn't think the soldiers would do anything bad to her without the Revinir's command, so she felt safe enough to obey. She strained against her harness, dragging the bones up the steep incline, and approached.

"Yes, ma'am?" Thisbe said as she got closer. None of these soldiers looked familiar.

"What are you doing up here?" asked the soldier. "This hallway isn't on your designated path."

"I know." Thisbe looked up with as much respect as she could muster as she tried to come up with a plausible reason. "I'm . . . I'm just really thirsty. So I thought maybe I could stop for a drink at the river." She tried not to appear like she was gauging the distance across the river and looking to see what it would take to get across it. It was far, that was for sure. Too far to swim with the water moving so fast.

The woman waved her away. "Get on with you. Drink your water in the testing room or your crypt."

Thisbe dropped her gaze. "I'm sorry, ma'am. I will." Her eye caught on a tarnished gold plaque on the rocky ground along the river's edge. There were two words on it.

"Aw, let her get a drink," said one of the other soldiers, a man this time. "She's just a pea, dragging twice her weight in bones. That isn't fair, if you ask me. We can at least afford her some water."

Thisbe hesitated, strangely touched that he'd noticed her heavy load, and kept her eyes down, glad for the extra time it bought her to check things out. She focused on the plaque. It said RIVER TAVEER.

"Watch it," the female soldier warned her fellow guard. "Don't be going soft."

"It's only water," muttered the man. "Forget it, then. Get on with you, kid."

Thisbe nodded and turned away. "Sorry."

"Aw, hang on," said the woman impatiently, apparently softening herself. "Hurry up and get your drink. If you try anything, we'll shove you in the river. Those bones will sink you in an instant."

"Thanks." Thisbe quickly moved to the river's edge as the two soldiers hovered over her. She knelt on the golden plaque and slipped her hand in the cold clear water, watching it rush over her fingers for a moment as it chased along. She closed her

LISA McMANN

eyes, feeling an unidentifiable pain of longing rip through her. It made her limbs tremble, and it almost took her breath away.

"Hurry up!" said the woman again, and shoved the toe of her boot into Thisbe's side.

Thisbe gasped and opened her eyes. She began scooping water to her mouth as quickly as she could, letting some of it splash on her face. She sucked it down, refreshingly cold and clean and delicious, like the water in Artimé. An unexpected sob escaped her, but the noise was covered by the roar of the river. She splashed more water on her face to cover all evidence of her sorrow. Then she rested her hand on the golden plaque, her fingertips slipping into the chiseled grooves of the letters, and another wretched sob came from out of nowhere. Thisbe's insides were breaking, and she had no idea why.

"That's enough," said the woman, not as harshly. "Let's go."

Thisbe choked and sobbed as she got to her feet. Tears and water blinding her, she shuddered in her overwhelming sorrow and stumbled blindly over the dragon bones, tangling up in her harness and nearly falling. The soldiers caught her by the elbows and set her on her feet.

"Thank you," she choked out.

The soldiers, not knowing what to think, quickly released her and stood back awkwardly, their expressions conflicted.

Thisbe dried her face on her sleeve and took a deep breath, trying to get her bearings. Then she yanked the bones around so they'd properly follow her. She fled as fast as she could, hurrying away with her head down and wondering how on earth she'd be able to escape this maze with that river so ominous. Why had the soldiers even let her get a drink in the first place? And what was happening to her insides that would force those sobs out at such an inopportune moment?

The soldiers were silent as they watched her go, their faces flickering in ways they hadn't flickered in years under the Revinir's rule. But Thisbe didn't have the faintest clue.

LISA McMANN

Breaking Down

That evening was long and lonely. Somehow Thisbe had missed Rohan on his way back from the extraction room—he'd probably gone past while she'd been by the river sobbing like a two-year-old. She still didn't know what had come over her. But there was a gnawing emptiness inside that wouldn't go away and seemed to be growing larger.

Of course she missed her sister and prayed she was alive, but she couldn't stand to dwell on Fifer, because it made her feel helpless and hopeless. And Thisbe felt so distanced from everyone else in Artimé—where were they? Why had they left her here? She wished she could send a seek spell, but she didn't have anything with her that was created by someone else—Fifer had the bit of script written by Seth. She was losing hope of ever knowing the answer. It made her feel numb all over. Perhaps that was how her body was protecting her—the numbness giving her the ability to survive and carry out her strenuous tasks. But today at the river a gaping wound had surfaced, and she hadn't been able to tamp it down. Would the edges of it heal eventually? Would her numbness ever wear away? Or was Thisbe supposed to be grateful for it?

She didn't have it in her to work on her magic tonight. Instead she lay listlessly on the floor in the bone dust, eyes on the ceiling, wondering how many feet of rock stood between her and the moonlight. Wondering what would happen if she tried to break through the ceiling. Would it fall in on her? Crush her? It seemed likely. Did it matter? Thisbe's eyes widened. Yes. Of course it mattered. She was not going to give up.

She thought about her options of escape. Would she be better off trying to overcome the soldiers at the elevator? But she had no idea how to control it. Even if she could kill all the guards there, could she figure out quickly enough how to make it shoot upward and out of the catacombs before more soldiers came running?

And what about Rohan?

Thisbe blinked. She sat up. What about Rohan? And why did she even care? This escape was about her, and only her. She couldn't worry about anyone else. Unless he could help somehow. But there was no way to really talk with him. No way to discuss a plan for any meaningful length of time. And she didn't know if she could trust him to keep her secret. All they had were her imaginings of things said through knocks on the back wall. Not exactly reliable.

And speaking of knocks on the back wall, there hadn't been any tonight. Thisbe looked up at the place where she usually pounded, as if that would magically tell her why there was no sound coming from it. It felt late—late enough that Thisbe should already be asleep. But maybe time was passing more slowly than usual this evening. It was hard to tell.

After a few more minutes, Thisbe felt sure it was much later than when Rohan usually pounded. Had something happened to him? She recalled that she'd seen him only once that day, when he'd passed her early in the morning. She got up, alarmed, and climbed up the bone hill. At the top, she picked up the dragon toe and pounded the wall three times. Then she waited, sure she'd hear a response.

Several minutes passed, and Thisbe grew more worried. She pounded again, hearing an echo as if there were a hollow spot in the wall between them. There was no answer. Thisbe wanted to call out his name, but she was scared to do that in case anyone else might hear. Was Rohan okay?

Maybe he was asleep—but why wouldn't he have pounded the wall first like always? Maybe he didn't want to be her friend anymore. But that was ridiculous. They'd had a connection— they just couldn't be seen acting like friends.

Maybe he was injured. What if the Revinir had done something to him today? Or . . . what if he had escaped?

That was ridiculous too. If he'd escaped, everyone would have been talking about it, rules tossed aside.

As the minutes passed, Thisbe grew more and more worried that Rohan had been hurt or punished. She pounded a third time, and again there was no answer.

Thisbe swallowed hard. She slipped and slid down the mountain of bones to her door and tugged at the cracks around the opening—there was no handle on the inside of her crypt. But it was useless trying to get out. There was no way to get the door open except from the outside.

She whirled around, sparks soaring from her eyes as her anger heightened. "If she's done something to you . . . ," Thisbe muttered, a warning. She didn't know what she'd do, but the Revinir would suffer.

Thisbe aimed her gaze at the doorjamb and began to pummel it with powerful sparks. Little chunks of the door flew every which way. But after a minute she stopped. Even if she could get out of here, she'd have to chisel her way inside Rohan's crypt too, and the soldiers would certainly get to her long before she succeeded. Plus, they'd hear her breaking down the door now and stop her from getting anywhere.

Slowly she turned and looked at the back wall. "Of course!" she muttered. She slapped her forehead, wondering why she hadn't thought of this before. Then she aimed her laser eyes on the back wall and thought about the Revinir. Fiery arrows flew and landed almost exactly where she wanted and left big divots—bigger than the kind she'd been making from close range, which seemed odd. She scrambled up the bone mountain and began to pelt the wall with sparks, but they appeared to have less power and less effect than when she'd been standing farther away. She went down again and backed all the way up to the door. Then she aimed for the wall.

Little chunks fell away, and then one particularly well-aimed shot split the rock wall and left a wide crevice over a two-foot space. "That's the way," Thisbe murmured. She kept summoning up her fury, pounding at the wall for several minutes until there was an indent more than a foot deep. But by then her sparks fizzled. She'd run out of energy and collapsed to the floor, exhausted. After she caught her breath, she climbed back up the bone mountain and used the dragon toe to pound inside the growing hole in the wall. A few pebbles and some dust gave way, but nothing more than that. She'd have to continue tomorrow when her strength returned and her magic recharged.

She piled a bunch of already-extracted bones in front of the hole so the crypt keeper wouldn't see what she'd done and slid wearily back down to her sleeping spot for the night. Worn out, she slept hard and woke up with a start when Mangrel opened the door in the morning. He gave her some water, pointed out the two bones she was to deliver that day, and left the door standing open as usual.

Thisbe took longer to get ready this morning. She stood and watched out the doorway as some of the other children walked past, but her back-wall friend wasn't among them. "Rohan—where is he? Do you know?" she'd whisper to the others, hoping they'd recognize his name, but they all shook their heads. The last one to go by was the girl who Thisbe had tried talking to early on. Her eyes widened in response. She whispered something in the common language, then brought her fingers to her neck and sliced the air across it.

"What?" cried Thisbe, loud enough to make one of the soldiers at the nearest intersection turn to give her a warning look. She lowered her voice. "What did you say? What does that mean? Is he . . . dead?"

But the girl, frightened by the soldiers, didn't reply. She hurried on.

Thisbe stared after her, more confused than ever. With a heavy heart, she set out.

A Shocking
Revelation

Thisbe's late start left her straining to pull her load faster to make up time. Her mind was plagued with thoughts and worries about what could have happened to Rohan. She imagined all sorts of things: Rohan being taken away forever. Or maybe he was still in his crypt, ill or injured or something? He couldn't possibly be dead. Or could he? Somehow, without him here, Thisbe became even more determined to figure out how she was going to get out of here and plot her escape. And to do that, she needed to be extra diligent and work on her magic even more. She was getting better and gaining control—she could tell that

LISA McMANN

much. She wished she had more variety in her abilities, but her inner magic seemed to be very focused on destruction using sparks and explosions. That didn't give her a lot of options.

As she dragged her bones through the catacombs, she planned her day. She would move as quickly as she could, and then as soon as the crypt keeper brought her dinner, she'd gulp it down and start working. One thing she wanted to accomplish was to be able to do her magic without having to work herself into an angry lather first. And she wanted to find out even more about what she was capable of—what was the scope of her power? Just how big an explosion could she create? She also needed her spells to be automatic, well placed, and lethal. It was the only way she might be able to get out of here.

Last night she'd figured out that the closer she was to her target, the weaker the effect of the spell, which seemed odd, but it was true. Being farther away made the spell more powerful and more accurate. She was limited by the size of her crypt in testing that out and didn't know if there was an optimal distance—she knew that there had to be some point where she was too far away from a target to hit it, right? But with no space to test it, it might be a while before she could find that out.

Perhaps if she reached a long stretch of passageway in the ca[tacombs where there weren't any soldiers or slaves she could t[ry] it out. Maybe if she snuck out in the other direction from h[er] crypt, toward the castle, she could find a passageway less trav[eled. But would the soldiers suspect she had no business going that way? She'd have to risk it. And she had a decent chance of being able to protect herself now. Her aim was improving. Though she didn't want to have to resort to that until she was ready to make her ultimate escape—it would most certainly get her captured if the Revinir found out just what she was capable of too soon. She needed to hide her abilities to keep the suspicion at a minimum.

A big part of Thisbe wanted to fold up inside herself when she truly thought about having to hurt anyone—even the ones who had hurt her. She didn't think it was in her nature to kill a person, even though she'd done it before by accident as a child. Indeed, there was a big part of her that denied she'd really have to go through with it. Perhaps there was another way to get out without having to leave any carnage behind. But if there was, she hadn't thought of it yet. So she was determined to prepare. Also in the back of her mind was the unsettling reminder

from the Revinir that she was more evil than good. Could it be true? Thisbe had lied multiple times, and it seemed like the Revinir could tell. Maybe being able to lie so easily really did make Thisbe an evil person—and here Thisbe had thought it was just her ability to be a good actor. But it seemed true—the Revinir had been somehow taking in dormant dragon magic for years, and that was one thing the dragons could tell about humans. Thisbe remembered how Hux had said Dev was exactly half and half. It didn't seem surprising that the Revinir would be able to pick up that ability from the magic in the bones. Which made it more unsettling.

Her mind lingered on Dev and their time together. Their relationship had been rocky, but they'd needed each other. They'd annoyed each other, done some rude things to each other, but there was something inherent in Dev that Thisbe had really liked. Then, abruptly, their relationship had ended without notice or fanfare. She'd probably never see him again. Now she'd made a friend who was nice and caring, and he was gone. Or dead. Or something horrible like that.

She was so deep into her thoughts and plans that her journey to the extraction room seemed to go more quickly than

usual. She was surprised when she reached the rushing sound of the river. Being nearly half done energized her, and she made the last leg of the journey at top speed. She deposited her bones next to empty stations, picked the two smallest of the ones that had already been worked on and hitched them to her harness, gulped downed a cup of water, and rushed out, nearly knocking someone flat in her haste.

It was the Revinir. Behind her were her soldiers.

"Ah, there you are," the old woman said, keeping her balance nimbly with the help of the doorway. "I've been looking for you." She narrowed her eyes. "Are you ready to work as my assistant yet? Opportunities abound. Mercenary options, no less."

"No way," Thisbe said with contempt, though she didn't know what mercenary meant. "Not in a million years."

"Ah well. It's a pity you're going to miss out. I'll have to make do with my newly acquired servant, then, though unfortunately he's not magically inclined. I would have preferred you." She hesitated, then leaned forward, her fingernails clicking together. "What sort of magic can you do, exactly?" The Revinir sounded slimy, and it made Thisbe want to avoid her even more.

"Nothing." Thisbe shrugged, then tried to push past her.

The Revinir put her scaly arm out to stop her. "I know you're lying. I've seen your sparks. Are you the one who killed the pirate captain? I think you are."

Thisbe said nothing, but her conscience twinged. She'd lied again like it was nothing. That was definitely something an evil person might do.

"Also," the Revinir went on, "I heard something very troubling about you. Sneaking around the river the other day, were you? Don't do that again. You're forbidden. And I've instructed my soldiers that if they catch you trying that again, they're to take any means necessary to stop you."

Thisbe's heart sank, but she tried not to let it show. "I won't. I was only thirsty."

"You know I don't believe you."

Thisbe looked at the woman with contempt. "You don't have to believe me." She started forward again, then stopped. "Where's Rohan?" she demanded, not expecting an answer. "What did you do to him?"

"Oh, he's busy elsewhere in the catacombs."

"He's alive?" Thisbe held her breath and failed miserably at trying to look like she didn't care.

The Revinir raised an eyebrow. "Hmm. Interesting. My hunch was correct. You seem to care a great deal. I'm glad I separated you two."

Thisbe scowled but didn't argue, and she tried more successfully this time not to let her intense feelings of relief be evident. "Did you make *him* your assistant or something?"

"Rohan? Please. He's only sixteen percent evil. Not nearly bad enough to work directly for me. Not like *you*. You're special." She laughed, and a puff of gray smoke came out of her nostrils. "I just needed to keep you away from him. I prefer you only be around other children with whom you can't communicate. That boy is just too educated and good to stay on this side of the catacombs. It means his work is much harder, certainly, but that couldn't be helped. I'll tell him you said sorry, since it's you're fault he's been moved—oh wait, no I won't. I'll tell him nothing of the sort. Perhaps I'll tell him you're dead." She cackled. "And he'll believe me, because he's so good. Oh, it's fun to play with the good ones."

Thisbe looked at her in horror, feeling the rage boil up. The Revinir was an awful, horrid person. She glanced at the soldiers, feeling terribly tempted to strike the woman down—did they think she was horrible too? She couldn't tell. Their faces were blank. It was too risky. Plus, hadn't the Revinir said that she was somehow indestructible now? That had to be something to do with the dragon-bone magic. But obviously dragons could die somehow, or there wouldn't be tons of their bones here. And Arabis and the others wouldn't have been threatened. Thisbe eyed the woman, wondering where to direct the spell once she was ready to do so. Her throat, perhaps. There weren't any scales there.

"You're thinking about trying to hurt me, aren't you?" said the Revinir, searching Thisbe's face. "I wouldn't try that if I were you. You won't succeed. It'll only get you thrown into the dungeon."

Thisbe's heart leaped to her throat, but she narrowed her eyes and tried not to let on. "What dungeon?"

"The one at the palace," said the Revinir. "I'm told you enjoyed your time there, though, so I'm not terribly keen on sending you back."

Thisbe was so angry she could hardly breathe. She lifted her chin and held back from letting any emotion show. After too long of a pause, she said through gritted teeth, "May I pass, please? I have work to do."

The Revinir smiled. "Of course, dear. Enjoy your day, and do tell a soldier whenever you are ready to work with me as my assistant. I assure you we'll make a good pair."

"It won't ever happen," said Thisbe. She pressed forward, leaning into her harness.

"All right," sang the Revinir, "if you say so. But you know what that means. Tomorrow you can start delivering three bones. Nice big juicy ones. The heaviest, which are overflowing with dragony magical goodness. It's past time to make another bone broth." She smiled condescendingly. "I'll convince you eventually."

Three bones? Thisbe felt like her brain was boiling. She closed her fists and her eyes to stop anything tragic from happening before she was ready and pushed past the soldiers, walking as fast as she could go and blinded by fury. But she couldn't escape the woman's laughter, which rang in her ears.

At least Rohan was alive. But how was she going to find him?

A Breakthrough

Thisbe didn't have time to wallow in her sorrows or wonder about how she was supposed to drag three bones to the extraction room the next day when she'd hardly been able to drag two. She didn't have time to whine about how her shoulders and back and knees ached from her job.

She took the time to eat, of course. She was slowly growing thin on one meal a day, though her tray today seemed to have slightly more food than normal. Perhaps when the crypt keeper had heard about the Revinir's insane order, he'd felt sorry for her. If so, she'd take his pity and the extra food. She needed all the fuel she could get.

Once she'd finished eating and was locked into her crypt for the night, Thisbe moved the stack of bones away from the hollow she'd made in the wall. Then she stood in the farthest corner away from it, near the door, and concentrated for several minutes, remembering the moment the Revinir had told her she had to take three bones tomorrow as punishment for not being willing to become her assistant.

Thisbe knew three bones wouldn't be the end of this punishment. The woman was trying to break her, to convince her to be her assistant, and so far it wasn't working. That wouldn't make the woman pleased at all. She'd keep adding more bones until Thisbe couldn't get the job done anymore and she'd have to give up.

But the Revinir didn't know Thisbe very well. She wasn't going to give up. As the food fueled her body, Thisbe's anger fueled her magic, and soon she could feel fire pulsing through her forearms. She opened her eyes, electricity sparking at her fingertips. She needed to test some things. First she tried the most minimal move she could think of. She flicked her fore-finger against her thumb, sending a line of sparks shooting toward the hole in the back wall. They hit a little left of center and made small divots. A bit of dirt trickled out. "Okay, so a flick of the fingers probably would hurt someone but not destroy them," Thisbe noted.

Next Thisbe decided to test her strongest move to see what the difference would be. She pulled her arm back, then took a few steps for momentum and flung her arm forward, pointing her forefinger at the hole and yelling "Boom!"

A fireball shot forth and slammed into the hole, making a small explosion that shook the walls and left a cloud of smoke and dust so thick Thisbe had to drop low to the ground to keep from choking. A piece of rock that had once been embed-ded in the wall came rolling down the bone pile at her, just missed, and slammed into the door behind her. Her sleeve was singed and smoking, and her forefinger burned in pain. She could see a blister forming on its tip. She cringed and sucked on it. "Well," she murmured, sitting on the floor and waiting for the smoke to clear, "that was pretty powerful."

After a moment she picked up a candle and climbed up the

bone pile through the haze. At the back wall, she felt around the hole and peered in. She couldn't tell how deep it went.

It was twice the diameter it had been before, easily wide enough for Thisbe to fit into if she curled up a little. She wrinkled her nose and shoved her head inside it, arm outstretched with the candle, trying to see what her magic had done. The candlelight flickered and shone in a circle, bouncing off the uneven walls of the hole. Thisbe crawled in and waved the smoke away.

Just then she heard a noise behind her at the door. She froze, then quickly backed out of her tunnel. She dropped her candle and began shoving the bone pile back in place to cover the hole.

Her door opened, and the crypt keeper looked inside. "What's going on in here? Did you make that explosion? Where did all this smoke come from?"

Thisbe stared down at him, hoping desperately that he couldn't see the gaping hole in the wall from his angle on the floor. "What?" she said weakly, stalling so she could think of an excuse. There was no use denying the smoke—it was obvious. "Oh, you mean this?" She waved her hand through the air and laughed a little. "It's . . . really . . . nothing. . . ."

"It doesn't look like nothing." He took a step inside and

tried to wave some of the haze out of the room so he could see better. "What did you do?"

"I—I accidently set my clothes on fire with the candle," said Thisbe sheepishly. "I've been trying to sort the dragon bones. Used ones over here, you see, and the ones that haven't been extracted go down toward the floor so they're easier to get to. Anyway, I knocked over my candle when I was moving today's bones up here and set my shirt on fire. Burned my finger, too. It hurts pretty bad."

"That wouldn't make that explosion sound," the crypt keeper said, looking suspicious. "It rocked this whole section of the catacombs."

"Oh, that! I have no idea what that was," said Thisbe. "I felt it too, but I didn't have anything to do with that. Maybe it was an earthquake. That's . . . actually . . . what made me knock over my candle." She coughed and waved the smoke aside. "Very startling."

The crypt keeper looked frightened, which puzzled Thisbe. But then his expression changed, and he narrowed his eyes at her. "The Revinir said you were more evil than good, which means you probably lie a lot."

Thisbe stared at him. He'd voiced her fears, and she didn't like the sound of them. She gathered her wits. "With all due respect, sir," she said, "perhaps the Revinir, who is the evilest person we've all met, is the one who is lying about my level of evilness. After all, you know she seems to have it in for me, don't you?"

The crypt keeper's mouth opened but then closed again. He frowned, then said, "That's true. And . . . it may be the smoke fogging my sensibilities, but I don't think it's fair what she's doing to you." He ducked his head and backed out of the crypt, then closed the door behind him.

Thisbe stood silent, letting his sympathetic words exist and ring about the room, almost as if they became stronger because they were the last ones spoken. She picked up the candle.

As time ticked forward without another interruption, she relaxed a bit and went back to rebuilding the bone pile, but she didn't quite dare to explore the tunnel again in case Mangrel returned.

She could hear little pieces of the wall continuing to break off and fall inside the hole behind her, but she ignored the noise and focused on swiftly finishing the bone pile. Since

LISA McMANN

the door had been opened, a lot of the smoke had dissipated, which Thisbe realized in retrospect had probably been what had prevented the crypt keeper from seeing the gaping hole before she could finish hiding it.

Soon Thisbe had constructed a significant cover in front of the hole. "There," she said, placing one last bone. She took her candle and got ready to head back down, when she heard a sudden rushing sound of dirt and pebbles from inside the hole. She bent down and peered inside. When her eyes adjusted to the darkness, she realized she could see a tiny crack of light from the other side.

After a moment, the crack split wide and someone pounded the rest of the wall away, revealing a candlelit face peering back at her. Rohan smiled wearily through the tunnel. "My good-ness," he said admiringly. "What a beautiful sculpture you've created while I was away. It almost appears as if you might have missed me a little."

A Heart-to-Heart

Throwing caution to the wind and her candle to the bones, Thisbe dove into the tunnel and helped Rohan clear out his end of it. "You should build a pile too, so the tunnel can't be seen from your door," she said. "I'll help you."

Together they made quick work of it. When they were finished, they climbed back inside the tunnel and sat with their backs curling to the curve of the wall, facing each other in the short passageway that connected their rooms. Thisbe retrieved her candle, relit it, and set it between them, then peered at her

LISA McMANN

friend. The shadows under his eyes seemed pronounced, and his eyes were weary.

"Are you okay?" Thisbe asked him.

"I'm pretty tired," he said.

"Do you want to go to sleep?"

"I'd rather talk with you."

Thisbe's face burned, and she shifted the candle away from her so Rohan wouldn't be able to see the color rise to her cheeks. He had such a strange way of talking, unlike Seth or any other boy Thisbe had known. Definitely not like Dev. The way he said whatever he meant with no hesitation was as intriguing as some of his word choices.

"Where have you been?" Thisbe asked.

"Have you missed my rapping on your wall?" A smile played at his lips. "I was so glad you responded. I thought you might be angry with me."

"No, I wasn't angry. I just didn't want to get you in trouble by talking to you. But it seems like you got punished anyway. I'm sorry. So . . . where have you been?" she asked again.

Rohan's eyes glistened in the candlelight. "To the castle."

"On foot? All that way? How?" Thisbe remembered

the lengthy ride she and Fifer had had from the castle to Dragonsmarche. It would take a tremendously long time to go that far on foot—at least a day.

"Yes, on foot. And in fact, these catacombs lead all the way to the castle dungeon. I'd never gone that far before in that direction."

"What's over there? Why did the Revinir have you go so far?"

"The crypts of the ancient human rulers are over there. Our ancestors."

"Oh." The statement weighed heavy on Thisbe. She'd never spent much time thinking about her ancestors before her time in the catacombs. She'd known little about her family's past, other than that her parents had died when she was a toddler. Her mother had black eyes, which was where she and Fifer had gotten theirs. Had their mother come from here? Or perhaps her grandparents? There was no record of such things in Quill. No history. No writings or stories—it hadn't been allowed. The only record of her parents' life and past had died with them.

Rohan touched Thisbe's singed sleeve. "Are you all right?"

Thisbe pulled away from her thoughts and looked up. "Yes," she said. "I'm just thinking about what you said. About your . . . our . . . ancestors being buried a day's journey away." She swallowed hard and looked at him. "I don't know any history of my family. Do you . . . I mean, are you sure . . . that I'm descended from rulers like you? I just don't really feel like my family was . . . you know. Strong and noble like that. They . . . they weren't. I'm pretty sure." All she could think about was how her parents had sent their creative son, Alex, to his death. How they might have done the same with her if that practice in Quill had continued. That didn't seem noble at all. It seemed cowardly.

Rohan pressed his lips together. "There was a time about forty years ago when our people were worried about being tortured and killed—the uprising was already happening. Some of our grandparents tried to save their children by sending them away from here. Perhaps your mother was one of them."

"But how would she have gotten over there? Across the gorge?"

"The worlds were connected back then."

Thisbe blinked. "They were?"

"Do you remember seeing the narrow waterfall that drops to nowhere off the side of the cliffs of Grimere?"

Thisbe nodded.

"It used to be a river that ran to the sea in your world. And your sea didn't end in a waterfall spinning around your world. It butted up against our cliffs."

"What split the worlds apart?"

"An earthquake. We have them now and then. Not to be confused with the volcano in the crater lake that rattles Grimere, of course." Rohan's voice was teasing.

"Of course," Thisbe said with a smile. "No wonder the crypt keeper looked freaked out when I suggested the big explosion earlier was an earthquake."

"Yes, you might get that stunned reaction from the older folk who remember the massive one. Sometimes they even react when the volcano in the lake erupts, even though they hear it all the time. According to my studies, a lot of people lost their lives." He yawned and rested his head against the wall. His eyelids drooped.

Thisbe wanted to know more about his studies, but she could tell he was exhausted. "When did you sleep last?"

LISA McMANN

137 « Dragon Bones

He murmured sleepily. "Two nights ago. My journey takes fifteen hours each way."

Thisbe stared. "With no sleep in between?"

"The soldiers at the castle end offered to let me take an hour's nap before I returned, but I said no."

"Why wouldn't you want to rest in between?" asked Thisbe. It seemed crazy to not at least put his feet up for a while.

Rohan opened one eye and looked at her with a lazy smile. "I needed to get back so I could knock on your wall."

The Birds

Back in Artimé, Fifer's abrupt change in behavior had Alex more than a little puzzled, but he kept himself as busy as possible in the following weeks to lessen the time he spent worrying over Sky and Thisbe. He and the team that was preparing to go on the rescue mission spent their days with Florence doing extensive Magical Warrior Training and exercises, and their evenings continuing to build the new larger wings for the dragons.

After delivering Crow, Simber spoke to the dragons about helping their effort, leaving them with much to think about.

LISA McMANN

They promised to have a decision by the time they came to get their new wings.

Then Simber spent a couple of days circling the area around the Island of Fire, knowing his search for Sky was probably futile but somehow feeling like he had to do it in order to be sure for himself. He even dove under the water and discovered Spike still combing every inch of the depths of the sea, looking for her too. But there was no sign of their beloved Sky. Eventually Simber made his way home, and Spike did whatever she usually did in the great sea while waiting for Alex to call upon her.

And then there was Fifer. She was rapidly regaining strength by the day until she was as good as new. Fifer's interest in the falcons had her venturing out in the mornings to the private area of the lagoon. With Crow on Warbler Island unable to keep an eye on her, and with Alex and Seth busy preparing for their quest, Fifer found herself left very much alone. Except for the birds, of course. They went with her everywhere, and their numbers grew as the days went by. She began to talk with them about her worries over Thisbe, her frustrations over Alex, her sadness over Sky, and her deep desire to be treated like a real mage. The creatures seemed sympathetic and always appeared to be listening, which gave Fifer some comfort, even though she knew it wasn't normal to think birds could understand her. Still, she wondered.

Whenever Florence trained the veterans and Seth on the lawn, Fifer watched secretly from the edge of the jungle and learned the various components and how to use them. And when Alex and the others worked on the wings, Fifer began experimenting with training the birds and soon discovered they were fast learners. The first thing she taught them was to stay outside when she went into the mansion. Using spoken words and the Warbler sign language, of which most mages in Artimé knew at least a little, Fifer commanded them to stop and put out her hand in a signal to the birds, and then she ventured to open the door. If they tried to follow her, she'd reprimand them and do the hand signal and verbal cue again. They soon caught on, and when they did it right, Fifer praised them.

The rest of Artimé was just glad the birds stopped trying to get inside the mansion, and they paid little mind to what else Fifer was doing.

Soon Fifer had the grand falcons flying to and away from her at her command. Next she taught them to fetch things—a leaf, a small branch, or anything Fifer could find to toss in the jungle. The birds eventually learned to act only when Fifer was speaking directly to them, and soon she was able to get a specific group of birds to do what she commanded while the rest waited, straining and eager to be addressed too.

She taught them to fly in a pattern following her hand movements. Sometimes she'd spend hours waving her hands like a conductor, directing the birds to swoop and soar and circle around. She got them to create shapes in the air—a circle, a triangle, a heart—and taught them all the hand signals and verbal cues that meant go, come, fetch, and more.

When she grew bored with those commands, Fifer taught the birds to take hold of her by her clothing and fly her around the lagoon close to the ground. It was great entertainment, especially when Fifer was feeling bad about everything. It never ceased to cheer her up at least a little.

In the evenings Fifer would leave the birds to roost in the trees. She'd go inside and retreat to her room, where she'd take her dinner alone because she didn't want to sit with Alex or hear Seth and Lani and Samheed and the others go on and on about the rescue mission.

She felt bad about it, but the truth was she just couldn't face Alex, especially after the way she'd left things with him. She knew he had to be hurting more than anyone about Sky, and of course he was worried about Thisbe. But Fifer couldn't seem to get beyond his refusal to let her join them. She just couldn't understand it. She'd already learned so much in her first trip away from Artimé, and she had so much magical potential, but Alex was treating her like a baby. Hadn't he noticed how much she'd grown since she and Thisbe and Seth had left? Didn't he grasp the amazing things they'd done while they were away? Clearly he appreciated what Seth had done, but Seth would've accomplished none of it without Fifer. Alex was being impossible. And she couldn't stand to be around him or Seth right now.

On the day the young dragons returned to get their new wings, much of Artimé gathered around to witness the transformation.

The first thing Alex did when they arrived was take Arabis aside. He had a question from the distant past that had been weighing heavily on his mind lately. "When you left our world ten years ago," he said to her, "did Queen Eagala somehow travel with you to the land of the dragons?"

"No," said Arabis. "We went alone. Her ship had sunk weeks before we left. When we were captured and until you told us, we didn't know Eagala was the Revinir—we'd never really had a good look at her before and hadn't realized the connection all these years."

Alex nodded, but appeared confounded by the answer. "Okay, thank you." He looked over the water toward the west for a long moment. "It doesn't make sense," he muttered to himself. "How did she get there?" Then he turned abruptly back to Arabis. "Have you had a chance to think about joining us? Can you risk coming along?"

Arabis nodded. "I've chosen to go with you. My brothers and sisters and mother and I have decided that one of us must go back and warn the ghost dragons in the land beyond Grimere."

"Ghost dragons?"

"That is what they are called," said Arabis with a bit of mystery. "They are in danger from the Revinir now that she has lost us. So I will help you get to your location and continue on a few hours' journey from there. I'll deliver my message and return to the forest outside of Grimere as quickly as possible to hide until you are ready to return to the seven islands."

It wasn't a perfect situation, but it was close enough. Alex poured out his gratefulness to Arabis, and she in turn voiced her thanks for the three children who'd freed them and given them the wings they needed to escape.

Only one, Seth, was standing nearby, and Alex called him over. Seth flushed bright red. "You're welcome," he said.

"Shall we put on your beautiful new permanent wings now?" Alex asked the dragons, standing aside so they could inspect them along the shore. The orange dragon nodded regally and moved closer so Alex and the others could start the job.

Fifer watched the gathering from afar, sitting on a log in the lagoon, her birds surrounding her. She couldn't hear what was being said, but the crowd seemed to be very excited about the new wings. It made her a bit glum to think about how everyone had been spending so much time on constructing them and making such a big deal over these beautiful new wings and cringing over the ugly ones Fifer and Seth had made. If Alex and the others had only had sapling branches and burlap

LISA McMANN

and a few scatterclips to pin the whole thing together, they would've made ugly wings too. It was an amazing accomplishment under really difficult circumstances, but nobody understood what they'd gone through. Maybe Fifer should start writing books about it like Lani had done so she could point out all the things everyone else thought were unimportant. And reveal the truth about Alex, who was nothing like the boy in Lani's books.

Kaylee, who had come with Aaron to see the event, noticed immediately that her young sister-in-law, Fifer, was nowhere to be found. She left baby Daniel with Aaron and sought out Lani near the edge of the shore.

"Have you seen Fifer?" Kaylee asked her.

"I spied her earlier heading along the shoreline in that direction," said Lani, pointing toward the lagoon.

They could just barely see a human blob shape sitting there, with birds fluttering about. "Thanks," said Kaylee. "I'm going to go talk to her."

"I'll come with you."

Kaylee strolled along the sand, and Lani rolled alongside

her. Aaron had designed and crafted Lani's sleek magical vehicle ten years before, after her legs had become paralyzed in the final battle, and he'd constantly made improvements to it in the years since so she could travel over a variety of terrains. The contraption embraced her around the hips and held her upright, giving support to the lower half of her body and keeping her hands free. Powered by concentration, it moved magically in compliance with her unspoken wishes unless she was particularly tired—then it sometimes veered off track. Now the vehicle struggled a little in the deep sand, but Lani powered it forward anyway, hopping up out of the sand to ride on the grass instead. Kaylee realized what was happening and stepped up on the grass too.

Before long they reached Fifer.

The girl looked up at them quizzically. "What are you doing out here?" The birds fluttered and settled.

"May we join you?" asked Kaylee.

"Sure, I guess," said Fifer.

Lani adjusted her wheeled vehicle and put her hands back to allow her to ease into a sitting position on the log next to Fifer. Kaylee sat on the other side of her and gazed out to where the crowd had spread in front of the mansion.

"I haven't seen you around much lately," said Lani.

"I've been here," said Fifer with a sniff. "Busy with my only friends."

Kaylee pressed her lips together to squelch a smile. "Aw, come on, kiddo. That doesn't sound like you, feeling sorry for yourself. Are you doing all right? You must be so anxious about Thisbe. I know I am. We're going to find her, though. I won't leave there without her, I promise you that."

"I should be going with you," said Fifer bitterly. "It's not right. I'll be sitting here helpless."

Lani put her hand on top of Fifer's. "I can only imagine how bad that feels."

Kaylee nodded. "Just so you know, I've talked to Aaron about it. He said Alex gets to decide these things because he's the one taking responsibility for you. He thinks Alex is saying no because he can't bear to lose anyone else, and I gotta be honest, I can't fault him for caring. Still, Aaron tried to convince Al to let you go, if that makes you feel any better."

"Thanks, but not really." Fifer blinked hard. "If you even manage to rescue her, I won't find out for days and days. It's not fair." She pressed the heels of her hands to her eyes to stop them from leaking, but it didn't work. "Who took responsibility for you, Lani, when you were twelve?" she asked, knowing the answer.

"I did," said Lani softly. "But that was a different time and a different situation. I would have loved to have had my parents and Henry in my life then. I know it feels like Alex is smothering you, but at least be glad you have him. At least he cares and would do anything for you. He had no one. When we were purged from Quill, he lost everybody. Everyone, Fifer. And his parents—your parents—didn't do anything to stop the governors from taking Alex away. It was horrible. I think he made a vow to himself to not stand idly by if you are in danger. To not be like your parents. So when you and Seth and Thisbe left, he fell apart. He thought he'd lost you. Now that he has you back . . . Well, he's going a little overboard in protecting you, but like Kaylee, I honestly can't say I blame him after what he's been through. Do you know what I mean?"

Fifer hadn't thought about it quite like that. She often forgot how real the Purge was—it was more than just a story in a book. And it made her feel softer toward her brother—at least a little. But then she grew frustrated again. "The thing is," she said impatiently, "I'm a great mage. I know how to do things now, only Alex didn't witness any of those things. It's because of *us* that those five dragons are here right now! Don't you get it? I'm not just able to do things—I'm also really powerful! But nobody sees that. Nobody understands. They're letting Seth go—why not me? Thisbe and I saved Seth's life like seventeen times!"

Kaylee, who was watching Fifer's impassioned speech, wore a troubled expression. "I suppose if Alex were in charge of Seth, he'd make him stay home too. But he's not, and Carina thinks Seth will be useful."

"Not for the Dragonsmarche part," Fifer argued, "which is where Thisbe is! Neither Seth nor Carina was there. But I was. I saw what happened." Fifer stood abruptly and whirled around to face the women, making the birds scatter. The leader falcon fluttered to Fifer's shoulder and began making a worried-sounding clicking noise by her ear, obviously sensing that she was upset. Fifer absently petted the bird and winced at how its claws pricked her skin, but she only felt more frustrated. "I can't stand arguing about this anymore. I should have my component vest—I've earned it. I should be training with all of you instead of sneaking around learning all the spells behind Alex's back—and yes, that's exactly what I've been doing, and I don't care who knows it. This whole thing is completely senseless, and you're all making a huge mistake by not bringing me with you." She blew out a furious breath and dropped her arms to her sides. "Thanks for trying to help. I mean it. But I give up."

With that, Fifer stormed into the jungle. Her flock of birds squawked and followed her, leaving Lani and Kaylee sober and thoughtful.

After a while, when the dragons had left to test their new perfect wings and the crowd had dispersed, the two young women went back to the mansion and found Alex. "You need to go after Fifer," Kaylee said to him. "And talk to that girl. She's distraught and you're not helping. Do it before we go. She needs you. Like, yesterday. So get a move on it."

Continuing Clashes

Ll right," Alex told Kaylee and Lani, though he looked like he couldn't do one more thing. The hard training and wing making and stress of the losses were taking a toll, and he wasn't sleeping well. But this was important. "I'll go look for Fifer."

Alex had been coasting on fumes for a few months, ever since Fifer and Thisbe had snuck off, and now he carried his weary body toward the jungle in search of his sister. His heart had been ripped from his chest and stomped on. First Thisbe, then Sky. He was having a hard time coping. He'd resorted to doing what he'd done in the past when things were overwhelming—put his head down and work. Try to overcome another enormous obstacle. That was the way it always went.

The last time something so personally tragic had caught him this unprepared was when Mr. Today had died and Artimé had vanished. But at least then he'd had Sky. Now . . . well, she'd dragged his heart with her under the sea.

He hadn't been able to face the fact that she was dead. Despite all the evidence, there were a few puzzling details that kept him from losing all hope. Perhaps his mind was trying to protect him from totally breaking down while he was dealing with Thisbe's abduction. But there was something concrete that left him with a shred of belief that Sky had somehow survived. A belief that stemmed from his archenemy, of all people—Queen Eagala.

Ten years ago, the giant squid who lived under the Island of Legends had followed Queen Eagala's ship and had watched it, with Eagala herself onboard, get sucked into the plunging volcano. Yet she was alive. If Queen Eagala had survived that, could Sky also survive? Or was she doomed without magic to help her?

Alex had always known that Queen Eagala was magical, but

he didn't know the extent of her abilities. What he knew of her—the ability to cast a silence spell over her island and send a flock of ravens to try to peck out the eyes of the Warbler children who'd found refuge in Artimé—seemed relatively tame compared to the magic of Mr. Today, or Alex, or the other mages in Artimé.

He also knew that despite being nonmagical, Sky, like many of Artimé's mages, could survive underwater for several minutes thanks to Ms. Octavia teaching them all how to utilize underwater breathing. So that added at least a little hope in her favor.

But even if she'd survived the plunge, where had she gone? Simber, Pan, and Spike had all been searching the area for weeks with no sign of her.

To the best of his knowledge, the ship Eagala had gone down in had never resurfaced. Even if it had, eventually it would've been seen by Pan or Spike, if not Simber. And they would have reported it. Perhaps the ship had been obliterated. It was the only explanation Alex could think of. But if it had been, how had Eagala survived that kind of beating? Especially when she couldn't swim?

Somehow she'd done it, which left the possibility that Sky could do it too. If the world's most evil person could survive, it seemed wrong that the world's best soul mate couldn't. Sky was pure goodness. When Alex was emotional, she was steady. When Alex was frustrated, Sky had quietly found solutions. When Alex had wanted to give up on the Island of Fire and consider it a disastrous place to live, Sky had wanted to figure out why it moved the way it did and do something about it. Well . . . maybe Alex had been right about that one—it had been disastrous. Though Sky had been so close to figuring out its systems.

"But how . . . ?" muttered Alex as he entered the jungle and began walking toward the depths to where the rock and Panther and the sharp-toothed dog lived. "*How* did Eagala survive *that* and get *there*? She'd had absolutely no means to do it. And, for that matter, didn't the pirates do it too? Didn't they say years ago that they traded sea creatures somewhere else?"

Alex was so lost in thought he walked within ten feet of Fifer, who'd been training her birds in a little clearing.

With no place to hide, Fifer watched him and overheard part of his muttering, and it made her think of something.

"There was a giant aquarium in Dragonsmarche," she said, startling him.

Alex looked up and spied her. "Oh," he said. "There you are. I've been looking for you. An aquarium? What of it?"

"You said something about pirates trading sea creatures, and that reminded me of the aquarium full of creatures in Dragonsmarche. Somebody else there said something about pirates trading sea creatures too. Do you think they're the same pirates who used to live inside the Island of Fire?"

Alex came over and sat down heavily next to her. "I don't know—we killed a lot of them in the last battle. But I'm really starting to wonder if there's another way to get to the land of the dragons other than by flying."

The mention of that brought something else to mind for Fifer. She recalled when she and Thisbe and Seth had been preparing to leave Artimé, they'd overheard Pan and Hux talking quietly about it. "I think there might be," said Fifer thoughtfully. "Before we left, Hux asked Pan if she would search for them. 'Like I told you?' he said. 'There has to be another way.' Then Pan told Hux if there is another way, she'd find it. Maybe we should ask her."

"That sounds like a good idea," said Alex. "Though she'd

probably consider that one of her many secrets." He leaned back against a tree and looked at her.

Fifer eyed him back. His face was scruffy and his eyes red rimmed. "So what do you want?" she asked. "You said you were looking for me. I'm not doing anything wrong. I didn't go deep into the jungle or anything."

Alex allowed a grim smile. "I know. It's not about you being out here. It's just . . . I feel like we need to clear the air a bit before I leave. I noticed you haven't been talking to me or eating dinner with me. And I . . . I miss you. And I know you're upset, and I understand why."

Fifer narrowed her eyes. "And so you've changed your mind? You'll let me come with you?"

"Oh, no. Not a chance. But I love you and I want you to know that. I can't bear to lose you and—"

"Alex, please. Knock it off."

Alex raised an eyebrow. "Wh-what does that mean? 'Knock it off.'"

"It means stop. It's a Kaylee phrase."

"Clearly." He folded his hands in front of him. "Anyway . . . I'm sorry. But I'm doing this for your safety."

"No, you're doing it because you don't want to feel guilty if something happens to me. Tell the truth, Alex. You're being selfish."

Alex's eyes burned. "I'm being selfish because I don't want to feel any more *pain* if something happens to you! It has nothing to do with guilt."

"People have to feel pain sometimes, Alex!" Fifer got to her feet, furious. "You can't keep me locked in Artimé forever!"

"I'm not going to! But you're *twelve!*"

Fifer sighed loudly. "Not this again."

"It's a factor!" said Alex. He got up too. "You don't get it right now. But someday, when you've experienced pain like I have—I hope that never happens, by the way, but if it does—you will understand. And we'll talk it over then."

Fifer fumed. "You. Are. Impossible!" Her yells startled the birds, and without thinking she yelled, "Attack!" and pointed at him.

To Fifer's great shock the falcons obeyed, and before she realized what she'd done, the birds were soaring at Alex, pecking him and grabbing at his clothing with their claws. "Aaargh!" Alex cried, flinging his arm over his face. "No! Release!"

"Ack! Stop!" shouted Fifer. "Retreat! Birds, come back!"

The birds obeyed again.

Alex cautiously lowered his arm. He straightened his robe and ran a hand over his disheveled hair. Then he gave Fifer a withering look. "So that's what you've been doing out here. Training birds to attack me."

"No, that's not—I'm sorry!" Fifer said. "I didn't mean it. I called them off. Are you . . . okay?"

Alex worked his jaw. Then he shook his head, like he couldn't stand to continue the conversation. They cared so much about each other, but they were miles apart in how they looked to the future. They were on complete opposite sides, and there was no backing down for either of them. As much as Alex hated to leave her on a sour note, he had little choice. "I love you," he said again gruffly. "I just wanted you to know that in case anything happens to me on the journey."

"I love you too," Fifer growled, kicking her foot against a tree root. "I just wish you weren't so stinking annoying."

"Likewise," said Alex. He shook his head, giving up, and turned back toward Artimé. "I'm going to talk to Pan like you suggested. I hope you'll be out in front of the mansion in the morning to say good-bye. If not for me, then at least for the others. This isn't a game. Some of us might not come back."

Fifer worked her jaw and didn't answer, but her stomach flipped. She knew it wasn't a game, but she hadn't really thought about *that* before. As she watched him walk away, she fought the urge to follow him, to jump on his back or hug him tightly. She wanted to tell him how sad she was. How scared she felt. But she and Alex had grown very far apart from all their conflicts, and she felt lost.

Just then he stopped walking and turned around. Fifer's heart surged. Had he changed his mind?

"I forgot to tell you," he said. "Aaron is going to stay behind so there's someone to take care of you and Daniel."

Fifer sighed heavily. "Believe it or not, I can take care of myself." All Alex had seen was her coming home bloodied and unconscious, and that wasn't even her fault—it was Simber's, for crying out loud. Alex hadn't witnessed how well she'd managed to take care of herself without anyone's help most of the time before that. She thought briefly about arguing, but the idea of starting that again just made her queasy. It was over, and he was leaving.

"Once we're gone," Alex continued, "if you could pack up and go to his island, that would be great. You can stay with him over there. It'll be fun—you can play with Daniel and help out with Ishibashi, Ito, and Sato. And hey—maybe they'll even teach you how to respect your elders."

Fifer's face fell at the slight. "Wow," she said. She sat down and reached for the nearest bird as her anger clouded up behind her eyes.

Alex dropped his gaze as if he regretted saying it. "Sorry," he muttered. He turned and walked away.

Maybe the best thing that could happen for them was to be apart for a while.

A Consolation Prize

Fifer hadn't kept track of everyone who was going on the rescue attempt, besides watching some of them practicing their magic and sword combat on the lawn now and then. In the morning, she reluctantly came downstairs and went to see them off.

The crowd was large, and Fifer could barely squeeze out of the door. Florence, standing just outside at the back of the crowd, saw her and helped guide her over. "Want to climb on my shoulders so you can see better?" the statue asked.

Fifer's eyes widened. Florence wasn't the "ride on my shoulders" type of warrior, so this was a rare treat. "Sure," she said.

Florence removed her bow and quiver of arrows and propped them against the mansion wall. Then she lifted Fifer up. Fifer scrambled to her shoulders and looked out high over everyone's heads. She was surprised to see Arabis the orange floating in the water near the shore. "Arabis is going?"

"Yes," said Florence. "There aren't enough seats on Simber, and she offered to help get them there. She's got to deliver a message to some other dragons in a neighboring region. Then she's going to hide out and wait for them to return. It's generous of her under the circumstances."

"Hmph," said Fifer. "What we did for them was pretty stinking generous too."

"Arabis said that—she thanked you yesterday. Didn't you hear?"

"I wasn't here—I was in the lagoon," Fifer admitted.

"She said later to Simber and me that she wanted to do this in your honor, actually. She was horrified to find out what had happened to you and to Thisbe after the dragons left."

That made Fifer feel better. "That's nice of her." When Arabis spotted Fifer sitting high above the crowd, the dragon bowed her head to the girl and offered a slow blink.

Fifer gave a sad smile and waved. They'd been through a lot together in the castle dungeon. "Who else is going besides Alex and Seth and Kaylee?" she asked Florence. "Samheed and Lani, right?"

"Yes, and Carina, Thatcher, and Talon. Oh, and Kitten."

Fifer smiled reluctantly at that. "Of course, Kitten. She's in someone's pocket, I'm sure. Is Fox sad to be left behind?"

"Devastated." Florence laughed and pointed to the middle of the lawn, where Fox was alone and heartbroken, howling at the blue sky.

"Maybe I should join him over there."

Florence turned her head to give Fifer a sympathetic look that became devious. "With Alex away, I suppose you could wander over to Magical Warrior Training anytime. I'll slip you some clips when nobody's looking and teach you a few things."

"Maybe." Fifer sighed. It was a great offer, and even though under normal circumstances she would be ecstatic, she couldn't muster up her enthusiasm at the moment. She watched as Alex and the other rescue team members, including Seth, looking quite proud and a little full of himself, secured their knapsacks, weapons, and supplies to Arabis. Then they climbed on, with

Samheed carrying Lani aboard since her contraption couldn't really navigate a dragon's back. Seth pointed out where the hollow was at the base of the dragon's neck, which was quite obvious in daylight, and they all settled into it.

On shore, Kaylee kissed Aaron and baby Daniel and hugged them both tightly, then climbed onto Simber's back.

Alex hugged his brother, patting him hard on the back, and the two spoke earnestly and quietly for a moment. Then Alex scanned the crowd over Aaron's shoulder, looking anxious until he spotted Fifer. He released his brother and fought his way through the crowd over to Florence, then reached up to grasp Fifer's hand. "Stay safe," he said. "And please don't do anything . . . dangerous."

Fifer sighed. He still didn't trust her. "Bye," she said.

"Bye, sweet sister. I love you."

Fifer's heart was heavy. "Me too," she mumbled. Of course she loved him, but she didn't *like* him very much lately.

"I'm going to find her," Alex promised.

Fifer nodded, a lump rising to her throat. "I'll be the last to know."

With a pained look and a squeeze of Fifer's hand, Alex

worked his way back through the crowd. He climbed on Simber and sat behind Kaylee, and after a moment of discussion with the team, Arabis and Simber took mightily to the sky, leaving Fifer and Artimé behind.

Fifer watched them for several moments, then dropped her gaze and rested her chin on the top of Florence's head. They'd done it—they'd gone without her. She sighed wearily, then slid off Florence's shoulders and thumped to the ground. With a word of thanks and a half-hearted wave, Fifer went against the flow of traffic and headed toward the jungle to mope before she had to pack up and go to the Island of Shipwrecks.

Birds flew in from all directions as she went, and they fell into step behind her. She didn't see Florence watching her go or disappearing inside the mansion with a consternated look on her face. She just went to her comfort spot in the lagoon and sat on her log and thought about life.

She tried hard to look at the bright side—sneaking into Magical Warrior Training would be fun. And finally getting to try out all the spells she'd learned by watching Alex would be a decent consolation prize. She might need a little coaching from Florence to really finesse her throw, but Fifer had all the components and their verbal commands memorized, and she'd been practicing the particular throw motions for each. Being one of the most naturally talented mages Artimé had ever seen had its benefits—she didn't have to go through months of practice in order to perfect the art of a spell like other new mages had to. At least she didn't think so—she hadn't actually tried very many so far. But she'd made dragons fly. There wasn't much out there that was harder than that.

"I just want to go," she moaned, and buried her face in her hands. As she sat there, the warm sun inched up her back through the trees, and the birds trilled and squawked around her. Fifer had become accustomed to their flutters and hardly noticed them anymore, but soon they grew louder and more insistent. She lifted her head to see what was going on.

The falcons were dragging brush from the jungle to her and laying it in a curious crisscross pattern on the beach in front of her. Fifer studied their work, wondering what on earth they were doing. Soon the project took on a netlike appearance. The lead falcon, Shimmer, came up to Fifer and chattered at her, while dozens of others joined in to pull more vines to the sand. Some of them pecked at the intersections and looked expectantly at Fifer, like they wanted her to do something.

"What in the world are you doing?" she asked them.

Shimmer squawked at her.

Fifer didn't understand.

Finally Shimmer began chattering to the other falcons, and soon at least twenty of them were flying up to Fifer and grabbing at her clothes. Before Fifer could realize what was happening, they had lifted her into the air like they'd done before.

Staying low, they flew a bit jerkily over the sand while the lead bird lectured Fifer.

"Okay, okay!" said Fifer. "I think I get it—you're making me a net hammock so I don't have to hang by my clothing. That's really nice, thank you. And, um, I mean, having you fly me around was fun and all the first time. But I'm not sure I want to spend the time tying all the net pieces together just so you can do that. I already have a winged creature to fly on if I want. I mean, when he's here, that is. But thanks. You can set me down now."

They let her down roughly and squawked and chattered,

making quite a racket trying to get Fifer to understand them.

And then she replayed what she'd said in her mind, and it dawned on her what they were doing. "Wait a second," she said, waving her hands to get the birds to settle down. "You heard me say I want to go with the rescue team?"

The birds reacted loudly—she was on the right track.

"And now you want to fly me places? Not just around Artimé, but faraway places?"

"Yes," the birds seemed to say.

"Like, to find *Thisbe*? But you have no idea how far that is. It's a super-long journey! It takes days! You'd never make it."

At that, the lead bird let out a high-pitched *spirrrr*. Within a minute, hundreds of purple-and-red falcons flew in and landed, standing almost in rank form in front of Fifer.

Fifer blinked. Was this really happening? Did she have a way to help find Thisbe after all?

A thousand fears rushed in. What if the birds couldn't fly that far? What if they dropped her in the sea, miles from anywhere? What if they got lost or attacked, or they starved to death before they got there?

But Fifer pushed all those questions aside. "Just . . . hold that thought," she said to the birds. She got to her feet and started quickly toward the mansion. Soon she was running at full speed and dodging Artiméans who were on the lawn enjoying the morning.

She ran inside and up the staircase, then darted down the not-very-secret hallway. At the Museum of Large, which was across from Alex's living quarters, she stopped and recited the spell that would let her in—she'd heard Alex say that one enough times. She pushed the grand door open and stepped inside.

To the left was the vast library, with all the books neatly categorized and alphabetized. Straight ahead was a pirate ship that had seen better days, and beyond it was the gray shack that would be the only thing left if Artimé disappeared again—which only happened when the head mage died. To the right was Ol' Tater, a mastodon statue who was currently magically asleep, being too dangerous a creature to roam the island.

Beyond these massive items was an area that Fifer and Thisbe had spent plenty of time playing in when Alex and Lani had undertaken the great task of organizing Mr. Today's personal library. It was an area where people stored their useful things that they didn't need very often. And one of the useful things Fifer remembered being in here was a sort of hammock that had been made many years ago and used to transport Seth's stepfather, Sean, home after he'd broken his leg on their journey. They'd constructed the hammock out of thick ropes and sturdy canvas sails, and they'd tied it to Simber's body so Sean could rest as easily as possible in his uncomfortable state.

Fifer remembered it now because that was a story Thisbe had always wanted to reenact when they were younger. Thisbe had loved the drama of the injury, and she always wanted to play the part of Sean, while Fifer got stuck playing the part of Simber, dragging Thisbe around the Museum of Large on this hammock.

Fifer ran to find it, and she pulled it out from under a bunch of other stuff that had accumulated over the years. The canvas was wrinkled and the ropes were a bit tangled, but other than that, it seemed as sturdy as ever.

Her hands shaking a bit with excitement, Fifer checked the thing over, making sure all the knots and connections were

LISA McMANN

solid, and laying it out to see how big it was. It was large enough for two or three people, and there was room for supplies, too.

Fifer smoothed out the canvas, her mind moving a mile a minute as she thought of the possibilities Shimmer and the other birds had presented to her. But could she trust the falcons? She had no reason not to—they adored her. They obeyed her. And together they made a fierce army.

Folding the hammock, Fifer blocked out all the doubts that crowded her mind. She picked up the unwieldy thing, letting a few of the ropes trail behind her, and fled the Museum of Large. Peeking carefully out of the hallway to make sure nobody was around who might get suspicious of her, Fifer ran to the girls' hallway and down to her room. She called out to her doorway so that it would open, and she rushed in, past Desdemona before she could surface and see what Fifer was carrying. Then she threw the giant hammock onto Thisbe's bed and sank onto her own, huffing and puffing and sweating from the exertion.

After a moment to catch her breath, Fifer went back to her living area, and to her tube, where she was planning to place a room service order so she could collect food for her trip. There, on the floor of her tube, was a package tied up in colorful paper and string.

"What's this?" Fifer whispered.

Desdemona pushed her face out of the blackboard. "It came up a little while ago," she said. "Anonymously. I guess you'd better open it."

Florence Sends a Message

Desdemona kept her head pushed out far enough from the screen to watch Fifer pick up the package.

"It's heavy," Fifer said. She pulled the string to release the bow. The wrapping paper fell open, revealing a note on top of a big lumpy cloth sack. Fifer lifted the piece of paper and read it.

Dear Fifer, you've earned it, the note read. *Do what you need to do. If you need more lessons, you know where to find me. Your friend Florence, Magical Warrior trainer.*

Fifer stared at the words in wonder. Then she opened the sack and peered inside. She reached in and pulled out something soft and brown. It shimmered a bit when she first touched it. She dropped everything else, the package hitting the floor with a *thunk*.

Fifer shook out the gift and stared at it. "My component vest!" she said, then shouted, "YESSS!" She hurried to put it on, her fingers trembling with the buttons. She smoothed it down the front and whirled around to face Desdemona. "How does it look?" she asked, breathless.

"Very smart indeed," said Desdemona, and she actually smiled to see Fifer's excitement. "It fits you perfectly. And did you see the shimmer? That's the magic protection activating. Mr. Today began adding that many years ago, and Florence continued it. You're very lucky to get yours early. And I feel lucky to have witnessed it. It's a big moment in a blackboard's career to see their human get a component vest." She almost looked misty-eyed. "You're growing up."

Fifer nodded, unable to speak. She ran to the mirror to admire it. She looked absolutely wonderful. "I'll never take it off," she said.

"Don't forget there was something else in the package in that mess on the floor."

"Oh!" said Fifer. "Right." She darted back to the living area, kicked away the wrapping paper, and picked up the heavy cloth sack. Reaching inside, she felt around and pulled out a handful of stuff. "Spell components!" she cried. Scatterclips, clay balls for shackles, little moss bits for magic carpets, yellow highlighters for light and to blind enemies with, backward bobbly heads, and real fire-breathing origami dragons, among others. There were tons more where those came from.

Fifer hopped up on her sofa and started jumping and dancing for joy and shrieking and laughing for the first time in forever. It was the best possible gift she could imagine.

She went back to the note and read it again. "Do what you need to do," she read out loud. Her heart rose to her throat. Was Florence somehow giving her permission to go after Thisbe? Fifer knew that Florence had disagreed with Alex, even though the statue hadn't ever disparaged the head mage. But Florence was openly defying his wishes by offering to let Fifer join in on Magical Warrior Training—she took her job seriously and acted as the final word on who was ready. "If you need more lessons . . ." Fifer stared at the words. "If." Florence knew very well that Fifer didn't really need lessons to make the magic work. She'd been teaching Fifer secretly while she taught Alex. But was Florence really saying what Fifer thought she was saying? Florence knew about the birds and their magical presence. Did Florence also know that Fifer would figure out a way to use them to go after Thisbe? And was she trying to help her?

It seemed to be so.

With that kind of permission, Fifer felt even better about her decision. She'd leave Florence a note and be off this very evening. Maybe she could even catch up to the others. Alex would have to let her join them, and if he didn't, Fifer would just continue on her own anyway. On second thought, there was little chance Fifer could catch Simber and a dragon at the speed of a hundred birds. How fast could falcons fly, anyway? It might take her weeks to get there.

She had to gather supplies and get it right this time.

With a final word of congratulations, Desdemona shrank back and disappeared into the blackboard. Fifer changed her mind about ordering food up and decided to go down to the kitchen to sneak some food. She didn't want to tip off the chefs by requesting two weeks' worth of meals all at once. She needed to be smart. Stealthily, she gathered as much sensible food as she could carry, like nut butters and fig jam and some fruit and cheese and crusty bread and slipped back to her room through the room service tube when no one was looking. She managed two more trips like it without being noticed and was able to hide everything in the bedroom with Desdemona only poking her head out and sounding suspicious once.

Next Fifer went back to the Museum of Large to find a big travel bag so she could carry everything. Her mind whirled. Was Florence really and truly giving her permission? Or was Fifer twisting the warrior's words to make them seem so? When she returned to her room, she picked up the wrappings and string and the sack full of components. A small slip of paper fluttered to the ground. She hadn't noticed it before. Fifer stooped to grab it. It was a drawing—an absolutely terrible stick-figure drawing—of Florence herself. Written alongside the picture: *If you ever need me, use my fabulous drawing with the seek spell.*

The seek spell was something Fifer was extremely familiar with since Alex used it constantly to try to track down her and Thisbe. It only worked if the spell caster held an item created by the person they were seeking. Florence wasn't particularly artistic, so her crude drawing made Fifer smile, but it also made it even more special to know the extra effort she'd put into it.

And seeing the gift and the note solidified in Fifer's mind that Florence wasn't going to stop her if she decided to strike out on her own. With a surge of fear and excitement, Fifer went into the bedroom and began packing her bag. She was going to avoid all the problems they'd had last time by taking plenty of food and water and extra clothing. And now she had all these spell components, too.

Florence trusted her. Now Fifer had to show her she hadn't made a mistake. She took a moment to write two letters. One to Florence, thanking her and explaining what she planned to do. *I'll stop at Warbler to see Crow so you'll know I made it that far at least. That'll keep you from worrying too much. I won't do anything dangerous until I'm safely with the others. Thank you for trusting me. Your friend, Fifer.* The other letter was for Aaron to assure him she was okay and there was no need to go after her. *I'll find the rescue team, and I'll stick with Alex no matter how much he annoys me,* she wrote. *I promise. I love you!* She signed her name at the bottom.

While Fifer waited for dusk and for the lawn to clear so she could sneak off unnoticed during the evening meal, she thought about other things that could be useful to have with her. She found a new rope that would help her out the window and down to the ground, and might come in handy on her journey, and added it to her bag. Then she remembered how Dev had fished for food, and she went in search of fishing tackle and flint to make a fire—though she had the fire-breathing origami dragons to help with that part now. Still, she didn't want to use her precious components if she didn't have to.

By the time most of Artimé was inside the mansion for dinner, Fifer was packed and almost ready to go. She ordered up her favorite meal through room service and ate, then sent the letters to Florence's room through the tube—she'd be sure to give Aaron's to him. Then she went back into her bedroom and closed the door.

Her breath came in short, excited bursts as she thought about what she was going to do. It was a thousand times scarier to do this alone than it had been to have Thisbe and Seth by her side. She calmed her nerves by reminding herself that she wouldn't be alone once she found the others in the land of the dragons. But doubts kept poking at her. What if she never found them? It was a huge land—much bigger than any of the seven islands. And what if she and the birds didn't make it? No one would ever know what happened to her. An uncomfortable chill raced through her.

"Stop," she chided herself, and released the glass spell from her window. It melted away, and she sucked in the cool evening air. She spotted several of her falcons on the lawn or in trees. "Ready for an adventure?" she murmured. She grabbed her travel bag full of supplies, hoisted it out the window, and let it drop. It hit the ground with a *thud*, and Fifer cringed. She hoped nothing had broken or smashed. But if it had, it was too late now. She threw the hammock out the window after it. Grabbing the rope, she tied one end to the invisible hook outside the window and flung the other end down. Then she slipped her rucksack over her shoulders and took one last look at her comfy bed. It would be a while before she felt so snug again—at least a week. But it would all be worth it to have Thisbe back.

She climbed out, hung for a moment while she replaced the glass with a spell, and went down the side of the mansion as stealthily as possible. When she reached the ground, she coiled the rope and put it in her pack. Then she made a soft scream to call the birds. She turned and was surprised to see hundreds of eyes glowing in the dusk. The birds were already there.

"Oh, my sweet birds," she said, and bent down to pet the nearest ones. "Are you ready for this? It's going to be hard."

They bobbed their heads as if they understood, and Fifer believed they did—for some reason, with Fifer's kind of magic, they could understand her. She unfolded the hammock and spread it out. "See what I found?" she said. "Do you think this will work?"

The birds chattered softly as they moved around the edges of the hammock, tentatively testing the ends of the many ropes to make sure they weren't too big for them to take in their beaks. Shimmer slipped its head into a loop of rope and wore it around its neck, prompting the others to do the same with the other loops, which had no doubt been hooked around Simber's appendages at one point.

While the birds figured out the hammock, Fifer loaded her travel bag and backpack onto it, and then, when the birds seemed ready, she sat down in the middle of the canvas. "Should we do a test run above the lawn just in case?" Fifer asked Shimmer. She didn't want to risk being seen, but with Alex and Simber away and Florence on her side, she wasn't nearly as worried about that as she had been the first time they'd snuck out. Anyone noticing her antics now might just think she was amusing herself with her flock of birds.

Shimmer chirped out instructions to the others, and together they began flapping their wings. They lifted the corners of the hammock off the ground, and then, almost as if Fifer and her goods were weightless, the whole contraption rose into the air. With the lead bird directing the others, they flew with the precision of dancers over the lawn.

Fifer slid to her knees so she could see over the edge of the canvas. It was like a picture of a hot air balloon she'd studied once in a book, only her basket was made of a ship's sail, and the balloon was made of red-and-purple falcons. Her heart soared with the creatures as they slowly circled the lawn. It worked! She looked up at the birds and noticed that only about a third of them were holding a tether. The rest were flying alongside and in front, creating a thick cover over Fifer's head.

LISA McMANN

She wasn't sure why, but she had a lot of faith in the birds by now and knew they must have a reason for what they were doing. She'd probably find out eventually.

"If you're ready, let's go!" Fifer called out to Shimmer. "First stop, Warbler Island." She watched as Shimmer let out a sharp *spirrr*, prompting the falcons to change course. After a few minutes, Fifer rummaged through her bag of goods. She pulled out a fizzy drink and got comfortable in the hammock. Soon they were soaring over the water toward Warbler.

Fifer Rides Again

The first ten minutes of Fifer's ride to Warbler were pleasant, but then the wind picked up over the open sea and began buffeting her around. The birds soared with it, reaching speeds Fifer had never imagined they could reach and zigzagging to catch the gusts. Fifer didn't know how to anticipate which way they were going to go, and soon her stomach was flipping with each turn. She put her fizzy drink away and tried not to throw up. Next she lay back and closed her eyes, focusing on rescuing Thisbe. Eventually she tried to sleep, and she managed to get a few hours. When she woke to the sound of Shimmer's *spiiiiiirrr*, she could see

LISA McMANN

in the starlight that the birds were switching out duties. The ones who had been carrying the hammock gave their ropes to the ones who'd been flying alongside. Some of the newly free group of falcons fluttered to rest on the edges of the hammock, while others flew in front and to the sides so the birds carrying the ropes could draft along with less resistance.

It was a magically smooth changeover, and it made Fifer wonder just what had gone into these birds when she'd touched them. Had she alone made them magical, or had they somehow been magical before? They weren't native to the seven islands, according to what Seth had learned from Grandfather Ishibashi. Had they come from some other magical land that no one had discovered yet?

She dozed again. By morning Warbler Island was growing close. Fifer peered over the cloth. "That's where we want to stop," she called out, hoping the birds understood. "That island there."

A few of the birds bobbed their heads. They headed for it. That's about the time Fifer first began thinking about landing.

By the time they reached Warbler, Fifer was worried. "Set me down gently," she said. They hadn't practiced this part with the hammock, and she was situated much farther below the birds than when they'd carried her by her clothing. She braced herself for a crash, but when the birds got close to the ground, Shimmer squawked out an instruction—or something—and they threw their wings up against the wind, then slowly lowered Fifer to the ground. Once she was down, they fluttered to drop their ropes in an outstretched direction so that it would be easy to lift the cargo again when it was time to go.

Fifer crawled to the edge of the hammock and slowly got to her feet. She felt a little wobbly after the ride, like the ground was moving. She stood there for a minute, taking in the lush tropical trees and white sandy beach, then made her way into the brush toward the entrance to the underground world of Warbler Island.

The opening in the ground was slightly hidden, but Fifer knew how to find it among the palm fronds. She pushed them aside and peered into the hole, then slid down into it. She landed in a hallway lit by magical orbs that some of the Artiméans had created for Sky and Crow's mother, Copper, who was the ruler of the island now that Queen Eagala had been killed. Or . . . maybe "replaced" seemed more accurate now.

The hallways echoed with the sound of voices from people working in various rooms off the main passage. Fifer didn't stop to see if she recognized anyone. Instead she went straight for Copper's living quarters, which had once been an elaborately decorated golden throne room. Now it had been toned down quite considerably to match Copper's more sensible preferences.

A young man around Alex's age, with orange eyes and scars around his neck, sat at a desk in the outer chamber. He smiled sympathetically when he saw Fifer come in. "Hi, Fifer. How are you?"

"Hi, Phoenix. I'm doing all right, I guess. Is Crow here?" Fifer asked.

"He's in the shipyard. Do you want me to take you there?"

"I know the way. Thanks." Fifer hurried back out to the hallway and kept on in the direction she'd been going before. After several minutes, she came to an exit and climbed the steep path that brought her outside on the opposite end of the island from where she'd landed.

All around her were ships in various stages of construction. Copper and Scarlet were balancing on the mast of one, repairing something, while Crow stood on the ship's deck holding a rope attached to a block. He pulled down, and a large sail rose and flapped in the air. Copper reached out for the end of it.

"Hi, Crow," Fifer called out, trying not to startle him. "It's me. Are you doing all right?" She meant all of them, regarding Sky's disappearance, but kept the question vague in case they were weary of speculating about her. Fifer knew well enough how hard it was to keep wondering about someone.

Crow turned sharply. "Fifer," he said, seeming alarmed to see her standing there alone. "What happened? Is everything okay?"

"Everything's fine. I just promised Florence I would stop here and see you on my way to . . . um, to find Thisbe."

"You're going after all? How did you convince Alex? And hey—nice vest! What's happening? Where's the rest of the team?" Crow secured his end of the rope and climbed down a ladder to the ground. Scarlet and Copper stopped working to listen, then started down to the deck railing so they could hear better.

Fifer explained everything about the team already having left, and what had happened with the birds, and fudging a little

LISA McMANN

when it came to her being officially permitted to undertake this journey alone. "Anyway," she said, "I just wanted to report that I'm fine and the journey is going well. The birds trade places when they get tired. Some even ride in the hammock with me if they need to sleep along the way. So if Florence checks in with you, just tell her I'm all good. Okay?"

Crow frowned. He glanced up at the deck where Scarlet and Copper stood, looking skeptical. Fifer squinted up at them and had a funny feeling they were going to ask a lot of questions. "Okay, well, bye!" she said, and took an uneasy step back.

"Wait," said Crow, moving toward her. "Just hang on a minute."

"My goodness, Fifer," said Scarlet, looking over the railing, concerned. "Are you sure you can go all by yourself? What if you can't find the others?" Scarlet was blond and fair skinned, and her cheeks were bright red from exertion and sun. She had scars around her neck like Crow and all of the other people who had grown up on Warbler under Queen Eagala's rule. The awful woman had used golden thorn necklaces threaded into their necks to keep them from being able to speak. Alex had long since magically eradicated the thornaments, as he'd called them, and now the Warblerans were left with scars in place of them. Some, like Sky, had hoarse voices to this day because of the awful devices.

"Yes, I'm sure," said Fifer with confidence she wasn't quite feeling. "I know my way around there better than any of them. And I have lots of supplies with me."

Crow remained skeptical. He'd spent many years with the twins, and he knew better than to believe that everything had happened the way Fifer had laid out. "Did Florence really tell you—to your face, in those exact words—that it was okay for you to go?"

"Well, no," said Fifer, shifting her gaze away, "not to my face. But she told me in a note to do what I needed to do, and she gave me a drawing so I can send her a seek spell if I need to. So that seemed pretty much like permission to me."

"Oh, Fifer," said Crow, like he'd said so many times in her life.

Fifer scowled and produced the note as proof. "Here, see?" She shoved it at him.

Crow studied it. "Well," he said, looking doubtful, "I have a feeling she expected you to maybe get in touch with her before you headed out, but . . ."

"It's too late now," said Fifer. She took another step back in case he was going to try to stop her, but he saw what she was doing.

"Look, just take it easy," he said. "I'm not going to send you home. I'm just . . . I'm trying to decide how I feel about it. I'm worried about you being alone over there. Like Scarlet said, what if you can't find them? With your black eyes you'll be in danger every moment."

Scarlet looked at Crow with a concerned expression. "Crow," she said. "Maybe you should . . . you know."

He glanced up at the women and nodded at Scarlet. "Yeah, I think so too. Mother?"

Copper nodded, and she and Scarlet started down the ladder to the ground.

Crow turned to Fifer. "Any chance you've got enough food for me in your pack?"

Fifer's eyes widened. "You're coming with me?" She wasn't sure how to feel, but surprisingly, the first emotion that came over her was one of relief. If any other person in the world had offered, Fifer might have stubbornly refused. But Crow was like a brother—not an overbearing brother like Alex, but the nice kind of older brother who takes you on adventures and lets you do things your real brother never would.

"May I?" asked Crow. "Is there enough room for me in your bird hammock? Can they handle an additional passenger?"

That was another thing, Fifer thought. Crow wasn't pushy or demanding. He asked politely. Fifer liked that in a brother. "There are so many birds," she said. "They should be fine to carry us and Thisbe, once we find her." And then she grew somber. "But we might have to fight once we get to the land of the dragons."

"Oh." Crow wrinkled up his nose as Scarlet and Copper joined him. "Boo fighting."

"I'll protect you, though. You don't have to do anything."

A smile played at Crow's lips. "Thanks, Fig. I appreciate that. Is there time for me to gather some things?"

Fifer glanced at the sun's position in the sky. "I suppose we have a few minutes. We can meet on the front beach."

As Crow turned to go, Scarlet gave him a secret sort of smile and touched his arm. He touched her hand and smiled back.

Fifer stared at them. They were acting weirder than usual. Everybody knew that Crow had a crush on Scarlet, but he'd

LISA McMANN

never done anything about it. What in the world was going on here? Then Scarlet kissed Crow's cheek, and he grew embarrassed. Fifer felt heat rise to her face. A kiss? Were they suddenly in love or something? Feeling super awkward, Fifer yelled, "Okay, bye!" and turned and ran for the entrance to the tunnel, which was faster than going through the brush aboveground. Since Crow had left Artimé to spend a few weeks here, everything had become weird. She didn't know what to think.

When she got back to the hammock, she told the birds that Crow was coming, and they seemed to be fine with the news of a heavier load. Several minutes later, Crow emerged from behind the palm fronds carrying a small kit bag and a few jugs of water. He stopped to take in Fifer's hammock-and-bird contraption and shake his head a little in awe. "How did you manage this? Actually, never mind. Sometimes it's better if I don't know the answers."

Fifer grinned. "Come on. Just sit here next to me."

Crow joined her on the canvas. Shimmer *spiiirrred*, and the other birds flew in from the trees where they'd been resting. This time half of the birds found spots holding ropes, clearly preparing for the heavier load.

Fifer was pleased to see it. "These birds are exceptional," she confided as they began lifting off.

"Exceptional, really? They do seem quite, um, capable. I hope."

"I made it all the way here, didn't I?"

"Very good point."

As they went up into the air, Crow looked back at the island, straining to see the shipyard. He waved his arm wildly at Scarlet, making the hammock sway. Fifer blushed again. In her mind Crow belonged to her and Thisbe, and it was strange to see him giving so much attention to somebody else—especially *that* kind of attention. But Fifer knew that Crow had liked Scarlet forever, so she supposed she was happy that he seemed to be getting closer to her. It just might take a little while for her to get used to it.

After a minute, Crow turned back around and settled in. "Oh my," he said as the birds found their wing rhythm and began riding the wind westward. "We're really moving."

"I know," said Fifer. "I didn't know falcons could fly so fast."

"You've really trained them a lot since I've been gone." He glanced at the water below them. "What happens if they drop us?"

"Oh, they'll probably come after us and fish us out of the water," said Fifer with confidence.

Crow nodded. "I hope you're right."

"They do whatever I tell them to do."

"Somehow I believe that," said Crow. "You've always had a way with birds. It's great you finally figured out what to do with them."

"Hopefully they'll help us find Thisbe."

Crow shrugged. Stranger things had happened with the magical twins—he was the last person to doubt Fifer when it came to this sort of thing. "As long as I don't have to learn magic, I'm good."

"Well," said Fifer doubtfully. "I mean, there are tons of soldiers everywhere, so you might end up in a fight. Do you have any weapons or anything?"

"I've got my slingshot and a pocketful of stones. Oh, and Scarlet gave me these." He pulled out a handful of red heart components. "She told me how to use them in case I really got into trouble."

"Heart attack components?" said Fifer in awe. Florence

hadn't given her any of those. Using one would knock some-body unconscious. Using three at once was lethal—Fifer had learned that from Lani's book in the part where Aaron had killed Mr. Today. Fifer wondered idly if she would ever use three instead of one. Unlike Thisbe, Fifer had never killed anyone. But she didn't think she'd hesitate too much if it was really necessary. Of course, that kind of decision was a long way off, since Fifer'd only been given temporary spell compo-nents. She could worry about that later.

Crow nodded and put them back into his pocket without giving Fifer any. She pressed her lips together, almost about to inquire if she could have just one, but it seemed like too much to ask since it was the only spell Crow knew. Maybe she'd bet-ter show him that she could do a simpler spell first before she convinced him to give her some.

They talked some more, Crow catching Fifer up on how he and his mother were doing after Sky's disappearance. "It's very hard," he admitted. "Sky and I have been through a lot together. We almost died on our raft when we escaped Warbler. We thought we lost our mother for good, but then we found

LISA McMANN

her. And now, when all was finally going really well . . ." His eyes became misty. "I miss her so much it makes my stomach hurt."

He went on to tell Fifer that his mother was handling the news better now than at first. She was feeling numb, and working on the ships helped her try to get back to feeling normal, at least a little. "My mother doesn't want to accept that Sky is gone, but I can't imagine there's any way she's still alive."

Fifer nodded somberly.

"Scarlet has been a good friend to us both through all of this," Crow said carefully. He glanced at Fifer, like he expected her to need to process this change in his personal status. "She's been there whenever I needed to talk."

"That's nice," Fifer said. "She's . . . nice. I like her." Still awkward but getting easier, Fifer noted. That would have to do for now.

"Yes." He resettled himself more comfortably in the hammock. After a moment he said, "It's odd, you and me being together without Thisbe. It feels like we're missing a piece of our group."

Fifer nodded, feeling suddenly melancholy. She tried not to

let her worries bubble up. That wouldn't help anything. She looked up at him and saw his easygoing grin as the wind caught his long hair and blew it behind him. She grinned back. Crow was so calm and gentle and good—he'd been such a big part of her life. Even though they were suffering so much over Sky and Thisbe, it felt like everything would be okay now that he was here. And together they were going to find their missing piece.

A Wrench in Thisbe's Plan

Rohan and Thisbe met in the tunnel between their crypts every other night after he returned from his long trek. Thisbe told him about her work and how she feared that someday soon she'd be dragging four bones a day. She showed him the cuts that the harness had made in her shoulders.

Rohan sympathized and pointed at his shoes, which were quickly falling apart from so many miles of walking. "The Revinir wishes me to bring her the bones of the most ancient human rulers," he said. "Conveniently kept in the crypt farthest away from here."

LISA McMANN

"Of course they would be. You said the catacombs actually connect to the castle dungeon? So you could get in there if you wanted to?" She wondered if that might be the best way to escape since she knew her way around the dungeon a little.

"There's a thick old door separating our side from theirs. But it's heavily protected by sentries. The Revinir's blue-uniformed soldiers on our side, the king's green-uniformed soldiers on the palace's side. I've started making friends with our soldiers at that end, and one told me that it's so heavily guarded to make sure none of the miscreants in the castle dungeon can get out—I guess there was some sort of uprising down there recently. The Revinir's captive dragons escaped."

Thisbe grinned to herself. She hadn't yet told Rohan about the part she'd played in that.

Rohan went on, his face concerned. "The problem is, the king didn't confess it to the Revinir right away, so she just found out about it a few days ago. She was positively boiling over it, Thisbe. Spitting fire. I worry . . ." Rohan hesitated and shook his head. "I worry for Grimere, and for us. If the king doesn't give proper restitution to the Revinir for the dragons he lost, the two leaders will be at odds. The Revinir isn't going to just forgive him. It's troublesome."

"What are you saying?" asked Thisbe.

Rohan looked up. "I suppose I'm saying this could spark a war between them." He noticed Thisbe's frightened face and relaxed a little, waving his hand to try to erase what he'd just said. "It'll probably never come to that. And the king has already started offering her things as payback, so they're sorting it out. I guess I just have too much time to imagine what-ifs on my journey." His smile was strained. "Please don't worry about it. Perhaps the king will come through with something tremendous to appease the Revinir."

"I hope so." Thisbe breathed a little easier. She wasn't sure what a war would mean for the black-eyed slaves—would they just stay down here or be forced to fight for the Revinir? Against the king?

"Anyway," Rohan went on, lighter now, "about the Revinir's soldiers stationed at the door to the dungeon— which is what we were talking about before I turned all grim and brooding—I'm sure they're trying just as hard to keep us from finding a way out as they are to keep their prisoners in."

He yawned and scratched his back on the rough rock wall, then slid into a more comfortable position. "I've heard it's a maze down there, though. Impossible to find your way through."

"I'll say," said Thisbe, a bit smugly.

"Oh, will you?" Rohan said, teasing her.

His teasing smile fell away when Thisbe told him about her time in the dungeon and about how she and her twin sister, Fifer, and their friend Seth had helped the young dragons escape . . . or at least she'd been hoping they'd escaped. "I don't want a war, but I'm glad to know the dragons made it out," she said.

"Oh yes. They're long gone."

Long gone. Like Simber. "How do you know all of this?" asked Thisbe after a time. "The dragons, I mean, and the stuff about the king?"

"I talk to the Revinir's soldiers, who talk to the king's soldiers."

"And they just tell you stuff so willingly?"

"I give them things so they like me. Bits of gold. Stuff I steal from the extracting room."

"Ah. So you bribe them with stolen items?"

LISA McMANN

"If you must call it that," said Rohan with an evil smile. "I'm not a hundred percent good, you know."

Thisbe laughed. "Okay, anyway, can you explain this gold thing to me? I never understood what the big deal was about it," said Thisbe. "The Revinir, back when she was called Queen Eagala on Warbler Island, used to make her people forge golden thorns. She would string them around people's necks to stop them from being able to talk."

Rohan blinked. "What a horror. She really did that?"

Thisbe nodded. "And she changed their eyes to orange so they'd be easily identified if they ever tried to escape."

"Like branding them," said Rohan. "She put her mark on them."

Thisbe nodded.

"And now she's put her new brand on us," Rohan said, running his finger over the back of his neck. "Does yours still hurt?"

"No." Thisbe touched her brand too. It was scratchy with dried scabs, some of which had already fallen off. "I don't understand why she has to do such violent things. I mean, she's got us captured and doing her work for her. Why does she need to brand us too?"

"She's obviously not right in the head," said Rohan. "To ingest dragon-bone marrow for its magical properties, and to delight in dragon scales growing thick on her skin? That's deranged."

Thisbe agreed, even though she wasn't quite sure what deranged meant. She wished for a library like the one in Artimé so she could look things up. But without that, she could at least guess what Rohan meant. It didn't sound like a nice word.

Rohan rested his eyes for a few moments while Thisbe thought through all she'd learned. After a while she sat up, startling Rohan awake again. "She's got a new assistant instead of me," Thisbe told him.

Rohan nodded as though he knew about it, but he didn't interrupt.

"Yet she still keeps trying to convince me to help her. She says . . ." Thisbe hesitated. For some reason she didn't want to talk about how the Revinir had told her she was more evil than good—besides, Rohan had heard her say it the first time. He knew the truth about her, and it didn't seem to bother him. Instead, she went in a different direction. "She's going to keep adding bones to my workload. I'm already struggling with three, but I'm due for another one any day now—I can feel it. I won't be able to do four. No way. I wonder if maybe . . ." She grew quiet, thinking.

"Maybe what?" prompted Rohan.

"Maybe I should give in. I mean, she's right. It's obvious nobody's coming back for me. Will I have more chances of getting out of here if I work with her? If I can get her to trust me?"

Rohan tapped his chin, thinking aloud. "Hmm. Interesting. And why *not* give in? Why not be her assistant? Maybe that will give you some power. And perhaps you can find out her weaknesses or even her secrets if you work with her all day."

"Exactly." Thisbe wrinkled her nose. "Working with her sounds awful."

"But like you said, it might give you a better opportunity to escape. Because you still want to, right? Even after you told the Revinir you no longer did?"

Thisbe looked hard at him. Again a ribbon of doubt sliced through her—could she trust him? Was he so good that he would feel compelled to tell the Revinir about her plans?

At this point, Thisbe decided, she couldn't *not* trust him. She had no one else in the world, and without help, she might never escape. Before she could change her mind, she blurted out, "Yes, I still want to escape. Do you? Will you help me? Will you escape with me?"

Rohan looked solemnly at her and nodded. "I never thought I could get out of here alone. But I believe if we work together, we might succeed. Especially if you can make your fiery magic work properly." He hesitated. "A lot of the guards already favor me, and I'm being extra good to them lately so they trust me more. If you can get cozy with the Revinir and find out some things, well . . . I think it's worth the attempt, anyway."

They stayed up late talking about the plan, and eventually Thisbe decided it was inevitable—she wouldn't be able to continue her job with more dragon bones. So she agreed to make the most of the situation.

As Thisbe stared off, thinking things through, Rohan dozed again.

"I wonder who the new assistant is," she mused. "Maybe he could be useful."

"What's that?" said Rohan, jolting awake.

"I said I wonder who the new assistant is. Is it one of the other slaves here?"

"No. He's actually part of the king's payback for the dragons that I mentioned earlier—one of his slaves. My sources tell me the king's daughter, Princess Shanti, got mad at her whipping boy and said she didn't want him anymore. So the king immediately offered him up when the Revinir found out about the dragons' escape."

Thisbe's stomach lurched. "What?" she whispered. "Princess Shanti's servant boy is . . . here? *He's* the assistant?" Her mind was spinning.

"That's what the soldier gossip is. I don't know his name, but I suppose you'll meet him soon enough."

Thisbe blinked, trying to figure out what it all meant. "Dev," she said softly, and then she looked at Rohan. "His name is Dev."

A Dark Venture

The next morning when Mangrel opened Thisbe's door, the Revinir was standing there with him. The woman didn't bother asking Thisbe if she'd be her assistant this time. She simply said, "Four bones."

Thisbe had to think fast. She hadn't prepared for the Revinir to show up at her door—she'd just intended to tell Mangrel she was giving up and have him show her to the ruler. Now she scrambled to make her plan work. She kept her chin up and gazed at the woman's pale, wrinkled face. "I can't do four," said Thisbe. "It's too heavy. It's too much." She dropped her gaze.

LISA McMANN

The Revinir didn't try to hide how pleased she was. "You could take two trips a day," she suggested. "You might still have time for a couple hours of sleep each night. Though you'd miss dinner. You wouldn't last many days that way."

Thisbe stared at the dirt floor and was quiet, as if she were considering it.

"Or you could work with me," said the woman. "Those are your options. Which do you choose?"

Thisbe glanced at Mangrel, who stood at attention, his face showing no emotion. Then she looked at the Revinir again and despaired. "I guess I have no choice. I won't live long without any meals."

"Precisely," said the Revinir. She grew more reserved and clicked her long fingernails against each other. "Come along, then. Bring three dragon bones with you. We're starting a new project today. How convenient to have you to help me and my new assistant just when we need you. I timed that quite well, didn't I?"

When no one answered, the Revinir glanced at the crypt keeper. "Didn't I, Mangrel?"

Mangrel frowned slightly, then answered, "Yes, ma'am."

Thisbe took her morning pitcher of water and drank it slowly, staring at the Revinir over the rim the whole time, which she hoped was unnerving. When she finished, she wiped her mouth with her singed sleeve and handed the pitcher back to Mangrel, then turned away and harnessed three bones to herself. She dragged them into the hallway and followed the Revinir in the opposite direction she'd normally go.

Thisbe watched the symbols on the walls, wondering which one of them pointed to the Revinir's quarters. Eventually she determined that a crown symbol next to a purple directional arrow was the one to follow. She noted that the red arrows that pointed to the extraction room would return her to the hallway where her crypt was, so she wouldn't have to worry about getting lost on her way back.

The path to the Revinir's quarters twisted and turned, and the woman walked briskly. Thisbe followed, falling several steps behind because of her heavy load. Eventually they came to a group of soldiers who were guarding the entrance to a side hallway. When they saw the Revinir, they parted to let her and Thisbe through, and the woman spoke to them while Thisbe caught up. This side hallway had gold stone walls rather than the gray rock walls of the rest of the underground. The doors were covered in jewels. It reminded Thisbe a bit of the castle, and for a moment Thisbe wondered if the Revinir was trying to turn the catacombs into a showy underground palace.

The woman went through one of the bejeweled doors and Thisbe went after her. The place shone with gaudy baubles and golden trinkets. Thisbe grimaced, finding it ugly. They passed through the entry room and continued into a huge kitchen, where enormous cauldrons sat near fire pits. Smoke curled up to the high ceiling and disappeared through a metal vent. Thisbe wondered if it led to the outside somehow, and if so, was the opening big enough for a girl her size? It didn't seem likely.

"You can unhitch the bones. You'll be working in here," the Revinir declared. "But first we're going to have a little chat." Thisbe slipped the harness off. They went back out of the kitchen and into a room nearby that had a throne in it, sitting atop a short pedestal. Thisbe nearly laughed at how ridiculous it looked. Did the woman actually sit there sometimes? If so, why? To feel important? Down here, there were only some soldiers and slaves around to be in awe over her—and Thisbe certainly wasn't impressed.

The Revinir stepped up to the throne and sat down ceremoniously. The hem of her robe rose up when she sat, revealing luminescent scales of all colors around her ankles. It was creepy. Thisbe stood on the floor, unsure of what she was supposed to do.

"Tell me about your magic," the woman demanded. "How did you destroy my birds?"

Thisbe almost corrected her like she'd done before, but then decided not to bother. The Revinir might as well think she'd done that, too. "I don't know how I did it. I was two."

"What else can you do? You sent sparks at my soldiers when they branded you. How did you do that?"

"It just happens. I can't control it," Thisbe said easily, even though it was no longer true. She'd repeated that line her whole life. "It's just some little sparky thing—it doesn't do much."

"And? What more?"

"Nothing much," said Thisbe. "Not without spell components."

The Revinir frowned and stared at Thisbe, like she was trying to determine if she was lying. Thisbe stared back, convincing herself to believe everything she'd just said—she wasn't sure what the woman could do with her dragon abilities, but it seemed like dragons might be able to know if someone was telling the truth. So she assumed the same for the Revinir. It was unsettling, thinking about how many lies Thisbe had told down here. There were a lot. If lies were evil, Thisbe was starting to wonder if the Revinir's assessment of her being more evil than good might actually be true.

She didn't want to think about it. "What can *you* do?" Thisbe asked her.

The Revinir seemed taken aback by the direct question. Her face clouded. "A lot more than you."

"I didn't know it was a competition," said Thisbe, feeling like she was talking to a child. She sniffed and looked around the throne room. "What do you want me to do here, anyway?"

"First you'll be helping me develop a new product to sell in Dragonsmarche. We'll see how well you do with that. Mostly I want you nearby so I can keep my eye on you."

"You could always just let me go. Then you wouldn't have to worry about me at all."

"Oooh no, my dear," said the Revinir. "You're much too valuable."

Thisbe stiffened at the term of endearment.

"Besides," said the woman, softening her tone a bit. "We can do great things together."

Thisbe's eyes narrowed. "Like what?"

"Well," said the Revinir, "to my knowledge, you and I are the only magical people in Grimere. Isn't that fascinating? And I'm growing more powerful by the moment with my dragon magic injections."

"You're injecting that bone marrow stuff?" asked Thisbe. "That's disgusting."

"Ah, but I'm a wonderful showcase for the new product we'll be creating, and soon I'll be richer than the king. Of course, we won't be selling the same strength of magic that I use for myself—that would be absurd to let anyone become as powerful as me."

Thisbe stared. "What?"

The Revinir continued. "I believe there's a way to reap the benefits of the dragon bones on a less potent level, however, through bone broth. I'm testing it out in my kitchen, and I've already begun experimenting on my test subject. It's risky, sure. But the bones are plentiful, and there is a great amount

LISA McMANN

of gold to be made if I'm successful. The pirates will pay top prices once they see what I've done, and the townspeople will be astounded and beg for more. But the timing is very important." She paused, deep in thought.

Thisbe silently freaked out.

"Once I buy the kingdom, or take it by force, we'll defeat my worst enemy once and for all. He'll never know what hit him."

"Your worst enemy?" asked Thisbe, suspecting she meant Alex, but hoping otherwise. "You mean the king?"

The Revinir eyed her. "The king is my pawn. He made a grave mistake in letting my dragons escape, and he'll pay for it. But I'll finish him off when his usefulness has run out. I'm talking about someone far more powerful. Someone from another land."

Thisbe didn't know of any other lands besides her own. "Do you mean the pirates? But you said you were going to sell this stuff to them."

"No, not the pirates." She smiled down at the girl. "I'm talking about your brother."

Thisbe stared as if she were shocked to hear it. "My brother? You mean Alex?"

"Yes. The one who left you here and never came back. That's what a horrible person he is."

Thisbe reared back at the inaccurate portrayal of her brother. "He—he's not—" she stammered. "He's not horrible."

"Then why, Miss Stowe, hasn't he come back for you? Why hasn't *anyone* come back for you? Surely *someone* would, unless the ruler of your world commanded them not to."

Thisbe fought with her words, trying to find the ones to protest what the awful woman was saying. "You don't know him at all!" she cried.

"Maybe he's trying to punish you," the Revinir said. "Teach you a lesson by leaving you here. Have you done anything wrong lately? Anything against his wishes?"

"I—I—you don't know what you're talking about!" Thisbe said. "You're a terrible person to say such things about my brother. He loves me! He's going to come for me." As she said the words, she felt doubt creep in. She'd told herself the same thing just the other night. It had been weeks, and no one had come. What did it mean? Why hadn't they found her yet? Where were they?

LISA McMANN

"There, there," said the Revinir. "I didn't mean to upset you. I just thought you'd have figured it out by now. After all, he didn't take this long to come after me with an entire army the first time we had a falling out. You'd think he'd come even quicker for his sister, but alas, he hasn't. It seems pretty obvious to me what's going on here, but if you're not ready to hear that . . . well, let's change the subject." She clicked her fingernails against the arms of her throne. "Are you ready to start working on the first batch of broth?"

Thisbe couldn't speak. Her face was hot with anger, and she feared she'd start shooting sparks everywhere if she wasn't careful. She turned away from the woman and stared at the door where the soldiers stood. "Sure," she said through gritted teeth.

"Let's get moving, then." The Revinir stood and clapped her hands. "Come with us, Dev," she called out, then turned to look behind her throne, where a small table was pushed up against it. Thisbe peered around it and gasped. Dev had been sitting there working quietly the whole time.

"Come out, Dev. Meet Miss Stowe and show her what a great assistant you are. My first glorious test subject."

Dev stepped slowly into view. He wouldn't make eye contact. Thisbe watched him, confused by what the Revinir was saying about him being a test subject. She looked harder at him, and then, with horror, she noticed that the skin below his ragged sleeves and pant legs was speckled lightly with dragon scales.

Doubt Creeps In

Thisbe listened numbly as the Revinir showed her where to find everything in the test kitchen. Dev didn't say a word. He looked like he wanted to disappear into the floor. When the Revinir had explained everything that Thisbe was to do, she turned to face the girl. "Do you have any questions?"

"No," Thisbe said. Then: "Yes. Why are you doing this here? Why not in the testing room?"

"I wish to keep this product private for now until I know how it works. Once I've determined the proper levels to provide the weakest visible effects, we'll produce a small batch to sell in the marketplace. I don't want it to be too plentiful—we want dragon-bone broth to become a craze. We want people to be searching for it. We want them to feel they must have it at all costs."

"But . . . aren't you afraid of people buying it and becoming magical and able to attack you?"

The Revinir laughed. "They won't have access to nearly enough magical product to make them anywhere strong enough to attack me. Besides, they can't get to me down here. And when I've gotten as powerful as I can be, and finished all I intend to do around here, we'll leave this place. I'll go back home to Warbler Island and take over the other islands like I'd planned all along. Especially Artimé."

Thisbe stared. "But how will you get across the gorge?"

The woman smiled. "I have my ways of getting back home. And there are the ghost dragons to the south and west of us if I should need to take them captive. But with any luck, I'll have my own dragon wings by the time I need them."

Even Dev reacted to that, repulsion evident on his face.

Thisbe could hardly take in what she was hearing. She didn't ask any more questions. Eventually the Revinir left her and Dev alone in the kitchen to start working on the magical dragon-bone broth. Three soldiers stood guard at the entrance to the Revinir's quarters, a whole room away from the kitchen. Thisbe and Dev were practically alone.

Thisbe turned to look Dev in the eye. "Hello again, thief," she said. "I didn't think I'd ever see you again. And now you've got dragon scales. How fashionable."

Dev closed his eyes and shook his head. "Shut it."

"Rude," muttered Thisbe. She hauled one of the giant pots across the floor to place on the fire, then hoisted one of the dragon bones into it. Then she began dragging buckets of water to pour over the bone. The Revinir had said it would need to simmer for many hours, perhaps overnight, in order for some of the magic to seep out of the bones into the broth.

Dev did the same with another pot and bone. He didn't talk to Thisbe.

She didn't talk to him, either—she was still reeling about him having dragon scales. Part of her thought through the idea of getting Dev on her side. He was maybe a little bit powerful now because of drinking the dragon-bone broth, which could be useful, though she had no idea what he could do—perhaps he just had the scales and that was it. The other part of her wanted to punch him in the face for what he'd done to her and Fifer and Seth. She wanted answers. But she knew she needed him on her side. She just wasn't sure how to get him there. And if she did, how would she even know? He wasn't trustworthy.

Once they both had their pots filled, all they had to do was sit and watch them, and add more water after a while to cover the portion that boiled off. The two sat awkwardly across the room from each other by their pots and stayed that way, casting veiled glances at each other.

Eventually Dev sighed and got up. He went over to Thisbe and sat down next to her. "Sorry," he mumbled.

Finding his apology surprising yet totally inadequate, Thisbe ignored him and chose instead to read the labels of the various ingredients on the pantry shelves next to her.

After a few minutes, Dev began to tremble and shake.

Thisbe didn't notice what was happening at first. But then Dev made a few weird squeaks. She turned and realized with a start that he was falling apart in sobs. She looked at him in alarm, and then she glanced out the door to make sure the soldiers weren't watching. After a long moment of uncertainty, she reluctantly reached out to him and gave him an awkward hug.

He held his body stiff, like he didn't know how to hug, but he stayed there, crying into Thisbe's dirty shirt like the world had ended for him.

Thisbe wasn't sure what to do. She stayed still and patted his back every now and then. Once she said, "There. It's okay." That made him cry harder. She didn't know what to make of it, but her sympathy for him grew as the time passed. She thought about what might have caused him to be so overwhelmingly crushed that he would fall apart like this with a practical stranger. Had he lost his precious piece of traitor gold? Or was he actually broken up about leaving the palace? This work in the kitchen seemed so much easier than the work he'd been doing—she'd think he'd be happy about that.

After a while he lifted his head and sniffed loudly. Then he wiped his face with his shirtsleeve. The uneven smattering of dragon scales on his forearm caught the light and shimmered. Maybe that was why he was crying. Thisbe hadn't fully processed how the Revinir might have administered the test product to him, but if she'd forced him to take it against his will, that seemed a strong enough reason to be upset.

"Are you all right?" Thisbe asked gently.

"I don't want to talk about it," said Dev. He pulled away and stared at his cauldron.

Thisbe made a frustrated noise, her sympathy flying out the door. "Are you kidding me? You get snot all over my shirt and you won't tell me what is so upsetting?" After weeks away from Dev, she was immediately as annoyed by him as she had been the day he'd stolen their food and eaten it in front of them.

"It's not that I won't. It's just . . . I don't want to start blubbering again." He said "blubbering" with a sneer, then frowned hard at the floor.

"Suit yourself," said Thisbe, her tone icy. "But where I come from, blubbering isn't something to avoid. It's a normal part of life to cry sometimes. And it makes you feel better. So maybe if *you* feel better, we'll both have a nicer time of it here."

Dev said nothing, but another tear dripped down his cheek. He swiped at it.

Thisbe sighed. She got up and went to check the bone

broth. "So . . . she made you drink this stuff? Is that how you got all scaly?"

"Yeah."

Thisbe peered at him. "Can you do anything magical now? Or dragonlike?"

"I . . . No. I don't think so."

"Do you feel anything different?"

Dev flashed an annoyed look. "My nose still hurts from when you broke it."

Thisbe frowned. Back in the dungeon, she'd planted a glass spell in his way and he'd slammed into it face-first. The reminder made her want to do it again. "So you don't feel anything different at all? You just grew some scales? Do they itch? They look itchy."

Dev sighed heavily and got up. He walked across the room to his cauldron and sat down on the floor over there.

Thisbe rolled her eyes. This wasn't going at all how she'd planned. She'd wanted to be friendly with Dev and try to get him to join her and Rohan in a revolt. But his bad attitude was extremely annoying, and Thisbe couldn't seem to let it go. Why couldn't he be decent?

After a while Thisbe sat down again by her pot. "I'm sorry about breaking your nose."

Dev shrugged and closed his eyes. "I lied. It wasn't broken. Just sore."

"Of course you lied," muttered Thisbe. What else was new?

Dev fell asleep, or faked it well, and Thisbe sat wrapped in her thoughts. When she grew bored, she concentrated on the fire and tried to flick sparks at it. She wanted her aim to get better from close range, but her flicks caused sparks to go in all sorts of directions. One flew up and came down on her head, causing a lock of her hair to melt and fall to the floor. She slapped the top of her head to make sure it went out. Then she scooted back from the fire to try sending sparks at it again from a distance.

The day continued with time moving extraordinarily slowly. Thisbe napped too. When she awoke to a nasty smell, she scrunched her nose and sat up. "What's that awful stink?" she asked Dev.

"It's the bone broth," he said, seeming less antagonistic after his nap. "The bones are releasing all the gunk inside them. It reeks enough to poison the gods. The Revinir said that'll make people in the marketplace want it even more. I don't get it, but she seems to know what she's doing."

"Is she going to keep making you drink it?"

Dev gazed at his forearms. His expression grew troubled again. "I think so."

Thisbe watched him. "Is there any way to make the scales go away?" she asked softly.

"I don't know." Dev blew out a breath. "It doesn't matter, I guess. Nothing that happens to me matters. We're not people. Not to her. Or to them."

"Them?" asked Thisbe, puzzled. "The soldiers?"

"Well, them too."

"But that's not who you meant."

Dev gave her a look. "You're not going to give up with the questions, are you?"

Thisbe grinned. "Not likely."

He threw his hands up. "Fine. The princess. And the whole kingdom, really. We're just . . . less than." His face screwed up. Then he stopped fighting the tears and let them go. He pressed his thumb and forefinger to the inside corners of his eyes, squeezing even more out.

Thisbe was quiet. After a while, she said, "I thought Shanti was your friend."

Dev didn't answer at first. Then he let out a shuddering sigh. "So did I."

So that was why Dev was so upset. Even though she knew some of what had happened from Rohan, she didn't want to let on. "What happened? Is she the one who got rid of you? Did she send you here?"

He stared at the floor in front of him and nodded. "She'd been mad at me for a few weeks."

"Why?"

After a moment, Dev looked up. "Because I helped your friends save Fifer's life."

LISA McMANN

Trying to Cope

Thisbe looked up sharply. "What?" she asked Dev. "Fifer's alive?"

"She was alive when I saw her," Dev said. "I showed Thatcher how to stop her bleeding. If he kept doing what I showed him, I would guess she survived."

The news of Fifer slammed into Thisbe, leaving her reeling. Over the past weeks she'd tried desperately to put Fifer's unknown fate in the back of her mind so she could get through each day. And now everything that had happened, everything she'd tamped down in order not to feel it, came rushing back. She slid her shaking fingers into her hair and gripped it, wanting to scream, but she couldn't with the soldiers nearby. She covered her mouth and tried to calm her breath until she could trust herself to speak quietly again. "Fifer's alive. You think."

Dev gave her a pained look that was not unkind. "I think so, Thisbe, but I can't say for sure. All I know is that she was alive at the point when Thatcher and that flying monster reached the forest. Thatcher and I started patching her up. She'd lost a lot of blood. And they had a long journey ahead of them, right? I told them to go right away—they weren't safe in Grimere with her."

The additional revelations rattled Thisbe again. "So they went . . . home? Without me?" She choked on the words as she pictured Simber, Thatcher, and Fifer flying over the gorge, away from her. She'd assumed it after a while, but now she knew it was true, and it hurt like a fresh stab to the heart.

Dev nodded. "Yes," he said quietly. "I watched them go. I think they *had* to—they had to do it to save Fifer's life."

Thisbe felt her body go numb. Of course they had to do

that. Of course they needed to save her sister, who was right there with them, rather than the one they couldn't get to. There was no other choice.

After a long while, Thisbe looked up. She swallowed hard. "You haven't seen them return?"

Dev's expression flickered, like he was realizing what Thisbe must be thinking—that they weren't coming back for her. "No," he said reluctantly. "I'd been watching. Before Shanti sent me here, anyway. That was three days ago."

Thisbe grew urgent. "No sign of anyone? Are you sure you'd have seen them?"

"If not with my own eyes, I'd have heard about it. Visitors from that direction don't often go unnoticed."

Thisbe felt something tearing through her chest. She couldn't breathe. Her head fell back against the wall, and she began to moan in pain like a wounded animal.

Dev looked at her in alarm. He glanced worriedly at the door, then back at Thisbe. When she continued the noise, he got up and went over to her. "Shh," he said softly, keeping an eye out for soldiers. "I know it feels bad."

Thisbe raked in a breath and started sobbing. "They should have come back by now," she cried, not caring who heard her. Her heart was breaking right there on the Revinir's kitchen floor, and she couldn't stop it.

Desperate, Dev reached out to put an arm around her shoulders. "Shh," he said again. "Shh. The soldiers will hear."

Thisbe covered her face with her hands and shook. Dev patted her back, looking terribly uncomfortable but growing more desperate to quiet her cries. "Thisbe," he said firmly. "It's going to be okay. It doesn't mean they're not coming. Maybe something held them up."

Thisbe shook her head in her hands. She knew better. Nothing could hold them up if they really wanted to go after something. She'd read Lani's books. The people of Artimé were warriors. And they didn't waste time.

After a while Thisbe lifted her head and saw Dev's concerned face in front of hers. She looked at him for a long moment. "Maybe the Revinir was right," she whispered. "They're never coming back."

"Don't listen to her," said Dev weakly. But his face gave

away his own suspicions. "How long does it take for them to get to your island?"

"A few days. They could have dropped Fifer off and turned around and been back here within a week."

"Oh." Dev looked away.

Thisbe could tell he believed what she was thinking and feeling too. They should have been back long before now. For an instant Thisbe wondered if the Revinir was right that Alex really was teaching her a lesson. If so, it was the meanest lesson she'd ever heard of. But deep in her heart Thisbe knew that couldn't be it. The Revinir was lying, making things up to get Thisbe to be on her side. Even as forgotten as Thisbe was feeling right now, she knew there had to be a logical reason for no one from Artimé coming back for her. And she refused to let the Revinir poison her mind against her brother—everything he'd ever done was out of love for her. She knew that. She began crying again, quietly this time. Because despite all that, she still had no idea where they could be.

Dev gave her a helpless look. After a while he got up to add water to his bone broth. He added some to Thisbe's as well while she sat grieving on the floor.

Hours went by in which neither of them spoke. Before they were done for the day and allowed to return to their crypts, Thisbe turned to Dev. "Thank you for saving my sister's life," she said. "And I'm sorry about Shanti."

Dev glanced at her, and for a moment they both felt the connection that comes when people are in pain together. "Thanks," he said. After a minute, he added, "She was my only friend."

Dev's Story

Thisbe spent a thoughtful evening alone in her crypt. It was a night Rohan was working, so he wasn't around. She ate her meal and worked on her magic half-heartedly, then went to sleep early.

The next morning Mangrel told her to bring three more bones to the Revinir's kitchen. She dragged them there.

The stench of the broth was permeating the nearby hallways now. When Thisbe arrived, Dev was already there with the Revinir, checking the cauldrons that they'd covered and left simmering over a slowly dying fire all night. Dev stoked the fires and added wood as Thisbe unharnessed her dragon bones.

"That's the last load you'll need to bring for this batch of product," said the Revinir, tasting the broth. She wrinkled her nose. "Disgusting," she said. "It's perfect."

Dev flashed an "I told you so" glance at Thisbe, and it was true—to the Revinir, bad was good. Scarcity increased demand. What other weird lesson would Thisbe learn today?

"Now we'll have to make the new broth equally as bad," the Revinir declared.

"New broth? Won't it all taste the same?" asked Thisbe. "It's just bones and water."

"You'll see soon enough." The Revinir took a cup and dipped it in the dragon-bone broth. She handed it to Dev. "Drink up," she said. "Let's see how strong it is."

Dev closed his eyes momentarily, as if he was resigned to doing this thing he didn't want to do. He plugged his nose, then took a few swallows. He almost gagged, but held it down. Then he took a few more breaths and finished the cup. "Blech!" he said when he finished. "That is just . . . the worst. It gives me a stomachache."

"Lift your sleeve," said the Revinir, who didn't seem to care.

Dev shoved his sleeve up, revealing the scales. As they

looked on, a few more scales appeared and blended in with the existing ones.

"Hmm," said the woman. She turned to Thisbe, her eyes narrowed, then scooped another cup of broth. "Drink it," she said, shoving it at her.

"Who, me? No!" said Thisbe, though she was curious about it.

"Soldiers," called the Revinir. Three soldiers came running. They pulled out their weapons. The Revinir turned back to Thisbe. "Drink it!"

"Sheesh." Thisbe, unnerved, took the cup in her shaky hand. She looked at Dev, who had dropped his gaze. Her heart fluttered in her chest, as if she sensed her life was about to change forever, and she gasped a little in fear. "I can't do it," she said.

One of the soldiers stepped closer, a menacing look on his face.

"Do it!" said the Revinir.

"Okay!" said Thisbe, shrinking back. She closed her eyes and pressed the warm cup to her lips. She tipped it and took a sip, swallowing it down. It was awful.

"Hurry up," said the Revinir. "I've got things to do today."

Now that she'd taken the first bit and there was no undoing it, the rest went down more easily. She took a few swallows, grimaced, and then finished it. It made her feel a little bit dizzy. Her arms and legs began tingling.

"Your arm," prompted the Revinir.

Thisbe pushed her sleeve up and held her arm out. A smattering of iridescent scales pushed out of her skin. She stared at them. "Oh my," she breathed, equally horrified and curious. They'd sprouted from her body, which was weird. But they were beautiful.

"It's too strong," declared the Revinir. "Dilute it with water to twice the volume. Then bottle it up to be sold. Don't spill any—not a drop!" With that, she dashed off.

The soldiers left the kitchen too and settled in their usual spot by the hallway. Dev and Thisbe looked at each other. Then Thisbe examined her arms and legs again and tried unsuccessfully to pull one of the scales out. "This is . . . horrifying. I think."

"I mean, you get used to it," said Dev, looking cautiously at Thisbe. "It's really sort of interesting. Unique, you know?"

But Thisbe was overwhelmed. Even coming from a magical world, she'd never seen or experienced anything like this. It was one thing to discover the larger-than-life Revinir sporting the scales, but to have felt them sprout from her own skin and to see them shining now—it was nothing less than extraordinary. She was forever changed. A human with dragon scales! And it had happened with such negativity and force, and so little fanfare or joy, which felt wrong for such a beautiful thing. It seemed like it could be so great to take on a dragon property like this, yet it had been done in such a degrading way that Thisbe was having a terrible time trying to figure out how to feel about it.

She crouched and looked at her legs, and slid her finger over her shin, feeling a surprising softness. This was so strange that she couldn't quite grasp what it meant for her. Would the scales ever go away?

"Are you okay?" asked Dev, looking at Thisbe curiously. "It's a little bit of an odd feeling, isn't it? Like . . . losing a tooth. It takes a couple days for it to feel normal."

Thisbe nodded. She definitely felt odd, not just physically, but mentally, too. Almost like she had gained an unspecified amount of knowledge, though she couldn't pinpoint any topics. She felt older, though that wasn't quite it either. "Wiser," she murmured.

"Yes," Dev said emphatically. He knew exactly what she meant. Then he turned quickly, embarrassed by his own enthusiasm over Thisbe's sudden change. Perhaps he felt less alone because of it. He fumbled with a cart filled with tiny empty bottles, then remembered they needed to dilute the broth first and went after a bucket of water. "I told you it tastes awful."

"Yes. It's like dirt and mustiness," said Thisbe, wondering if her fate had been instantly changed by this. Perhaps not. All she knew was that her desire to escape was stronger than ever. Would this newfound wisdom help her understand the Revinir a bit better? Could she anticipate the woman's motives more successfully now? Maybe it could help her get out of here.

Her mind turned to that dilemma as she absently stroked her arm, trying to get used to the surprising softness of the scales. When she brushed her hand down over them, they lay smooth and flat. But when she brushed upward, they stood uncomfortably, tugging at her skin. She didn't like that feeling, so she smoothed everything downward again.

LISA McMANN

Dev's water bucket clanged against the side of his cauldron, bringing Thisbe back to the task at hand. She realized that he was doing all the work while she had just been standing there. "Sorry," she said, and began helping to dilute the broth. She could feel the scales slice the air.

"It's okay," said Dev generously, going back for more water. "I get it."

Thisbe marveled a bit longer, but her thoughts eventually returned to escaping again. She knew with certainty that she needed to work on Dev some more—and with the new scales, they had something extraordinary in common. That could serve to bring them closer. And he was being decent today, at least, so she wanted to take advantage of it. As they worked, she thought about the previous day and realized she'd never gotten the whole story behind why Dev was sent away from the castle. Maybe talking about that would also serve to strengthen her trust in him a little.

"So . . . what actually happened to bring you here?" asked Thisbe. "You said Shanti sent you away because you helped Fifer."

"Yes," said Dev. "That was part of it."

"Why wouldn't she want you to help her?"

Dev shrugged. "Shanti assumed Fifer would die. She was mad that she wouldn't get the money from selling her at the auction after she was counting on her."

Perhaps because of the Revinir's teachings about the marketplace, or because of the wisdom from the dragon-bone broth, Thisbe, who'd never spent money in any form before, was beginning to understand how and why it was used to trade for things. But she still thought money was a waste of time. "In Artimé, we don't use money. Nobody buys or sells things. We just have them. Or we give each other things if we need something. I guess we don't need gold if we have magic." She thought for a moment, landing back on what Dev had said about Shanti. "Wait. The princess didn't want you to help a severely injured person because she was losing money over it?"

"Basically."

Thisbe was incredulous. "And you went against Shanti's wishes to save my sister? You risked that?"

Dev looked uncomfortable. "Of course. Fifer was going to die otherwise." He started to fill the tiny bottles.

Thisbe wasn't quite sure what to say—Dev had been a

hero, and she'd had to drag the information out of him. That wasn't what she'd expected from him. "Then what happened?" she asked.

Dev started from the beginning and told her about how he and Shanti had been heading for Dragonsmarche to see what would happen at the auction when they noticed Simber flying toward them. After Dev had done what he could and the Artiméans flew away, he and Shanti continued to the city. "Dragonsmarche was in chaos when we got there. Carts were overturned, people trampled, the giant aquarium was cracked and flooding the square, and some of the sea creatures were sure to die. There was nothing we could do for them. Some were captured and stolen. I hope the rest of them made it to the lake."

"That's horrible." Thisbe remembered pointing out the aquarium to Fifer before they'd been tied up on the auction stage. There had been a creature inside that had looked familiar. But it was all a blur now.

"We hung around the square listening to the story about what happened to you. I tried looking for you, but of course there's no way I know of to make the Revinir's elevator come up when you're on the outside. Most of us didn't even know that entrance to the catacombs existed. She must only use it in the dead of night or something."

Thisbe had figured as much when the crowd seemed surprised to see it come up in the square. "You really looked for me?"

Dev's expression flickered. "I mean, I couldn't, obviously—you were underground, and the other entrances are far away from where we were in Dragonsmarche. But I looked around a little, in case the townspeople were wrong."

"Interesting," said Thisbe. She almost smiled, but the memory of being snatched away by the Revinir was too heartbreaking—that moment marked Thisbe's estrangement from everything she knew, or might ever know again. "Did the Revinir pay Princess Shanti for me? Or did she just steal me and get away with it?"

"I think she paid the princess something afterward. But then she got really mad when she found out the dragons had escaped."

Thisbe nodded, saying nothing to give away the fact that she'd learned some of that information already. She felt an emptiness growing inside whenever she thought about people buying and selling other people. And she wondered if Alex and the others would have to *buy* her in order to get her back. The desolate feeling led her to wonder once more if the Revinir was right about Alex not sending a rescue party for her. Why? The question pounded in her ears, unanswered. Maybe he'd had enough of her. Maybe he'd actually just thrown his hands in the air in frustration for the last time. But wouldn't someone try to talk him into going back, like Florence or Lani? Wouldn't anyone else come back for her? Not even Fifer? Maybe they didn't know how to get money.

It was all too confusing. As much as Thisbe tried to convince herself that she was being ridiculous in thinking any of those bad thoughts, she still couldn't come up with a good reason for Alex not sending someone for her. And that continued to sow more and more doubt in her mind as she began to bottle the magical bone broth.

"So you stayed with the princess?" Thisbe said eventually, picking up Dev's story again and prompting him for more.

"Yes, but she was mad that I'd defied her. I apologized, and things got a little better. Then, about a week ago, the Revinir

LISA McMANN

finally discovered that her dragons had escaped—she hadn't heard about it since she was underground, I guess, and the king wasn't about to admit it. But word worked its way underground to the Revinir's soldiers, and she came storming into the castle to talk to the king."

"If the Revinir owned the dragons, why did the king have them?"

"The Revinir didn't have a place to keep them. The original dragon entrance to the catacombs, which was used to bring in the dead ones, collapsed a long time ago with the big earthquake, and they don't fit into any of the other entrances. So the Revinir had made an arrangement with the king, which allowed him to use the dragons infrequently to transport building materials and jewels and junk like that in exchange for keeping them captive and feeding them."

"Oh."

"Anyway, when the Revinir found out the dragons were gone, she was really mad. There was a huge shouting match, and the princess got hauled into it because the king found out that she was the one who'd ordered the gate opened, which allowed them to escape. Naturally Shanti was boiling mad at me, since it was sort of my idea to release them."

"It was—you?" Thisbe was surprised again.

"Yeah. I couldn't stand that they were locked up and muzzled like that. Anyway, when the Revinir demanded payment from the king, Shanti suggested . . . me." He grew quiet. "So. That's how that happened."

Thisbe dropped her gaze. "I'm sorry." She had so much to process, so much she wanted to say. Dev was more complex than she'd ever imagined, and she wasn't sure what to think about him and how the things he'd done and all he'd experienced in his life had shaped him. He was one surprise move after another—maybe that's what happened when you were exactly half-bad and half-good. Whatever the case, Thisbe was mystified by him.

They worked the day away, scooping all the way to the bottom of the giant cauldrons and pouring the smelly liquid into tiny bottles, then capping them tightly and putting them on a cart. When they finished, they began the broth-making process all over again, each with a new bone in their pots, covering them with water and stoking the fires to bring them to a boil.

After a while, a soldier came in. "The Revinir told me to tell you that you're to stay late tonight to add water to the cauldrons for the next five hours. Then you can cover them for the night and go."

"Five more hours?" Thisbe looked up at the woman. "Why can't *you* just put some water in these pots? Why do we need to sit here?"

The soldier pointed her weapon at Thisbe.

"Okay, okay," Thisbe muttered. She wasn't happy about this development. It meant she might miss her secret evening time in the tunnel with Rohan. She was looking forward to seeing him, and she wanted to show him what the Revinir had done to her. Every time she moved, she felt the breeze slice through the scales, and it reminded her again of this incredible thing that had changed her. She still hadn't quite gotten over the shock of it. Now and then she rubbed her hand over them, always expecting them to be sharper. But they remained soft and pliable. They didn't itch.

As she and Dev continued their jobs into the evening, they chatted on and off. Things had grown comfortable between them, and they sat together in between the times they were adding water to their cauldrons. The horrid smell grew as the bones boiled and released their bits of magic into the liquid.

Dev explained to Thisbe the parts of the dragon-freeing story that she'd missed while being chained in the castle dungeon. And he told her how he'd led Seth out. Eventually he also confessed that he'd intentionally put Thisbe in the prison chamber with Maiven Taveer because he knew the old woman would be decent to her.

The surprises about Dev didn't end. He'd done some really thoughtful things. Maybe he wasn't all bad. Thisbe laughed to herself at the joke, but then realized he could have changed for the worse or the better by now, and it seemed like he was heading in the better direction. But was he good enough to trust him with her secret to escape? He'd burned her before. She was tempted to tell him, but she just couldn't. Not yet. She needed to be absolutely certain he wouldn't betray her.

As they were about to leave for the night, there was a noise at the door. Thisbe turned and sucked in a sharp breath when she saw Rohan coming toward her, dragging a huge sack of small bones into the kitchen. He looked exhausted and ragged.

"Rohan," she whispered. Then her eyes landed on the

bones. Her sight wavered for an instant when she realized what they were.

"Who are you?" Dev asked him, looking alarmed at the delivery. "What are those for?"

Rohan glanced at Thisbe, telegraphing a warning look. Then he turned to Dev. "The Revinir told me to deposit these here."

Dev narrowed his eyes at the pile. "Those . . . aren't dragon bones."

"No, they aren't," said Rohan, looking disgusted. He unhooked his harness from the sack, which fell open and flattened on the floor, leaving the bones in a pile. "You're to make broth from these once the dragon-bone broth is done." He looked defeated. "May the gods of our ancestors forgive us all." With that he turned around and walked heavily out of the room.

Despair

That night Thisbe and Rohan huddled in the tunnel between their crypts. Rohan's mood was unlike any Thisbe had witnessed. He seemed beside himself in desperation. "Unearthing the dragon bones was bad enough. Making broth from them for profit—even worse. But now, taking the bones of our ruling ancestors who came before us . . . It's absolutely beyond the pale. I feel like filth. Like I've lost all sense of decency."

"But it's not your fault," Thisbe said. "The Revinir is making you do it."

Rohan buried his face in his hands and sighed heavily. "I complied. I didn't resist. I should have."

"She'll torture you if you resist! You're trying to stay alive. We're trying to get out of here."

Rohan shook his head. "On my walk back, I saw my future in those bones, Thisbe. And it was one of complete disgrace. What good is living under the weight of that?" He dropped his hands and looked at her, his passion evident. "Tell me if you know the answer. Make up something. I'm grasping for an excuse. For anything that will allow me to sleep tonight, because I can't rationalize this any longer." A noise of frustration escaped him. "I have too much time to think."

Thisbe looked at him with solemn eyes. A long moment passed in silence as she rolled the words over in her head. These bones didn't quite have the depth of meaning to her as they did to him, but he was right. And while discovering her history was new and strange to her, Thisbe felt the horror in her gut too, growing more powerful since she'd taken the broth, as if a stronger sense of right and wrong had begun to shred away her innocence.

"I don't know the answer," she said. "But look." She pulled up her sleeve and showed him her arm with its dragon scales.

Rohan sucked in a breath and held his candle closer, examining her arm. "She made you drink it too?"

Thisbe nodded. "She brought in the guards to threaten me."

"Oh, Thisbe." Rohan didn't seem to know what else to say. "I'm sorry."

"You can touch them if you want. I don't . . . I don't hate them."

After a moment Rohan drew his finger lightly down Thisbe's arm. "Can you still feel things?" he asked.

"Yes."

"They're softer than I imagined."

Thisbe nodded. "Do you think they will ever go away? I tried to pluck one, but it's stuck fast."

"I don't know."

"Dev has had more than me. She's been testing on him for a couple days."

Rohan shook his head and closed his eyes, a pained expression on his face. "And now the ancestor bones. We can't . . .

LISA McMANN

We just can't . . ." He let his head fall back against the stone wall.

Thisbe didn't know how to comfort him. She didn't know how to stop what was happening. But she had new information to share, so she turned to that. "Dev said the Revinir paid the princess something after she snatched me from the auction, trying to be fair about it and not stealing me. So that might be why she was so angry when she found out about the dragons' escape and learned that the king kept it from her at first. Now she really doesn't trust the king."

Rohan sighed and let his head fall forward. "That's not encouraging in the least. The stability of Grimere is about to crumble."

Thisbe didn't know what to say, but fear clutched her throat. War was such an unknown to her—she'd only known peace in her world.

After a few minutes, Rohan opened his eyes. "I'm so tired, but we have to fight this. Are you ready to escape? Can you be ready soon?"

Thisbe pressed her lips together. She'd been practicing her

magic, her aim, her concentration for some time now. She'd grown steadily better, but she knew her ability was limited. Her explosive spells would work for a time, but did she have enough in her to fight everyone they'd come across as they ran to the exit? She wasn't confident.

"How will we go?" she asked. "When is the best time? Do we try to kill the Revinir or focus only on escaping? What about Dev? And what about our black-eyed brothers and sisters? Do we leave them here? Or try to tell them what we're doing?"

Rohan blew out a breath. "This is complicated," he said. "If we tell too many, word will leak to the Revinir. Do you trust Dev?"

Thisbe closed her eyes, feeling a faint electricity buzzing over her scales when she thought of him. She was torn in half trying to decide. And as much as she wanted to give him the benefit of the doubt, she didn't have any room to make a mistake just because she felt sorry for him in a weak moment. "I'm not sure. Do you know how to swim?"

"Yes, a little. Why? The river?" He looked scared but didn't voice his fear.

"Yes. I think we two should go alone and head for the river exit. We can figure out how to come back for the others later. Shall we plan it for two days from now, when you return with your next load of ancestor bones?"

Rohan nodded. "We'll go that night, at midnight when the slaves are locked in and the soldiers are feeling at ease. You can break through the door, and we'll go no matter what happens."

Thisbe nodded.

"We can't continue on like this," Rohan said, as if to reassure himself that this was the right plan.

"And if we die in the river," said Thisbe, "at least we'll die honoring the lives of our ancestors."

Rohan agreed. "I can't bear to go on desecrating their remains—it will rest on my conscience forever. So it's settled: In two days we'll run for the river at midnight. And we won't stop for any reason."

Thisbe's eyes shone in the candlelight. She grasped Rohan's hand, and they nodded solemnly together. It was settled. They stayed up late planning and then said their good-byes before going off to sleep—they wouldn't see one another again until the escape. But no matter how tired she was, Thisbe tossed and turned. They had a plan. But how were they going to get across that river?

In the middle of the night Thisbe awoke with a start, her scales standing on end. She was panting as if she'd been running for the exit in her dreams. And in the pitch blackness, an idea began to form.

A New World

Morning was dawning when Alex and his team flew over the gorge, giving them a spectacular view of the gaping space between the worlds. Behind them the wide waterfall of the seven islands, which they'd once been swept down, rolled neatly under the world and disappeared into the mist. In front of them soon appeared the narrow waterfall that fell infinitely off the cliffs of Grimere. The sun hit the highest castle, next to it, making it sparkle.

"That's the castle where the dragons were chained up," announced Seth, sitting up a little on Arabis's back and acting

LISA McMANN

as a tour guide for the others. "There's a horrible dungeon with lots of prisoners and the dragon stalls." As they reached the other side of the gap, Seth went on to describe in graphic detail how Hux nearly hadn't made it, and how he and the twins had been hanging by slipping vines above the great nothingness.

"That's a lot more than I needed to know," remarked Carina. Alex nodded in agreement.

"The twins saved me, pretty much," Seth admitted. "If it hadn't been for them, we wouldn't have been tied together. Thisbe was able to hang on to Fifer and me until Hux could pull us up." He paused, remembering, then added, "I like this way better."

Arabis, Simber, and Talon landed safely on the mountainside near where Seth and the girls had been before. The Artiméans climbed down to stretch. Kitten crawled out of Seth's pocket and began sniffing the air all around them.

Arabis turned her head to address the group. "There is an entrance to the catacombs from the castle Grimere's dungeon," she said. "I've never seen it, but I know the passageways go on for miles and miles underground. The entrance in Dragonsmarche would be near the center. There is a third entrance beyond Dragonsmarche, near the crater lake. I've flown by that one. It's a cavelike opening high on a rock wall that drops down to the lake's edge."

"A cave opening?" asked Simber. "That might be easierrr to access than trrrying to figurrre out how to rrraise that moving cylinderrr in the middle of the squarrre."

"It would be if it were big enough," said Arabis. "Unfortunately neither you nor I would be able to fit. I don't think anyone uses it except for fresh air. There's a sheer drop-off to the shore of the lake, and it's quite impossible to access for most anyone." She eyeballed Talon. "Though Talon might be small enough to enter that way."

"The castle entrance doesn't seem like our best option either," said Thatcher. He recounted to the others his narrow escape when the portcullis came down. "There are soldiers everywhere who would see us coming and close the drawbridge. Besides, I don't ever want to go near that dungeon again, much less through it, even if we did manage to get past everybody."

"Mewmewmew," said Kitten sweetly.

"So that leaves the center entrance in the middle of Dragonsmarche," continued Thatcher. "Which is going to be very difficult since we'll have to try to find it and then figure out how to make it come up so we can go in there."

"Mewmewmew," said Kitten again.

"Perrrhaps we need to collapse a larrrger arrrea of the grrround arrround that entrrrance," Simber mused. "We'd have to do that at night so we'rrre not obvious about it to the townspeople. And we'd rrrisk hurrrting people below. I don't like that." He glanced at Kitten. "Wait. What did you just say?"

"Mewmewmew!"

Simber tilted his head slightly as if deep in thought. "That's a verrry long way to rrrun for a tiny kitten, though."

"Mewmewmew."

"Trrrue." Simber looked thoughtful.

"What's she saying?" asked Alex.

"She says we should drrrop herrr off at the castle, and she can find herrr way thrrrough the dungeon and into the catacombs without anyone noticing herrr." Simber looked at Kitten. "But then what? How does that help us get in?"

"Mewmewmew," said Kitten confidently.

Simber looked at the others. "She says she'll trrravel to the Drrragonsmarrrche entrrrance and brrring the cylinderrr up forrr us."

"But, Kitten, how will you know when we're ready?" Alex asked.

"Mewmewmew."

"Hmm," said Simber. "Good point—we could send you a seek spell once we arrre quite surrrre you'd be therrre. Do you have anything you've crrreated that you can give us?"

Kitten reached her tiny paw into a tiny tuft of fur and pulled out an even tinier something. She held it out. Seth opened his hand, and Kitten dropped it on his palm. It was a silver square.

"What is it?" asked Seth, straining to see.

"Mewmewmew," said Kitten with pride.

"It's a locket," said Simber. "She made it in jewelrrry class."

"Mewmewmew," said Kitten.

Simber rolled his eyes. "She wants you all to know it has a picturrre of Fox inside it."

"Aw," said Seth. "That's pretty cute, I have to admit." He looked around. "Do we have some fishing line? I can wear it around my neck so I don't lose it. It's so small."

LISA McMANN

Carina reached for the supplies and found a piece that was the right size, and Seth poked the line through the locket's miniscule ring, like he was threading a needle. Then he tied it around his neck. "Maybe Talon can be ready and waiting at the cave entrance at the same time. We could send him a seek spell too, to let him know it's time to attack."

"That's a good idea, Seth," said Alex. "Then we'll go in together." Simber nodded his approval.

Alex regarded Seth thoughtfully for a moment, his esteem for the boy rising. Seeing his sharp problem-solving skills surprised him, not having witnessed them before. It made him wonder if the girls had become that sharp too. He thought about Fifer back at home and how hard she'd tried to convince him that it was so, and felt a pang of guilt. He'd been so busy training he'd never given her a chance to show him or even tell him much about what she'd been through.

Seth didn't notice Alex. He was working through the rest of the plan. "How are we going to get Kitten to the castle? We don't want any of them to see Arabis or know that Simber is back, do we?"

"That's right," said Lani. "Let's not tip them off."

Talon stepped up. "I'll take you, Kitten. I can fly above the clouds so no one sees us coming and put you down on one of the turrets. Do you think you can figure out how to get to the dungeon from there?"

Kitten nodded.

"It'll take Kitten quite some time to travel the distance," said Arabis. "You'll want to head due west, Kitten—as much as you can, anyway. If what the guards have said is accurate, your path should be slightly uphill the entire way."

Kitten bowed graciously to the dragon. "Mewmewmew."

"She intends to sneak rrrides along with anyone going in that dirrrection," Simber interpreted.

"Good. Likely just a day's journey, then." Arabis glanced around, assessing their safety on the hillside. "Perhaps we should make our way into hiding, just there," she said, nodding and pointing with her tail toward the forest. It had been many hours of walking for Seth and the twins over rough terrain, but flying wouldn't take long at all.

"Talon, can you find us at the edge of the forrrest?" said Simber, pointing with Arabis to where he wanted Talon to go.

"Fear not," said Talon. "I shall see you there by afternoon."

With that, Talon set off with Kitten for the distant castle. The rest of them climbed onto Arabis and Simber and took off to the shelter of the forest. To their right they could see the tiny village waking up. Seth told everyone how Fifer and Thisbe had made the bamboo prison bars come alive, how he'd gotten hooked on them by accident, and how the girls had then saved him.

"Wow," said Alex. "They did all that? I—I didn't realize." Somehow seeing the place where his sisters had been brought all sorts of questions to his mind. He regretted that he hadn't thought to ask Fifer more when he'd had the chance. Had he made a mistake not letting her come? "What else happened, Seth?"

Kaylee and Lani glanced at him and then at each other. Lani rolled her eyes, but they kept quiet, and Alex didn't see her.

Seth pointed to a hill rising between them and the castle. "Over there is where Thisbe killed a poisonous snake and saved Dev's life. And Fifer helped me walk after I twisted my ankle."

Arabis, who'd heard by now that Fifer hadn't been allowed to come, sensed that reinforcements might help the girl's case for next time. She added to what Seth was saying. "Fifer and Seth were heroic in saving us. I was about to be killed. They stayed levelheaded, even after Thisbe was thrown into the dungeon, and performed the most amazing magic I've ever seen, given what they had to work with." She snorted. "Some saplings and a bit of burlap they found in the dungeon—I would never have believed they could make true working wing extensions come alive from that. And Fifer's ability to comfort and work with Drock, who was exceedingly upset as he often is, was a lesson in patience for the rest of us." She paused. "I commend them both."

The words brought tears of pride to Carina's eyes, and Seth lowered his head. "Thanks." He knew telling these stories was the least he could do for his friend Fifer, to say these things in front of Alex where he could actually see for himself what odds they'd been up against. It was his way of making up for Fifer being stuck at home. Maybe he could play a part in Fifer getting to go along in the future. Or at least getting Alex to understand that they were not just simple inexperienced kids. They were real and true mages.

Alex remained thoughtful and quiet as they descended to

the edge of the forest. They all followed Arabis into a clearing that both she and Simber could squeeze into.

They ate a meal and refilled their water jugs from the river while waiting for Talon. As the day wore on, Carina and Thatcher told more tales from the dungeon where they'd spent time in the cell next to Thisbe, and Kaylee asked for more details about everything, trying to get to the real heart of what it was like out here for the three children—not only to inform Alex but also so the team would have as few surprises as possible.

Finally Talon was a glint in the sky coming toward them. But the stories continued. In the middle of Seth recounting how Fifer had to race against the clock to make the magic wings come alive without Seth there to help, Alex let out a long, troubled sigh. "Okay, okay," he said, holding up his hands in surrender. "I know what you're doing. And I know why you're doing it. And you're right." He hesitated for a moment, struggling for the right words. "I'm deeply disappointed . . . in myself. I am. And it's hard for me to admit that. It's hard for me to not get defensive or to accuse you all of ganging up on me, even though you haven't said a word about me refusing to let Fifer come along. I guess . . ." Alex picked up a small stick and began breaking it into pieces. "Seth, I guess seeing this new land and hearing about the various struggles you and the twins overcame makes it real, and it brings me back to when we were your age. I still want to protect my sisters, but I'll admit it. I think . . . I made . . . a mistake."

Everyone was quiet, and Lani didn't roll her eyes now. Solemnly she locked her gaze with Samheed, remembering those times when they were twelve and thirteen too. Carina, Thatcher, and Kaylee exchanged glances, then nervously watched Alex's bowed head. Had they gone too far with all the stories to try to make this point?

Finally Alex looked up, resigned. "It was a big mistake. As much as it breaks my heart with worry, I should have let Fifer come with us. And . . . I hope I haven't compromised our mission by not allowing her to be here."

On the Right Track

Fifer and Crow crossed over the space between the worlds at sunset. Like Seth had done a half day earlier with his team, Fifer pointed out the various places she'd been to and told Crow all about her adventures with Thisbe and Seth. Crow was appropriately shocked and impressed. It seemed surreal to Fifer now, reliving all the close calls and near disasters. It almost made her feel like Alex had been right to be overly worried, but she quickly brushed off that feeling. Along with the familiarity of the terrain, having Crow with her gave her added comfort.

They stopped on the hillside, wanting to stretch and give

the birds a rest, but there wasn't much for the birds to eat or drink among the rocks. So soon they were off again. Fifer directed them toward the forest and river, where they could safely settle down for the night.

When they reached the edge of the forest and landed, Fifer took the supplies and Crow folded up the hammock. Fifer lit a blinding highlighter to guide them closer to the river, and soon they came upon a large clearing that had been recently and quite magnificently trampled by what had to be very large creatures. There was a spot that had held a fire, though it was fully extinguished now. The birds chattered noisily over it all.

"I'll bet Arabis and Simber and the team stopped here for a bit," Fifer said. "We're not too far behind them."

"We'll have to set out early to catch up," said Crow. "I'm sure they've stopped somewhere as well for the night." He pulled out a couple of prepared meals that Fifer had taken from Artimé's kitchen and quickly ate his.

Fifer ate too, though she wasn't very hungry. She began to feel butterflies in her stomach when she thought about meeting up with the rescue team. It would no doubt be a huge surprise for them to see her. "I wonder if Alex will yell at me when we find them," she mused as they made beds out of the brush. "Actually, there's no 'if' about it, because I'm sure he will. But how badly?"

"There's not a lot he can do about it," said Crow with a shrug. "We're here. I know it's early to go to sleep, but we can't do much else now that it's dark. We may as well rest up so we can make ourselves as useful as possible tomorrow." He lay on the grass and put his hands behind his head. "Have you thought about what you'll tell Alex?"

Fifer set the glowing highlighter between them on the grass and rummaged through her travel bag. "A little. I'll say I couldn't stand to be away from Thisbe a moment longer. And if that means he loves me less, then that's the way it goes. I'll take her over him any day."

Crow smiled wryly. "I'm not so sure that technique will endear you to him. You might want to leave out that last bit and stick with the first. I think he might understand that, especially since he's chosen his twin over some other things in the past. Try to see things from his perspective, and use what you have in common with him instead of getting immediately hot and butting heads. If you attempt to do that, and he sees your effort to understand him, maybe he'll realize you're more mature now and do the same thing for you."

Fifer pulled a thin blanket from her bag and lay down, draping it over her. "I remember in one of the adventures Lani wrote that Alex could feel it when Aaron was badly injured after the pirates captured him. That made him want to go after Aaron."

"Yes," said Crow. "I remember that. He was totally driven by that feeling that Aaron was on the brink of death. Do you have that kind of twin bond with Thisbe? Or those prickly feelings about each other when you're separated?"

"I'm not sure," Fifer admitted. "This is the first time we've ever been separated. I don't have some weird sense that she's about to die or anything, though." She paused, thinking it through. "Maybe our bond isn't as close as Alex and Aaron's."

"Or maybe Thisbe's not in life-threatening danger," Crow suggested. He yawned and rolled to his side.

"Mm-hmm." Fifer nodded sleepily. Crow's words comforted her. She was glad they'd talked this out. She'd thought worrying about it might keep her up all night, but she felt better now. Almost good enough to face Alex tomorrow.

Now all they had to do was find him.

LISA McMANN

A Tragic Turn

By that evening, Thisbe was growing nervous. The ancestor bones lay on the kitchen floor where Rohan had left them, and they'd soon be using them to make a new broth, which was unsettling enough. But adding to that, in just over twenty-four hours she and Rohan would be breaking out of here. *No matter what.* That phrase repeated in her head unendingly, like one of Fox and Kitten's songs they'd sometimes play at Artimé's annual masquerade ball—it was annoying, but you couldn't stop it. All she hoped was that she could get through the remaining time without the Revinir making her drink ancestor-bone broth. Because she wouldn't do it.

"What's wrong with you?" Dev asked her when he caught her paused in filling the last of the dragon-bone broth into the bottles.

Thisbe blinked and continued working slowly. "Nothing." She felt guilty for not telling Dev the plan, but she had to protect herself. She'd learned her lesson with him.

Dev frowned and helped Thisbe finish. They cleaned out the cauldrons and replaced them on their fires. Then they both turned slowly and looked at the pile of ancestor bones.

"I can't do this," said Thisbe.

"Me either. It's horrible."

They continued to stand there, trying to figure out what to do. "We could tell the soldiers we're done for the night," said Thisbe. "Then we wouldn't have to start this until tomorrow. Maybe . . . maybe something crazy will happen that will stop everything." Thisbe glanced sidelong at Dev.

"They won't let us go." Dev went to the door and looked at the entry room.

"Get back in there," growled a soldier. "The Revinir is coming."

Dev scooted back into the room. "She's coming."

"I heard," said Thisbe, growing panicky. She and Dev scrambled to look busy as the woman came into the room.

The Revinir assessed the kitchen and saw both cauldrons empty and the fires low. "Get started on the new bones," she barked. "What are you standing around for?"

"Well," Thisbe began, stalling for time, "I don't understand what you are trying to do with the ancestor bones. I mean, the dragon bones have magic in them. What do these have?"

"Nothing, I assume," said the Revinir. "The broth we make from them is just the placebo for after we sell out of the batch of dragon-bone broth."

Dev and Thisbe were more puzzled than ever now. "What are you talking about?" asked Dev.

The Revinir looked at the children like they were stupid. "We'll sell through the first batch of dragon-bone broth at the market tomorrow. People will take it home and drink it. They'll see the changes and show their friends. Everyone will get excited, word will spread, and hundreds of people will come to our booth next week seeking it. But we don't want anyone to have a second dose of dragon-bone broth—they could get too powerful. So we're making this fake magical broth to replace it, and increasing the price dramatically. The people will buy it anyway, but they won't know it's not dragon-bone broth when they spend all their money on it, trying to become stronger. Once we have their money, our booth disappears without a trace before we're discovered."

Thisbe was disgusted, but she wasn't surprised. The Revinir was going to knowingly give the ancestor-bone broth to hundreds, maybe thousands of people, while passing it off as magical dragon broth. She hardly knew what to say at first. Then she whispered, "I see."

"So get moving," said the woman. "We'll need a lot more of this fake dragon broth so we can sell as much as possible. Half the bones to each pot, cover with water, bring to a boil. And don't leave until you have a full cauldron simmering on a healthy fire that'll last until morning. Then we'll test it to see if there might be some ancient magical component to them. After all, the bones are intact after all these years. Something must have preserved them."

She turned to Dev. "I want you to report to my throne room an hour earlier than usual in the morning," she told him.

LISA McMANN

Dev didn't ask why, and she didn't explain. The Revinir turned and left Dev and Thisbe to get started.

"I wonder who is going to the marketplace to sell this stuff," Dev said. "I'm worried it might be me since she wants me here early. She knows I have experience in the market because Shanti told her—that's what convinced her to take me as partial payback for losing the dragons."

"Everything about this is horrible," said Thisbe, absently stroking the scales on her arm, which she was starting to get used to having. "She's horrible. And I'm not drinking this stuff."

They did what they'd been told to do. A few hours later their giant pots were completely full and simmering properly, and the fires were going strong. They left after the soldiers checked their work and went their separate ways back to their crypts.

That night, after her meal, Thisbe spent every waking moment working on her magic and her aim. Her stamina seemed to be improving a bit, probably helped by the less physical work she'd been doing lately. But she was afraid to try anything too powerful for fear it would summon the crypt keeper again. She wouldn't know until the actual escape how much the powerful spells would drain her energy—she'd only ever done one at a time before. She'd have to use her magic wisely and sparingly in case they were faced with more obstacles than they'd planned.

Early in the morning Thisbe went into the kitchen. The Revinir was there with a handful of guards. Before Thisbe knew what was happening, three of the guards stepped in front of the doorway behind her, blocking the exit. Another stood by the cauldron.

Wary, Thisbe glanced around and saw she was trapped in the kitchen with the Revinir. "What are you doing?" she asked. "Where's Dev? What's happening?"

The Revinir calmly picked up a cup. "I've tried this new broth, and it seems worthless," she said. "But I want to test it on you."

"No," said Thisbe, eyeing the soldiers and trying to remain calm. She took a step back. "I don't want to drink that."

"Oh, but you will," said the woman, stepping toward her. "It's not a big deal. I don't think it'll do anything to you, either."

"No," said Thisbe, more firmly. "I won't do it!"

The Revinir narrowed her eyes at the girl. Then she sighed heavily, annoyed, and looked sideways at one of the soldiers. Without a word, the soldier stepped up to Thisbe and grabbed her arm while the Revinir dipped the cup into the boiling broth.

"I said no!" Thisbe cried out. She wrenched her arm out of the soldier's grasp.

"Drink it!" shouted the Revinir, holding the steaming cup toward her. "Here. You can hold it. Just take your time. Just a small sip."

"I won't!" Thisbe darted to keep the guard from grabbing her again, then lunged at the Revinir, trying to knock the cup out of her hand. The soldier stuck his foot out to trip Thisbe. She screamed and flopped to the floor hard on her back. "Stop!" she yelled. The soldier backed off, but the Revinir swooped in and splashed the cup of hot broth in Thisbe's face.

Mid-scream, Thisbe gasped in surprise, sucking some of it in. She choked and sputtered and felt it scald her lips and tongue and the back of her throat as it went down. Coughing, she swiped her eyes to clear them and rolled to her side. "I hate you!" she said bitterly, and tried to spit the taste from her mouth. But it remained.

Satisfied that Thisbe had ingested at least a little of the broth, the Revinir backed off and held the soldiers at bay, watching Thisbe carefully.

Thisbe stayed low, feeling strange. Slowly she wiped her face with her shirt. Her mind spun as odd new thoughts entered it—but none of them made sense. A flash of an ancient stone road, an army of soldiers, a blaze of silver dragons in battle. A broken land, a destroyed forest, a river stretching out and falling into a sea. Bodies in heaps. A pirate ship sailing away. A barrage of meteors and a devastating earthquake. Children being sent away in the dead of night. A young woman dragged off by soldiers.

The images kept coming, flashing behind Thisbe's eyes, making her dizzy. She stared blindly at the floor of the kitchen, feeling the Revinir staring at her and knowing she couldn't let on that anything had changed. She didn't want the horrid woman to think she had felt anything at all.

Her stomach roiled, and she clutched at it. She lifted her head weakly, then gagged and retched at the Revinir's feet. The woman exclaimed in disgust, and the soldiers yanked Thisbe away from her. Still dizzy, Thisbe couldn't see anything beyond the images flashing, too many to keep track of. Sometime during all of this, her dragon scales had risen painfully of their own accord. They stood on end as burning tears poured from her eyes, trying to flush the broth. She coughed again. "Leave me alone," she whispered when she could speak again. Her body ached.

After a few moments the flashing images subsided. Thisbe's coughing fits settled, and the tears slowed. She lifted her head and tried to focus on the boiling pot of broth nearby. Her vision steadied, and she glanced at the soldiers near the door, seeing that a few of them didn't try to hide their discomfort at witnessing the Revinir's actions. Then Thisbe turned and looked up at the woman with more contempt than she'd ever felt for anyone in the world. "Are you happy now?" she said sarcastically, her voice ragged. "You got your way again by being horrible. You must be so proud of yourself."

"Did anything happen to you?" the Revinir asked, clearly having no qualms about what she'd just done.

Thisbe clenched and unclenched her fists. Her face blazed. She spat on the floor again, then wiped her mouth, the taste of vomit overshadowing the broth. "No," she said as civilly as she could muster. She focused on remaining calm. She had to, or she could ruin her plans for escape. With all the soldiers nearby, Thisbe couldn't let a single spark escape or they'd be all over her.

"Nothing at all?" asked the Revinir, a tiny line of gray smoke coming from her nostrils. She stared into Thisbe's eyes as if she could read if she were lying.

Thisbe stared back defiantly, no longer caring what the Revinir could do with her dragon powers. "Nothing at all." She worked her jaw, then moved to clean up the mess on the floor since she knew no one else would do it. She glanced at her forearms and saw the dragon scales were lying down again.

"Good," said the Revinir. "Start bottling it up. Dev can take it to the market next week."

"Unbelievable," Thisbe muttered. Then she narrowed her eyes. "Is that where he is now? Alone?"

"Of course not alone. I sent soldiers with him."

"Why didn't you send me and leave him to drink that horrid stuff?"

"Because you don't have the first clue about money. Besides, you'd try to escape."

"Wouldn't Dev try?"

"No. He's been a servant his whole life. He wouldn't dare. He knows his life would be in danger if he's not with someone in authority." She gave Thisbe a warning look. "Yours would be too."

"Because of our eyes," said Thisbe.

"Obviously. You're safe down here. And you can gain more power over the others by sticking with me. Despite your horrendous behavior and lack of respect, I'm holding out hope to be able to trust you." She folded her arms. "I promise we can go far together."

Thisbe glared. After all the woman had done to her, she still thought Thisbe would leap at the chance to work with her over the long term. "Right." Thisbe shook her head. "What do I have that can help you?"

The Revinir began to pace. "You have the magic and the ancestry. I've got the dragons. Together we're the right combination to take back this land."

Thisbe narrowed her eyes. "You have more dragons? Where are they?"

The Revinir gave a condescending smile. "I *am* the dragon.

But we have access to other dragons if we need them. You'll find out more in time if you commit to working with me."

"How do you know I haven't already?"

"I can read your thoughts."

Thisbe knew the woman had to be lying, because if she could read her thoughts, she'd know a lot about what she and Rohan were planning to do. "What am I thinking right now?"

"You're thinking that I'm right about your brother and the people of Artimé. They aren't coming back for you."

The words struck Thisbe like a spear to her heart, and she couldn't stop her gasp in reaction.

The Revinir seemed pleased to have hit her hard. "See? I'll convince you eventually. We're better together. We could rule this entire land, beyond the depths of the forest," she said, pointing north, "and far beyond the lake." She pointed west. "But only if we work together. There's a lot to overcome."

"I'd rather die than work with you," said Thisbe.

The Revinir grabbed Thisbe's arm and said in low, sinister voice, "If you attempt to escape, you just might."

Fifer Catches Up

The birds had begun rustling early near the hammock, seeming to understand the need to get off to a good start before the light of day. Fifer shook Crow awake, and the two of them packed up and climbed onto the hammock. "We need to find Alex," Fifer told Shimmer. "You know who that is, right? And Arabis the orange and Simber." Shimmer and several others bobbed their heads, and then Shimmer called out instructions in its usual way. Soon they were rising above the trees and soaring over the forest.

"They seem to understand everything you say," Crow

mused. "I wonder how long it would've taken you to find this out if Thisbe had been around."

"I might never have," said Fifer. "I hope she can learn to like them. Especially since they're really well trained now. I'll teach them to not flutter up at her."

"She'll probably get used to them," Crow agreed. "I totally have, and I used to be terrified of Queen Eagala's threat of sending the birds after us Warblerans. When she actually did it, I thought that was the end for me. Then you broke the spell with your scream. It was amazing. I was there with you, hiding in the giant rock."

"I remember," said Fifer, though she meant she remembered the story as Lani had written it, not from her own memory.

"It seems odd that these falcons started turning up after that, doesn't it? I've been thinking about that. Ishibashi told Seth that they'd never seen them until about ten years ago. And the scientists have been there over sixty years now I think."

"That is odd," said Fifer. She looked down and could see a road leading from the castle to the west. It was the one she and Thisbe had traveled on in the back of a vehicle. "Maybe when

LISA McMANN

I broke the spell, the ravens turned into these magical falcons."

"And maybe that's why the birds obey you," said Crow. "Because you broke the spell."

"I'll bet the Revinir will be really mad if she finds that out," said Fifer. "I hope I get a chance to tell her."

Crow smiled. In general he could tell that Fifer was maturing, and she seemed to be putting a bit more thought into her actions. But she still had her moments of recklessness, and this was one of them. "Again, you might want to think that through before you do it."

"I know, I know," Fifer muttered. "Sometimes I just say things that are in my head to see how they sound out loud. Sometimes they sound good, other times not." She didn't say whether she agreed with Crow and instead sat up and looked out. The birds were taking them safely above the trees so there was little chance of anyone noticing them. She wondered how far Alex and the others had made it. Maybe they'd even rescued Thisbe already. While Fifer would hate to miss that action, it would be more than worth it to have her sister back safely.

After a while, in the distance they could see the big city of Grimere and the Dragonsmarche square in the middle of it.

Shimmer uttered a sharp call to the other birds. They changed course slightly and headed for the edge of the forest that lay closest to the city.

"I think the birds found our rescue team." Fifer shifted nervously, then peered out but couldn't see anything through the cover of trees. The birds carefully maneuvered their cargo to fly above the river, where they could descend below the branches and find a place to set everything down. Crow and Fifer shaded their eyes, trying to see any sign of Alex's team.

The birds clipped a huge treetop, which slowed them down sharply, throwing Fifer and Crow off balance. The two tried desperately to lean in the hammock this way and that to avoid branches, but the ground came up fast and the birds screeched and fluttered to a halt. A few of them were forced to drop their ends to avoid smacking into trunks. The hammock tipped and spilled its contents onto the forest floor. Fifer and Crow tumbled out and sprawled awkwardly on the ground, unhurt.

When they could pull themselves to their feet, they looked up and around. Twenty feet away stood Alex and the others, staring at them.

"Oh," said Fifer, pulling leaves from her hair. "Hello."

Finding Common Ground

Carina, Thatcher, and Kaylee stared. Seth's mouth fell open in shock. Simber, who'd been ready to pounce, stood down and nearly smiled, but quickly looked stern instead. Arabis appeared startled but pleased, and Talon seemed unsurprised, though if he'd expected anything, he'd kept it to himself.

Alex's face went from shock to fury in about half a second. "What the— How did you—" he sputtered, and then, "Fifer, honestly! I don't know what to do with you anymore."

Fifer smiled meekly and inched closer to Crow for protection. But Crow looked at Fifer expectantly—it was up to her to explain.

"Take it down a notch, Al," murmured Kaylee, putting her hand on her brother-in-law's shoulder, lest he go barreling at his sister. "Let her talk before you go shooting off your mouth again and wrecking everything. Remember what you said yesterday."

Alex clenched his teeth and muttered, "That was when I thought she was in Artimé."

"Are you really that surprised to see her, though?" Carina asked him. "She's got more tenacity than all of us put together. It's admirable."

"*I'm* not surprised," said Seth. He grinned and ran over to Fifer and embraced her. "How did you do that? You got them to fly you this whole way? That's incredible! They must be really tired."

"They took shifts," said Fifer, keeping one eye on Alex. "Some of them would rest on the edges of the hammock when it wasn't their turn."

"*Cooo-l.* Ha-ha. Get it? Bird joke." Seth chuckled to himself and bent down to look more closely at the magical falcons.

"Hi, Alex," Fifer said finally.

He nodded. "Fifer."

"Look," Fifer began, remembering Crow's advice, "I know you're mad. But I couldn't stand being so far away from Thisbe. She's . . . she's my other half, like you and Aaron. Plus, I can help you all. And I know you'll never believe me unless you see me do it. So I'm here. To . . . to show you."

"Hey!" cried Seth suddenly, standing up again. "You're wearing a component vest! Who'd you steal that from?"

Insulted, Fifer smoothed the wrinkles from her vest. "I didn't steal it. I would never do something like that."

"Someone lent it to you?" asked Alex.

Fifer blew out a frustrated breath. "No, Alex. I earned it the way everyone else earns it. From the Magical Warrior trainer."

"Florence gave it to you?"

Fifer pinched her lips together. She didn't want to name Florence outright, though everyone knew that's who she meant. She didn't deny it. "Every other person in Artimé has earned their vest on their own merit. Nobody goes around asking the parents or guardians if it's okay to give a kid a vest. It's up to the trainer to decide. And she did. So."

Alex scratched his stubbly chin, his eyes narrowed and still on Fifer. He sighed and shook his head slightly, and then he emitted what almost sounded like a reluctant laugh. "You drive me crazy, Fifer," he said. "You really do."

Fifer nearly spat out an angry retort about how he drove her even crazier, but Crow touched her shoulder. She glanced up at him, and he frowned.

"Look," Crow whispered. "He's smiling. Don't blow it."

Carina, Thatcher, and Kaylee all seemed to be saying the same thing with their strained expressions.

Fifer closed her lips and dropped her gaze. She took a couple breaths. "I know I drive you crazy," she admitted. "It's like I can't help it, you know? Because I'm so worried about Thisbe. I can't stand not knowing. Like, remember when you thought Aaron was dead that one time? You said you could feel that part of you was gone."

Alex's smile faded as he remembered. He could almost feel it again just thinking back to those days. "I remember," he said quietly. After a moment he came over to her and knelt, putting his hand out to pet one of Fifer's birds. "I've actually been thinking a lot on this journey. And I get it now."

"You do?"

"Yeah. I'm still mad you disobeyed me. But . . ." He glanced at Lani, who raised an eyebrow at him and nodded encouragingly. "I think maybe you and I should take a little walk. Okay?"

Fifer nodded. "Okay."

Alex stood, and he and Fifer set out through the forest away from the others. Fifer glanced over her shoulder, and Kaylee gave her two thumbs up in encouragement.

When they were out of earshot of the others, Alex glanced at Fifer. To his surprise, she was a few inches taller than his shoulder already. "When did you get so tall?" he asked sheepishly.

Fifer shrugged. "I don't know. I'm strong, too. Want to see?"

He nodded. Fifer lifted her arm and flexed her biceps. He reached out and tested it. "Wow," he said, impressed.

Fifer dropped her arm, then said, suddenly impassioned, "Alex, I want to tell you things. Secrets. Confessions."

Alex looked surprised. "Okay," he said. "You can talk to me about anything. You know that, right?"

"I've tried to tell you things before, but you haven't been hearing me."

Alex opened his mouth to retort, but then he closed it. "That's fair. Will you give me another chance?"

Fifer was surprised and encouraged by his question. She nodded and began. "First confession: I watched out the window when Florence was training you on the west lawn."

Alex cringed. "Oh. I see."

"I was so proud of you, Alex." Fifer's voice hitched. Suddenly tears were surfacing in both their eyes. "I was there," she went on, "and Florence knew about it. And I learned how to use the components that way, as Florence retaught you. But mostly that time by the window was so important for another reason. Because I saw bits and pieces of the Alex from Lani's books for the first time. And I feel like I know you better now."

Alex stopped walking and stared numbly at the ground cover. "I haven't read them," he confessed.

Fifer stopped too and faced him. "What? How could you not?"

"It was too hard."

"What was?"

He pursed his lips, a pained expression crossing his face. "Reliving all of those losses. The battles, and my friends. It was too hard to see myself as I was before . . . and realize I'm not that person anymore. And the person I am now is someone I don't . . . really . . . like as much." He let out a breath. "It was too hard to be painted as some sort of hero when I wasn't feeling like one. It was easier to shove all of those memories away where they couldn't gnaw at me every day. Easier to pretend that 'fearless leader Alex' was just a character in a storybook I hadn't read."

Fifer was quiet for a moment. "But here you are again."

"Yes," said Alex. "I suppose." He slipped his hand inside his robe, pulled out a handful of spell components, and looked at them. "Here I am again," he said softly.

"Do you feel good about it?" asked Fifer. "About deciding to retrain and go? And about fighting again after so long?"

Alex looked at her for a long moment, revealing vulnerability in his eyes. Then he nodded. "Yes, I do." He replaced the components, then asked, "Do you?"

Fifer looked puzzled. "Do I feel good about myself fighting? Or about you?"

Alex gave her a crooked half smile. "Both."

"Yes," she said. "To both."

"Good."

They continued walking a few steps, and then Fifer stopped. "So . . . do you maybe want to throw scatterclips at each other?"

Alex frowned and looked like he was about to say no, which he would have automatically done in the past. But then he tilted his head and eyed her mischievously, one brow raised. "Yes. I do. Fifteen paces. Avoid the trees. Go."

Fifer almost shouted in delight—she'd never expected him to say yes. They turned their backs on each other and counted their steps, then faced each other again. Fifer pulled out a handful of scatterclips from her vest, praying she'd get the spell right, because if she messed up now . . . Well, she didn't want to think about the consequences.

Alex slipped his hand into his robe and took out a full set of scatterclips. He tossed them confidently in his right hand. "You're sure you want to mess with me?" he said. "I'm the head mage of Artimé, you know. Somebody even wrote a book about me once."

"I'm sure," said Fifer, laughing nervously. Her stomach flipped. This was the first actual component spell she'd be doing. What if it didn't work? Would Alex forbid her from fighting? Would he send her home?

LISA McMANN

"Wait," said Alex, holding up his hand. "You don't know the deadly verbal component to scatterclips, do you? I only ask because . . . well, talk to Aaron about that sometime."

Fifer's eyes widened. "I don't know that verbal component," she said.

"Okay, good," said Alex. He dropped his hand. "Ready?" He took a quick glance at what was behind him and drew his arm back, poised to throw.

"Ready," called Fifer, doing the same.

"Go!"

Alex and Fifer flung their scatterclips at each other. The two sets of components soared straight and true and had to dodge out of each other's way in the center of the distance between them. Fifer closed her eyes and stood firm as Alex's clips soared into her, grabbing her clothing and yanking her backward through the air until she slammed into a tree with a *thump*. The scatterclips hooked into the trunk, leaving Fifer hanging. She peeked out of one eye, cringing at the same time, hoping she hadn't done anything wrong with her throw.

Alex was pinned as well and laughing. "You did it!" he

called out. Fifer had nailed it. Just like with other spells, she'd picked up how to do it with hardly any effort.

"Release," said Alex, and he and Fifer both fell to the ground. Alex got up and ran over to her. "That was really good," he said, helping her up.

"Thank you," said Fifer.

"I'm impressed. How many times have you done that?"

Fifer wanted to lie and tell him that she'd done it dozens of times so he'd have more confidence in her. But she told him the truth. "That was my first time."

Alex shook his head, awed. "How did you get the throw right?"

"I watched you," said Fifer. "And I practiced the movements a lot. I just haven't done it with the components before."

"Do you want to show me some more?" asked Alex.

"I do," said Fifer, "but I don't want to waste my components."

"I'll reimburse you from our stash," said Alex. "Show me what else you can do. I really want to see."

Fifer grinned. They spent the next little while going through Fifer's vest pockets and having her try out each new

LISA McMANN

component she pulled out. Fifer knew Alex needed to see her do them—and she was okay with that. She needed to see what she could do too. And it was nice that they were actually having a conversation without either of them arguing.

After Fifer had tried out everything successfully, the two walked back to the group, talking about magical strategy as if they'd been fighting together for years.

Kaylee watched them return and smiled as she saw them in animated conversation. "Looks like you two are seeing eye to eye," she remarked.

Fifer grinned. "Alex let me try out my new components on him."

"And she didn't even kill me," Alex quipped.

Crow flashed a thumbs-up at Fifer. It was heartwarming for all of them to see the two Stowe siblings getting along for once. Things were looking up, and the team was growing anxious to move.

"When do you think Kitten will reach the exit?" Alex asked Arabis, who was holding her mouth open in the river and scooping up fish.

The dragon swallowed them down and lifted her head. "She

probably won't make it there until sometime after midnight. It's a lengthy journey on foot."

"I think we should be cautious and wait until morning to send the seek spell, then," said Alex. "So Kitten will certainly be in the right place."

"But if we're to be stealthy, we don't want a lot of people roaming about in the square," Thatcher pointed out.

"We'll go before dawn," said Alex. "Before the townspeople start their day. How does that sound?"

Everyone agreed it was the best option.

"Also, after dark this evening," said Lani, "I was thinking some of us could check out the area and maybe see if we can find the exact location of the cylinder. Perhaps there's an outline visible in the stone."

"That's a great idea," said Seth.

"I agree," said Thatcher. "I'm not positive I can find the exact location, especially if the stage they put the girls on isn't a permanent fixture in the square. Everything is such a blur."

"I could find it," said Simber, "but I don't think I should rrrisk being seen."

LISA McMANN

"I can show you all exactly where it is," said Fifer. "I stood there long enough."

Kaylee smiled. "It's good we have you here, then, isn't it?"

Fifer grinned. She glanced at Alex, and he shrugged, then grinned back. It felt good not to be so frustrated and angry all the time for once. Now if they could just get Thisbe back without anybody getting hurt or captured, that would be truly amazing.

A Shocking Turn

The rescue team shared a late-afternoon lunch in the cover of the forest while a small group of them made plans to venture out, hoping to find the Revinir's cylinder entrance to the catacombs in the square.

In her packing and planning, Fifer had been thinking ahead, and she'd brought along clothing and accessories that would disguise her black eyes. She dug through her travel bag and pulled out a scarf and some stage glasses with tinted lenses that Thisbe had worn in a recent play. Samheed glanced twice at her when she put them on, then smiled when he realized what she was doing. "Incognito," he said. "Very nice."

LISA McMANN

"I don't want anybody to notice me. I was up for auction out there once—I don't want to be again!"

Before they left, Arabis bade them good-bye and good luck. As soon as darkness fell, she'd be on her way to warn the dragons in the land beyond the forest. "I'll be swift," she promised them.

Simber and Talon chose to stay in the forest so they wouldn't draw attention. "Maybe I should stay back too," said Lani, looking down at her contraption. "Does this look too magical? Will people suspect?"

"I've never seen any wheels that look that advanced in my world," said Kaylee, skeptical. "If this world isn't magical at all, you might want to wear a long jacket that will hide some of it."

"Stay toward the middle of our group," Fifer suggested. "We'll cover you."

Lani agreed. Soon the humans were heading toward the road that led into the square. They went up the road in two groups. Fifer, in disguise, led the way with Alex and Kaylee. Seth, Carina, Thatcher, Samheed, and Lani went behind them. It was a lengthy walk, but when they got close, Fifer filled in the others on some details.

"The soldiers in green are the king's soldiers. They're from the big castle. If you see any soldiers in blue uniforms, those are the Revinir's. They sort of seemed to work together when Thiz and I were on the auction stage—though I'm not positive if they are friendly or not. The green ones let the blue ones come in and surround the stage. So I think that means the Revinir and the king aren't enemies, but I don't think they're friends, either."

"Maybe they just warily tolerate each other," said Lani.

Alex nodded. "Arabis mentioned that the Revinir would be furious at the king for allowing the dragons to escape and she'd demand something in return. That could create a problem."

"So tomorrow," Thatcher clarified, "we're most likely going to end up fighting the blue-uniformed soldiers. Leave the green ones alone unless they attack."

Dragonsmarche, the weekly market in the center of Grimere, was teeming with shoppers. The Artiméans looked on curiously as people traded gold nuggets for other goods. Kaylee explained to those who were puzzled by the exchange that the gold nuggets were the currency and they were worth something—at some point someone had decided gold was valuable, and people began to seek it and collect it, and they could use it to get other things.

"Why doesn't everybody just share everything like we do?" asked Seth. "If they need something, get someone to make it for them, or do it themselves."

"It's easier to do that in magical worlds, I suppose," Alex mused. "We have everything we need. But when Artimé's magic was broken and we were starting to starve, people began fighting and stealing from each other. It was ugly."

"Dev stole our fruit on the mountainside," said Seth, remembering his severe hunger.

Fifer glanced back at him and nodded. They'd had their eyes opened to a different world with Dev. "I wonder how he's doing," she said. "Princess Shanti was so mean to him."

"Yeah," said Seth. "I hope he's . . . okay." They both had ambivalent feelings about Dev, but he'd helped them at least as much as he'd hurt them. He was intriguing, at a minimum.

As they neared the center of the square, an explosion in the distance rocked the ground. Most of the people of Grimere ignored it, but the Artiméans startled. Fifer and Seth remembered they'd heard it before, and they looked to the west. "Look that way," said Seth, "beyond that hill. There'll be smoke rising up." Sure enough a plume of gray smoke rose.

Alex narrowed his eyes, puzzling over it. "It sounded like . . . like . . ." He shook his head as if he couldn't quite figure it out.

They meandered and weaved through the crowds, trying not to look like foreigners, though their clothes were quite different from everyone else's. Fortunately it was crowded enough that not many seemed to take note. Fifer led the others toward the center of the square. The stage wasn't there now, so it was hard to figure out exactly where the girls had been. Fifer looked around, trying to remember if there were any other landmarks she could recall. Then she spied the huge aquarium in the far corner of the square. It looked like the glass had been broken and repaired, and there were fewer sea creatures inside than before. Once Fifer found that, she could remember how the stage had been set in relation to it and about how far away from it she'd been. She moved toward the area where she thought the stage had been.

"It was here," she said in a low voice. "We faced this way, right, Thatcher?"

"Yes, from what I can remember. Simber and I circled and

flew in from that direction." He pointed toward the aquarium.

Fifer envisioned the auction and the way the crowd had grown and spread out. "It's got to be somewhere nearby."

The group, attempting to not appear suspect, milled around the area looking at the ground and tried to detect any sign of cracks that would indicate a break in the mortar. But the uneven cobblestone was covered in cracks, and there was no apparent pattern.

As Fifer and Seth worked their way around a stand where someone was selling tiny bottles of liquid, a blue-uniformed soldier stepped out and nearly knocked Fifer over. She stumbled and caught her balance on the edge of the table. The bottles shook and threatened to spill off.

"Watch it!" snarled the boy behind the table.

"Sorry," said Fifer, pulling her hand back. She glanced at him and nearly gasped. "Dev?" she said before she remembered her disguise.

The boy behind the table looked startled but didn't seem to recognize her.

Seth came up behind Fifer. "Are you all right?"

Dev froze in fear. "Seth," he said, then glanced at the blue-uniformed soldiers behind him, who were talking quietly together. He leaned forward and squinted, taking in Fifer's scarf and glasses. "Fifer? Is that you? You're okay?"

A musical fanfare began at the mouth of Dragonsmarche, and the three moved closer so they could hear one another.

"What are you doing here?" Dev said sharply. "It's dangerous!"

"Have you seen Thisbe?"

"I—I—" Dev seemed frozen in his ability to tell them everything that had happened. "Yes!" he sputtered. "She's down there! In the catacombs. Same hallway as the elevator."

"She's alive?" Fifer exclaimed, and Dev nodded.

"Elevator?" asked Seth. "You mean that cylinder thing?"

"Yes," said Dev.

The blue-uniformed soldiers stepped toward the group, suspicious. "If you're not purchasing any dragon-bone broth, be on your way!" shouted one over the noise of the band. He moved closer, looking menacingly at them, and Fifer and Seth turned and rushed away.

Dev watched them stiffly as another soldier came and stood

behind him with a dagger pointed at his back. He was help-less to do anything. But he consoled himself with the news he could share with Thisbe later—that her people had finally come back for her. She'd be so happy.

It almost made Dev feel emptier inside. Part of him wanted Thisbe to be with her family, but that meant he'd have no one again. He closed his eyes as pain washed through him, and then took a deep breath and opened them, ready to sell the dragon-bone broth. The sooner he could move everything, the faster he could get back inside to tell Thisbe.

Seth and Fifer found Alex and the others again and hurried to tell them what they'd found out—Thisbe was alive! They exclaimed their relief at the news as the marching band got closer and louder. And then the crowd parted and the band pushed through. Behind the band was a small chariot that was drawn by two jewel-adorned tigers.

Sitting in the front, wearing a petite crown that sparkled in the waning light, was Princess Shanti. All around her chariot were soldiers with green uniforms who looked about uneasily, almost as if they were assessing the number of the Revinir's soldiers in the area.

Shanti was looking around too, but not at the soldiers. Finally she spied Dev and halted the tigers, then ordered the band to be quiet. When the band ceased playing, the townspeople looked over to see what was happening.

"There he is," Shanti announced loudly to her soldiers. She pointed at Dev. "I want him back. Now! Seize him!"

On the Run

Fifer and Seth hid behind the others so the princess wouldn't recognize them. But Shanti was focused on Dev. "Bring him to me now!" she ordered. The soldiers in green marched over to Dev, who was beginning to quake with the dagger point pressed in his back. He quickly grabbed something off the table and slipped it into the money belt around his waist, then put his hands in the air. "Shanti, no!" he said. "What are you doing?" One of the Revinir's soldiers whistled for help, and more in blue came running. They pushed Dev around the table and out into the open.

The princess's soldiers drew their swords, prompting the blue-uniformed soldiers to do the same. "Help!" cried Dev, caught between them. "Princess, please!" he pleaded. "Does the king know what you're doing? The Revinir will be furious. Don't make this mistake."

Shanti jumped out of the chariot and stormed toward Dev, unafraid. "Stop this nonsense," she said to him, then chided the soldiers on both sides. "Put these swords away. I want my servant back. I am the princess. Therefore, you must give him to me."

The soldiers in blue stood firm around Dev—they took their orders from the Revinir. "Stay back," one of them ordered her. "This slave was given as restitution and belongs to the Revinir."

"Perhaps we should take the princess as the final payment," jeered another of the Revinir's soldiers.

Shanti's eyes burned. She continued forward, acting like she couldn't imagine anything bad ever happening to her. Her soldiers followed her, staring down the ones in blue.

"Shanti, stop!" shouted Dev, his eyes wide and fearful. "I mean it! Just go back to the palace before you start a war!"

"Don't speak, Dev," said Shanti coldly. She stood between the two groups of soldiers and began telling them what to do like they were five-year-olds.

The Artiméans shifted uneasily. "What should we do?" asked Fifer, peering between Alex and Kaylee.

"I didn't bring my sword," Kaylee muttered.

"I've got components, but we can't do anything," said Alex. "It'll jeopardize our chances of rescuing Thisbe. Besides, I'm not sure whose side we're supposed to be on. Are you?"

Fifer and Seth looked at each other. "I guess Dev's," said Fifer, "but why is he being guarded by the Revinir's soldiers? It sounds like the Revinir took him after what happened with the dragons."

"That would explain how he knows where Thisbe is," said Seth.

Shanti reached out to grab Dev by the collar and pull him with her. A soldier in blue struck the princess's hand away, then pointed her sword at Shanti. It glinted in the sunlight.

"Don't touch her!" shouted the captain of the king's soldiers. They drove the Revinir's soldiers back, and Shanti grabbed at Dev again.

"Come on, Dev," she said angrily. "Soldiers!" she shouted. "Take care of this."

Swords clashed.

"Shanti, please," Dev begged. "Stop them." A few soldiers in blue shoved Shanti away from the booth.

The princess screamed, and the king's soldiers charged to protect her and fight back. Some of the Revinir's guards grabbed Dev, who struggled to get away, but all he could do was watch, terrified. From the chariot, the tigers growled.

The skirmish became a fight. The king's soldiers attacked full on and knocked over the table of dragon-bone broth, sending the glass vials smashing to the ground, the broth spilling everywhere. The Revinir's army charged.

"No!" shouted Dev, and with a huge effort managed to escape the soldiers' grasp. He shoved Shanti out of the line of fire. Losing his balance, he tried to roll out of the way, but the soldiers kicked and stepped on him, leaving him squirming and unable to get up. Shanti stumbled and fell against one of the Revinir's soldiers, who turned sharply and slammed the pommel of his sword into her stomach. She doubled over and yelled out for Dev to help her as another blue soldier swung wildly

LISA McMANN

with his sword, swiping at her. His blade left a deep gash in her neck. Her eyes widened in fear, and then the blood started flowing. She dropped to the ground, her princess crown falling off her head and rolling over the uneven pavers. Another of the Revinir's soldiers slammed his sword down on the princess. She stopped moving.

The tigers growled and yanked at their tethers, and the crowd of townspeople pushed back, many of them running for their lives. One of the tigers bucked and broke free of the chariot, then began stalking random people around him. The blue soldiers fought the green, swords clashing, blood and bodies flying. Shanti lay still in the midst of it all, bloody and broken. Dev got up and fought his way to her, shoving people aside even as they trampled her limp body. He knelt next to her. Reaching for her shoulder, he shook her gently and called her name. But he could see the truth. Shanti was dead.

Dev clutched his head, beside himself, and yelled, "You killed the princess!" His face awash in terror, he got up and stumbled into the fighting, numb and disoriented and yelling in the Revinir's soldiers' faces. "You killed the princess!"

Running townspeople stopped and turned. "The princess

is dead," they murmured. "Killed by the Revinir's soldiers!"

"Surely the king will declare war."

The Artiméans watched in horror. "Run, Dev!" screamed Fifer before she could contain herself. "Get out of there!" Hearing her, Dev looked wildly around. He came to his senses, dashed through the remaining onlookers, and disappeared.

"Look out, friends," muttered Carina to the others. "One of the tigers is loose and it's coming this way. Time to get out of here!" She and Alex found everyone from the rescue team and sent them running toward the forest.

But Crow stayed back as the royal tiger continued attacking injured bystanders who couldn't get away. People screamed. Crow reached into his pocket and pulled out his slingshot and a handful of stones. With a troubled look on his face, he loaded a small stone and took aim, then fired. It got the tiger's attention.

Crow stepped toward it and reloaded, this time with a big rock. The tiger recognized its enemy and stalked him. Crow waited. The rest of the rescue team turned from a distance to see what was happening.

"Crow!" screamed Fifer. "No! Look out!"

Crow took careful aim and pulled the stone back as far as he could, his hand shaking. The tiger came at him. He let the stone fly.

It hit the creature between the eyes. The tiger roared angrily, then retreated to nurse his wounds. Crow turned and ran to join his team.

"At least he's distracted," said Crow when he reached them. "Enough to give the people a chance to get away."

"Wow," said Seth. "That was really brave."

Crow didn't answer. Instead he cringed as he watched the battle, his face drawn. He hated fighting. But he'd do anything to protect his friends, just like they'd done for him so many times in the past. Soon one of the king's uniformed soldiers was able to stun the loose tiger long enough to reattach him to the chariot.

The rescue team retreated farther to the edge of the square, where the buildings began. There they watched from behind an abandoned wagon as the king's soldiers fell at the hands of the Revinir's soldiers.

Eventually the Artiméans slipped away to the forest again, all together this time.

After the blue soldiers had fought off the last of the green and declared victory, they descended on the princess's chariot and looted the jewels that encrusted it. Leaving the dead scattered, one soldier lifted and turned a particular cobblestone in the square near where Dev's market booth had been. The Revinir's elevator rose. The victorious soldiers piled in, helping their wounded.

The last one in grabbed Princess Shanti's crown and held it high in triumph. They left her dead body on the ground in the middle of the square.

A Change in Plans

The end of the day drew near, but Thisbe's work wasn't done. She bottled the new liquid alone, lost in her thoughts. The images of her ancestors that had overwhelmed her after taking in the bone broth occasionally flitted through her mind, making little sense. Yet the Revinir hadn't experienced anything after drinking the ancestor broth. Why hadn't this same thing happened to her? Thisbe wondered if it was because the woman wasn't a descendant of the royal black-eyed people.

It made Thisbe thoughtful—was her lineage the real reason the Revinir wanted Thisbe to join her in taking over the land? To use her somehow because of who her powerful ancestors were, like she wanted to use the dragons' power?

It had to have something to do with her magical abilities, too, or the Revinir could have chosen any of the other slaves. The woman desperately wanted to be great at something, even if by association. Since she wasn't royalty, having Thisbe as an assistant—and more importantly, a *willing* assistant—was of the utmost importance to her. That much was clear. Perhaps she wanted validation. Perhaps Thisbe represented some sort of proof that she was powerful and respected because this black-eyed servant thought good of her. Knowing the incredible ego that the Revinir had, this made the most sense.

Thisbe wasn't having any of it. But she was extremely nervous. She'd nearly gasped when the woman had mentioned escaping, as if she knew full well about the plan. Was the dragon-bone marrow really that strong that the Revinir would have gained such strong intuition? Or was it just a random threat that happened to be accurate? She'd find out soon enough. She and Rohan were breaking out in a few hours. *No matter what.*

As she finished up for the day, she kept looking anxiously

LISA McMANN

for Dev. Maybe he wouldn't have to come back here after working in the market all day. She wished she'd said a more meaningful good-bye to him. And had somehow been able to hint to him that they'd be coming back for him and the others eventually. If they survived the escape.

Just then there was a ruckus among the soldiers at the door. A moment later Thisbe could hear faraway shouts from the main hallway. The soldiers ran out, and Thisbe went to the doorway. Rohan was nearing with his load of bones. He was clearly agitated.

"What's going on?" Thisbe whispered.

"Something terrible has happened," he said. "The princess came to the market and ordered the Revinir's soldiers to stand down," he said in a low voice. "She demanded to have Dev back. There was a fight, and the princess was killed."

"What? *Killed?*"

"Yes, and Dev ran off."

"He did?" She clutched her throat, feeling sick for him. "I hope he's okay."

"He ran toward the forest is what I've heard, not back to the castle. The Revinir is fuming. And I'm afraid my fears of

LISA McMANN

the past weeks will be realized. The king will surely declare war on the Revinir after this. I have no doubt. And after losing the dragons and now Dev, she will certainly welcome it. We're in for it, Thisbe. All of us."

"Oh no," Thisbe said under her breath. Stunned, she couldn't imagine what Grimere would be like in the middle of a war, or what it would mean for the black-eyed slaves.

"It's chaos in the square," said Rohan. "And it soon will be down here. It'll only get worse as time passes."

Thisbe searched his eyes. Then she peered down the hallway. "We should leave now while everyone's distracted."

"You read my mind," said Rohan. "Is that the dragon ability?"

"No. I'm just smart. Let's get out of here."

Rohan flipped his load of bones onto the kitchen floor and rolled up his harness while Thisbe put her things away in the kitchen as usual, so nothing would seem suspicious. At the last second, Thisbe grabbed a few bottles of the ancestor broth and slipped them into her pocket. She wasn't sure why she'd taken them—perhaps they'd hold some value down the road. Then the two snuck out toward the main hallway. They could hear soldiers shouting. They reached the main passage and peered in all directions.

"We'll pretend like we're walking back to our crypts," whispered Thisbe. "It's the right time of day. We'll go one at a time so we're not seen together. And we'll just keep going."

"Maybe we should grab dragon bones to drag toward the extracting room so we look like we have a purpose for going that way," said Rohan.

"Perfect," said Thisbe. "Though it'll seem a little odd to go in that direction in the evening. But we could say the Revinir is punishing us for something. Maybe we can get by everybody without having to fight at all."

Rohan slipped his hand in hers and gave it a squeeze. "Whatever happens . . . ," he said, and trailed off.

Thisbe turned to look at him. She saw the worry in his expression. "We keep going," she said, finishing his thought.

He flashed a crooked smile. "That's not what I was intending to say, but all right."

"What were you going to say?"

"I'll tell you once we make it out of here."

With no time to waste on words, Thisbe nodded and stepped into the hallway, then moved toward her crypt like normal. Rohan waited a few minutes, then followed.

The trek back to their crypts went smoothly enough. Thisbe turned off to her hallway and Rohan to his. A few soldiers ran past Thisbe toward the elevator exit, and she could see a larger crowd of soldiers there. She slipped into her crypt and drained the last of her water from the pitcher. Then she climbed up her bone pile, sending a small dragon bone tumbling to the floor to use as an excuse. She slid down after it and reached for her harness.

As she did so, Mangrel appeared and pushed a food tray inside the room. He slammed the door shut, locking Thisbe in for the night. "Wait!" Thisbe stared at the door. "Buckets of crud!" she muttered, using one of Alex's common expressions. For a split second her heart fell, and she thought all was lost. But then she remembered.

"Rohan, wait!" she cried, turning toward the tunnel. She quickly attached the bone to her harness and started climbing again, but became hindered by it getting caught on the other bones. She had to stop to unhook it and carry it, and her panic increased. Had the crypt keeper been to Rohan's room already? Or was he gone? "Rohan!" she called again, growing frantic. She finally made it to the top. She reattached the bone to the harness and dove into the tunnel. "Rohan!" she called again, and crawled through.

Emerging into his crypt, Thisbe looked out. There at the door was Rohan . . . being held fast by the Revinir.

Breakaway

Thisbe stared at the woman.

The Revinir sneered when she saw her and realized what the tunnel meant. "Aren't you clever?"

"Leave him alone!"

The Revinir shook her head. "You've been very devious, teaching this good boy to do evil things."

"He hasn't done anything!" Thisbe said, feeling her scales rise and her body's fiery magic heat up. "Let him go."

"I will," said the Revinir. "But only if you stop your nonsensical escape and share just one of your secrets with me."

"What secrets? Which one?"

LISA McMANN

"I want to know what you learned from that broth. I know you were lying. Something happened to you. Tell me what it was!"

Rohan looked confused. Thisbe hadn't had a chance to tell him about *that* yet. She let out an exasperated noise. "It was nothing. Let go of Rohan. I'm warning you." Thisbe raised her arm and pointed at the woman. She could feel the electricity pulsing through her, ready to explode.

"Don't make me kill him," said the Revinir. "He's so good."

Rohan gulped and gave Thisbe a wild look. Thisbe realized that behind the folds of her robe, the Revinir was holding a knife to Rohan's chest. Didn't the Revinir have any dragon powers to threaten him with?

Thisbe felt her heart beating wildly. She didn't know what to do. Rohan was so close to the Revinir—what if she fired and hit him by mistake? "What do you want me to do?" she asked the crazed woman.

"I want you to join my effort to take over the entire land of the dragons. Then we'll fight against the people who betrayed you in the seven islands."

"I think you have a lot of other trouble you're going to have to deal with first, lady," Thisbe said.

The Revinir jabbed the knife against Rohan's chest, making him yelp. "Tell me what happened to you when you drank the ancestor-bone broth!"

Rohan gulped down a breath, and his eyes stretched open even wider. He gave Thisbe a hard look, and without him saying a single word, she knew he was telling her it was okay to say no.

Thisbe swallowed hard and tried to be brave. "And if I don't join you or tell you—what then?"

"I'll kill Rohan right here in front of you."

Thisbe's fingers wavered. "Okay, then," she said. Then she slowly dropped her arm, carefully watching every move the woman made. "I'll tell you."

The Revinir looked appeased. She relaxed her grip a little, and Rohan inched to one side. Quickly Thisbe threw her arm forward and pointed at the woman's neck, fingers dripping sparks. "Boom!" she cried.

A fireball burst forth and flew across the crypt. Rohan dove. The spell hit the Revinir in the chest. She flew back into the wall and dropped to the floor, but she didn't break into dozens of pieces like Thisbe had expected.

Thisbe stared for a moment, then started skidding and sliding down the dragon bones, her harness dragging the extra one along with her. Rohan scrambled to his feet and checked the woman's pulse. "She's not dead," he said wildly.

"It's her dragon scales," Thisbe muttered. "They protect her." She thought about trying to finish the woman off, but didn't want to waste an ounce of energy—she had a lot more fights to be ready for. If they started moving fast now, the Revinir might never catch up. "Let's go. We'll lock her in."

"Brilliant." Rohan grabbed his harness and slipped it on; then they went out his door as quickly as possible and closed it behind them, automatically locking the Revinir inside the crypt. Staying together now for safety, they moved as fast as they could with their cargo.

"That was quite a powerful spell," said Rohan, a bit breathless. "Thank you for saving me."

"I wasn't about to go along with her," said Thisbe. "Not for any reason. Even if nobody ever comes back for me—which is what she keeps reminding me about." She frowned, thinking about how the people of Artimé had left her here. It was deeply painful and probably always would be. But she didn't hate them for it. Not the kind of hatred the Revinir seemed to feed on and expected Thisbe to feel. Thisbe shook her head. "I don't care how evil I am. I'm not like her."

"Is she still selling you that bunk? You're nothing like her. Besides, I think she makes up half of her dragon abilities to scare us. She's got scales and a little smoke and that's all. That's my guess. Otherwise why would she need to hold a knife on me?"

"I wondered about that too." Thisbe thought the woman might have a bit more dragon power than what Rohan had suggested—some sort of mental advantage that Thisbe had felt the tiniest bit of herself ever since she'd drunk that cup of dragon-bone broth. There was no telling the quantity the Revinir had ingested to produce such a full blanket of scales on her body. But Thisbe was quite sure the ancestor-bone broth hadn't done anything for the woman like it had for her. It was intriguing that the Revinir wanted to know so badly what had happened after she'd forced it down Thisbe's throat, as if she expected it to be something very important. And perhaps it was. Thisbe hadn't had time to contemplate the images she'd seen, but they remained burned in her mind as solidly as her own memories. But she might never know their significance now.

They passed through an intersection with only a few suspicious glances and hurried on toward the river. When the soldiers were out of earshot, Thisbe looked at Rohan. "She made me drink the ancestor-bone broth."

"So I gathered," Rohan said gently, and studied her face. "How ghastly that must have been. Are you okay?"

"I'm—I'm not sure. The Revinir threw it in my face. I didn't swallow much, but enough, I guess. It felt . . ." She recalled the dizzy feeling and stumbled in the hallway. Rohan reached out and steadied her arm. "It felt weird," Thisbe said. "I saw some things. Like images of things I've never seen before, but now I feel eerily like I've experienced them. It's hard to explain."

"I'm really sorry."

"Thanks." Thisbe was quiet for a time as they moved along as quickly as they could. They were both hungry and weak, not having eaten since dinner the previous day. How Thisbe wished she'd grabbed some food off her tray after the door had closed. But she hadn't thought of it in her panic. She had the ancestor broth, but she'd rather trade it for food than drink it.

Her mind turned back to the day. "The Revinir told me there are other dragons somewhere."

"Yes, I believe that. When I was a child, my mother and father told me about the ghost dragons beyond the forest—they were something to be feared. Is that what your dragons were like? Wild and fierce?"

"Not to us, because we are at peace in the seven islands. For now, anyway. The Revinir wants to take over the rule there, too."

"She makes a lot of plans," said Rohan. "But she's barely conquered one city here, and now that's in jeopardy."

"I thought everyone was afraid of her."

"They are. It's because she's so secretive and sneaky. She managed to capture dragons and build an army right under their feet—the people up there fear the unknown. How big is her underground army? How strong is she? How rich? How many dragons are under her control? No one knows because they can't get in."

"How did you find that out? From the soldiers?"

Rohan nodded. "And other newer children when they come in—I try to find a way to question them."

"You are very popular. I wish I could learn the common

language so I can speak to the others. I've only picked up a few words so far."

"I can teach you once we're out of here."

Once we're out of here. Thisbe bit her lip anxiously. They both grew somber and hurried on, knowing they might not ever get out of here. And now that the Revinir knew of their secret tunnel, they'd most certainly be kept far apart if they got caught.

At the next intersection, two soldiers stopped them, a man and a woman. "Where are you going at this time of night?" the woman asked.

Rohan smiled to appear sheepish. "The Revinir is punishing us again. I'm too friendly—it's really becoming a hazard to my rest time." He laughed, and the male soldier gave a reluctant smile. The female soldier remained stern but didn't press him.

"Has anyone found the traitor who ran away?" Rohan asked them.

The woman remained suspicious. "Not yet. What do you know about him? Did he tell you of these plans?" She looked at Thisbe. "How about you? You worked with him."

"I had no idea. I despised him. We barely spoke."

The woman studied Thisbe, then stepped aside. "Go on, then. Don't let the Revinir catch you talking together or you'll have even more work to do."

"You make an excellent point," said Rohan. "Thank you for the advice." They continued on in silence, with Rohan dropping back from Thisbe for appearances until they made the next turn. All they had left now was the group of guards at the river exit, and there was no telling how many were there—with any luck at least some of them would've been called away to help with the wounded soldiers from the square and the search for Dev.

Thisbe was quiet, wondering if Dev had known about the princess coming for him. She doubted it greatly—his earlier heartbreak had been too real to fake. Thisbe could tell that much just from her time studying acting with Samheed. It took a lot of studying to appear that realistic when pretending to cry. She was sure Dev hadn't ever had the opportunity to act in his life. He was manipulative, sure. But he'd tried fighting off those tears with all his might, and he hadn't succeeded. She believed the princess must have surprised him by showing up at the market. The thought made her angry. Princess Shanti hadn't been nice to Dev. She'd used him as a whipping boy, making him take punishment for the wrongs she'd done. That wasn't a friendship. If Dev considered that to be what friends do to each other, he had no understanding of the meaning of the word.

In that moment, thinking on friendship, Thisbe's heart wrenched. She missed Fifer and Seth. She missed her writing class with Lani and her dance class with the lounge band and her fencing class with Kaylee, which she'd only just begun. She longed to see Aaron again—he'd always made her feel better when Alex had been angry with her and Fifer. And even as confused and upset as she was about no one coming to rescue her, she still missed Alex, and she felt terrible about leaving like they'd done. She knew he loved her and Fifer dearly. A little too dearly, but was that all bad? She bet Dev would give anything to have someone care so much for him. Something had to have happened for Alex and the others not to have come after her. "I hope you're okay out there," she said under her breath.

By now Rohan had caught up with her. "What's that?"

"Nothing." They continued on. When the sound of the

river became evident, Thisbe began flexing her fingers and trying to work up some anger to cover the melancholy feelings she had. It didn't take long—she just needed to think about that morning, when the Revinir had ambushed her with the broth.

Rohan glanced sideways at her and stayed quiet, seeing she was concentrating. Soon they came up to the narrow hallway where they'd need to turn. They stopped to look all around, and then Rohan, growing anxious, asked Thisbe what she thought the best plan was.

Thisbe had forgotten that she'd never told him. She'd thought of it two nights ago but hadn't seen him since then, and with the excitement about Dev and with the Revinir, she'd forgotten all about the fact that he was approaching this without insight or instructions.

"When we get within sight of the soldiers," Thisbe said, "unhook your dragon bone and leave it behind, but keep your harness on. We'll need it later."

"Okay," said Rohan. "To get across the river?"

"Possibly. If not that, we'll need them eventually for

LISA McMANN

something, I'm sure." She tapped her lips, then said, "We're going to have to fight them. I'm not sure how many good shots I have before I start shooting worthless sparks. I should have several, but I haven't eaten anything since yesterday, so I'm not feeling terribly strong. We'll just have to wait and see. I'll go for the biggest ones first. Stay out of my line of fire, but if you can do anything at all to help, that would be grand. I wish you had a weapon."

Rohan bent down and pulled up his pant leg. There was a dagger, tied to his leg. "Like this?"

"Where'd you get that?"

"I lifted it off a soldier yesterday. I figured we might need it."

"Well done," said Thisbe. A spark of hope grew inside her. Maybe they'd have a chance. "Stay back until they come at us. We may need to make a break for it past them. Then stick close to the left wall. If we're lucky, we won't get wet at all."

Rohan raised an eyebrow while Thisbe detailed the rest of her plan. When Rohan was clear on the procedure, they locked eyes for a moment, then moved forward and went around the corner.

There were five soldiers there, guarding the river exit. As Thisbe headed toward them, Rohan turned sharply. "Thisbe!" he whispered.

She looked back. The two guards from the last intersection were running toward them from behind, and the five in front of them had noticed them coming. They were surrounded.

The Plan Backfires

I t's now or never," Thisbe said quietly. "Let's go!" She stayed far away from the soldiers, hoping the distance would give her better aim, then shot a ball of fire at the largest soldier by the river. It exploded on his chest and, like the snake in the desert, he flew into dozens of pieces that mostly landed in the river. "Whoa," said Thisbe. She let out a breath. "Okay. That's one down."

The soldiers tried to figure out what had just happened, but they were flabbergasted and couldn't make sense of it.

Thisbe felt terrible. But she had to continue. She used a little less power on the next one, knocking him to the ground almost as easily. Even if the remaining three didn't understand magic, they knew enough to rush at the source of it. The closer they got, the poorer Thisbe's aim was. She pointed again, her finger burning and throbbing, and shot off another fireball. It slammed into a soldier's legs and flipped her up into the air. She crashed to the floor, conscious and crying out, but unable to get up.

Meanwhile Rohan took on the two advancing from behind. He yelled out an apology, then punched the woman in the face, dropping her. He looked at the other guard, who was one of his friends, and just gave him a pleading look. "Please, Gustav," he said. "Just give us a chance."

The man looked uncertain for a long moment, then sighed heavily. "All right. Go, before I change my mind." He dropped to the ground, faking an injury.

"Thank you," said Rohan. He turned quickly to help Thisbe with the remaining two soldiers.

Thisbe's finger was black with soot and searing with pain. She tried her other hand and shot off another medium-size ball of fire. It missed wildly. She wished she'd practiced with that hand. She tried a second time and missed again as the two soldiers closed in.

Rohan came running, brandishing his dagger. The soldiers had swords and ran at them, leaving Rohan trying to dodge and weave without getting hit, and trying desperately to get close enough to get a jab in himself. He had no experience, though he was pretty good at avoiding the sword.

Thisbe slipped past them toward the river and turned around, shooting off sparks with her eyes when the guards spun around to go after her. A pair of sparks slammed into a soldier's eyes and he cried out, covering them and moving about in serious pain, unable to see. Thisbe quickly dispersed some more sparks at the remaining guard, aiming for and hitting her hand. She dropped the sword and Rohan moved in, slamming his knee into her stomach and grabbing her sword. But she dropped to the ground gasping for breath, and he held off hurting her further.

"Come on!" said Thisbe. "Quickly!"

They ran to the river and stood at the edge. Thisbe quickly cast invisible hooks, like the one outside her bedroom window in the mansion, just above the water line, putting them all the way across. Then she cast another line of them at shoulder height.

"One of the soldiers is getting up," said Rohan under his breath.

Thisbe glanced back. "You go across first. I can swim better than you in case they knock me in. Just feel around on the wall for the hooks, and trust me. They'll hold you fine. Step on the low ones and grab on to the high ones and walk across." Thisbe turned and shot sparks at the soldier coming at them. The woman cried out in pain but kept coming.

Rohan reached out, feeling for the first hook. When he found it, he grabbed on, then moved his foot above the water along the rock wall, trying to find the foothold.

"No hurry or anything," said Thisbe, seeing another soldier stirring.

"I'm trying to go as fast as I can," said Rohan.

Thisbe tried a wrong-handed throw and ended up accidentally shooting an invisible hook instead of a fireball at the woman. It apparently struck her, and she yelped and reached for her nose. Blood streamed down.

Thisbe was getting tired. She didn't have any sparks left. She glanced over her shoulder at Rohan, who was reaching for the next hooks. He needed to go faster. But if he faltered and slipped, he'd be dead. Thisbe didn't want to rush him.

A second soldier was getting up now. Thisbe ran at the man, who swung his sword at her. She jumped, but the blade caught her in the lower leg, slicing into her. "Ouch! Hurry, Rohan!"

"I'm trying!"

Thisbe summoned all her strength and sent a weak fireball from her burning finger. It hit its mark, dropping the man temporarily. But the woman soldier was moving more quickly again.

"Okay, Thisbe!" Rohan shouted at the last set of hooks. "Come on!" He jumped to safety.

Thisbe ran for the wall, then placed a glass spell in front of the woman who was chasing her. She banged into it and recoiled, giving Thisbe enough time to turn and reach for the first hook. Her fingers were growing numb from the burning pain, but she swiped them along the wall, desperate to find it. Finally she felt it and grabbed on. She put her foot out and slid it along the wall.

"Look out, Thisbe!" shouted Rohan.

Thisbe couldn't look. Her foot struck the first hook and

she pulled herself onto it, then, shaking, reached for the next ones. Stretching precariously, she turned her head to see the man maneuvering around the glass barricade and coming toward her.

"Thisbe!" screamed Rohan.

The soldier lifted his sword and batted the side of it against Thisbe's hand on the first hook. She shrieked in pain and let go, balanced for an instant on one foot. Then the soldier struck her again, and she plunged backward into the rushing river.

More Trouble

Thisbe hadn't had time to take a breath. She choked and sucked in a mouthful of water and flailed as the river's current whipped her upside down. She couldn't find her bearings. She couldn't tell where the surface was. All she knew was that she didn't have much time before she'd be swept under the wall.

Finally she righted herself and surfaced, the wall coming fast at her. Coughing and sputtering, she lifted her arms and turned her face, and slammed into it. Her fingers raked at the sheer stone as she tried to find something to hold on to. It was that or be forced under.

"Hook," she cried, but it didn't appear where she needed it. She was slipping, her legs and midsection already pulled beneath. The only thing holding her here was the pressure of water against her back, pressing her face and chest against the wall just above the surface. But the river's grasp on her legs was strong. She took a deep breath and continued to struggle as it pulled her down an inch at a time.

"Thisbe! I'm here!" Rohan yelled. "Reach for me! Grab my harness!" He was safely on the far bank, throwing the end of his harness to her, but it was too far away. Thisbe couldn't get there, and she couldn't let go of the wall to reach for it.

When her hands slipped, she submerged and was swept under the wall. She cast a glass spell in front of her and immediately slammed into it feetfirst, her knees buckling. It stopped her and kept her from being swept away, but she couldn't swim upstream against a current like this, and she wasn't sure how far under the wall she'd gone. Blindly she cast another glass spell in front of the one that was there, making the glass twice as thick and putting her a half inch closer to where she needed to be.

She could hold her breath for a long time, but was it long

LISA McMANN

enough to cast enough glass spells to inch her way back into the hallway?

She tried again to cast hooks, and this time she managed to place two of them on the rock above her. She reached for them and pulled herself against the current. Then two more. Once again she could hear Rohan shouting—he had no idea that Thisbe could survive underwater for so long, and she knew he must be beside himself. But she couldn't think about him right now. She hung on to the hooks and pulled her legs up to her chest, then cast another glass spell to push off against with her feet and to stop her from losing the ground she'd gained. Then she cast two more hooks and nearly reached the hallway wall. She gripped them and pulled with all her might, until finally her head was back in the hallway. She used her chin as leverage and her face broke the surface. She sucked in a big breath, then quickly cast more hooks on the wall. Reaching up, she found them and grabbed hold. She pulled her body along with her, casting another set of hooks just above the surface toward Rohan's side of the river. She moved sideways one hook at a time, fighting the current, her arms aching. She could hear his muffled shouts, and then she felt something hit her in the head.

It was his harness, in a loop. Thisbe grabbed on, trying to slide her arm through the loop, and managing to hook it around her elbow. "Got it!" she cried, her voice ragged. When it grew taut, she let go of the hooks.

Rohan pulled her to his side of the river. When she reached it, he got on his knees and yanked her up and onto the passageway floor. He rolled her over.

She looked up at him and coughed. "Thanks."

"How are you possibly alive?" he exclaimed. Then he glanced across the river at the soldiers, and his face changed. "Oh no," he muttered, getting up. The one who had batted Thisbe into the river was coming across on the original invisible hooks like Rohan had done. "Get up, Thisbe. Look!"

Thisbe lifted her upper body and turned to see what was happening. Then she held her hand up at the hooks. "Release!" she said weakly. The invisible hooks apparently disappeared, for the soldier plunged into the water and was swept away, never to be seen again.

"Gods of nature!" muttered Rohan as he watched the soldier disappear. "Who are you?" His face was stricken, and he looked to Thisbe to know what to do next.

Safe for the moment, Thisbe released the other spells so the soldiers couldn't use them, and slowly got to her feet, dripping wet. Together she and Rohan moved toward the fresh air. By now it was nearly dawn, and they'd made it across the river.

When they reached the exit, they peered out to see where their journey would take them next. The sheer wall of rock, almost perpendicular the ground, landed at the edge of the crater lake, hundreds of feet below them. Thisbe's stomach turned—her fear of heights hadn't magically gone away. She swallowed hard and stepped back. "Blurgh," she muttered, trying to calm her butterflies.

"Now what do we do?" asked Rohan, still rattled. He didn't look excited about the prospects either. It seemed impossible.

Thisbe took a few deep breaths and shook out her arms, which felt weak after performing so much magic and struggling in the river. How was she going to climb down from here? She glanced back at the soldiers, two of whom were helping the remaining injured ones now. The one that had let Rohan go was one of them, and he refused to look up at the escapees. It seemed strange that no new soldiers were coming to this area. Hadn't anyone gone to summon help? Or had they given up on the two and simply considered them a loss?

Perhaps there would be soldiers waiting for them by the time they reached the bottom. Then again, Thisbe imagined the soldiers would never expect them to make it down alive. So it seemed most likely that they'd ended pursuit to spare their own lives.

Thisbe took another deep breath and let it out, collecting her thoughts. "Okay, well. We have to climb down, that's what. And it would be best to make it down before it's bright enough out for anyone to see us. Hook your harness to mine."

While Rohan connected the harnesses, Thisbe got on her hands and knees at the edge of the opening. She assessed the situation, with only shadows to hint at the variations in the wall, then carefully placed four invisible hooks directly to one side of the opening, where she expected she'd need her hands and feet to go in order to swing out of the mouth of the cave.

Thisbe glanced at Rohan. "Are you ready?"

Rohan's gray face was tinged with green, but he nodded.

Thisbe reached out sideways for the first handhold. She found it and grabbed on. "Watch where I go so you have an idea of where the hooks are. Okay?"

Rohan nodded again and gulped hard.

"And we'll move one at a time. If one of us falls, the other has to be hanging on tightly if we're going to have a chance of surviving this."

"My God," whispered Rohan. "You don't seem scared. Why in the world aren't you petrified? I'm shaking."

"I'm terrified," Thisbe admitted. "But we don't have any choice. Unless you want to go back?"

"No. We need to continue."

"Okay. Here I go. Watch the harness ropes so we don't get tangled." Thisbe sat on the edge and let her feet dangle out. Hanging on to the first hook, she slowly slid out, reaching her foot to find the invisible hook that was there somewhere. She felt the blood drain from her face and tried not to think about the height. She'd done something far worse before with Hux and Fifer and Seth. Now at least she'd remembered this spell.

As she slipped farther and farther off the edge of her seat, she began waving her foot, trying to find the hook. Finally her toe struck it. She relocated the hook and rested her toe on it, then eased her upper body out and started to reach toward the other handhold. "This is the absolute worst thing I've ever willingly done in my life," she muttered, then gasped and swung out. Her foot stayed solid as she pivoted and reached wildly for the other hook, slamming her hand into it hard. Fingers stinging, she found it again and grabbed on, pulling her face and body close to the rock wall. "Phew," she breathed. Then she found the second foot hook. She rested for a moment, her cheek against the cool rock, then turned her head and looked at Rohan. She blew out a breath from deep in her chest and tried to smile.

He looked back at her, fearful.

With her body frozen in terror, she wasn't sure if her smile had translated. "Everything's great," she assured him. She made another set of hooks next to the first set, and began the process of moving sideways, lifting her line of harness over one of the hooks to help in case either of them fell. "Eventually we'll go down one below the other, like

LISA McMANN

descending a ladder," she explained, "but let's just get you out here first."

Rohan nodded. He found the first handhold, then began sliding out and searching for the first foothold like Thisbe had done. "This is utterly grim and horrifying," he muttered. "I'm not sure why I've become your friend."

Thisbe laughed softly, glad he was trying to make a joke. "You've really gotten yourself into a mess with me," she said.

"I had no idea you could do all of this magic," said Rohan. "You are a goddess, and I am but a mortal boy of no significance who will surely die in moments." He connected with the foothold a little easier than Thisbe, as he was taller and it wasn't quite as far of a reach for him.

"You're fine." Thisbe watched him and realized the conversation seemed to be helping him cope. "Just wait until you see me make things come alive. I didn't try it with the bones for obvious reasons."

Rohan managed a smile before he swung out and dangled precipitously for an instant, then hit the rock wall chest-first. He made a noise and flailed, panicking a little.

"Your handhold is right next to mine," Thisbe said, trying

to stay calm. "You're doing great." If he fell, she wasn't at all certain she could support his weight. The points of the hooks dug into the soles of her shoes a bit, but it wasn't the most uncomfortable thing Thisbe had ever endured, though it might be by the time they neared the bottom. Rohan found the top hook and gripped it tightly. He was breathing hard. "Was it really necessary to make the hooks invisible? What was the thinking there?"

"Not my spell," said Thisbe, eyeing him. "Are you doing okay?"

"Yes, for now," said Rohan, panting. "Tell me more about something. Anything. Your world. I don't care what." He pushed his face into the wall and couldn't slow his breathing. "Help me," he said.

"Try taking one deep breath," Thisbe said. "That's what my friend Seth would suggest. He has trouble breathing sometimes when he panics. It just happens. It's real, though, and he says it feels awful, but it's going to be okay. One deep breath, if you can, and blow it out."

Rohan tried to do what she suggested.

Thisbe told him a little bit more about Seth while she

planted two more sets of hooks, one set directly below each of them, equidistant apart like a ladder so it would be easier to find them. "The hardest part is over," she told Rohan. "You made it out. Still okay?"

Rohan nodded. He took in a couple more breaths and blew them out as slowly as he could. "My arms . . . and legs . . . are rubber."

"That's just how they feel on the outside. Inside you have strong muscles from all the work you've done. They won't fail you now." She watched him for a moment as his breathing evened out. "Your next hooks are just a couple feet directly below the first set. Let's do this together. Which foot do you want to start with?"

"Left," said Rohan.

"Okay. Here I go. Did I ever tell you about the Island of Graves? It's covered in saber-toothed gorillas." Thisbe found her left foot hook and moved to the right foot.

"No," said Rohan, copying her when she was solidly in place. "I'm quite sure I'd remember that. Tell me."

As Thisbe talked about the Island of Graves and how

Kaylee had lived there in a tree for a year before Alex, Sky, and Aaron had rescued her, they moved down another set of hooks. Thisbe kept planting new ones directly below the existing ones as they went, and soon both of them became a bit more comfortable.

"How did you stop yourself from being swept down the river back there?" asked Rohan after a while. "I thought you were lost for good and I was stuck forever."

Thisbe told him about the glass spell and how she'd used it to make walls to push herself back against the current. Then she told him how most people in Artimé could hold their breath for several minutes.

The edge of the sky tinged orange, and while the two of them remained in the shadow of the wall, at least they could see the ground. But their limbs were growing weaker. It became harder for Thisbe to tell stories because it was wearing her out, so she stopped. Every step required concentration on their shaking legs.

By the time they were two-thirds of the way down, they were spent and beginning to really worry they wouldn't last.

Thisbe couldn't place her hooks properly anymore, and both of them slipped at least once. The bottoms of their feet became tender and painful.

But they couldn't stop. Eventually, because of how taxing the magic was becoming, Thisbe stopped making double ladders and moved over to Rohan's ladder. That helped her magic fatigue, but they were exhausted all around. They'd been up all night and hadn't eaten in ages. At one point, the volcano in the lake erupted with a huge blast of water, scaring them both—they'd never been so close to it when it had gone off before. After the water had slapped the lake, a fireball flew out. The spout spewed lava and a second fireball. Then after some time, the volcano plunged into the water and disappeared. "We have one of those in our world too," said Thisbe. "Pirates used to live under it in a big glassed-in world." The image of a pirate ship flitted into her mind—the same one from when she'd taken the ancestor broth—but it disappeared, and with her exhaustion, she soon forgot about it.

Rohan couldn't respond. They continued, fighting through pain and weakness.

Finally they made it to the ground. The sun was coming

up. They looked around for soldiers but saw no one. Then they crawled on shaky limbs to the edge of the lake to drink some water. Soon they took to the thick foliage beside it and collapsed under some bushes, unable to go any farther without rest.

Before they fell asleep, two giant shadows passed over them, heading straight for the opening to the catacombs. But the brush hid everything from view.

Mass Confusion

The Artiméans had spent a troubled night in the forest, with Talon and Simber keeping careful watch over the others while they slept. They'd all hoped Kitten was safe after the unexpected ruckus and would make it to the elevator sometime during the night. They were comforted by the fact that she was so tiny she wouldn't be noticed, and even if someone stepped on her, she had more lives left.

Before dawn the first wave of the rescue team set off toward the cave entrance: Talon flying with Alex, and Fifer and Crow in the hammock being carried by the falcons. They rose above the trees and swept over the quiet city and the empty square. Few signs of the previous evening's fight remained. Talon and Alex headed to the hill beyond the city square, in the direction of where they'd seen the smoke. Fifer commanded the falcons to follow Talon's lead. It took them quite some time to reach the far side of the hill where the cave entrance was, but Crow and Fifer didn't speak much. They were anxious and focused.

Fifer was a bit perturbed not to be going in the elevator entrance, which, according to what Dev had said, was much closer to where Thisbe's crypt was. But she and Seth had told the others where to look for her. Plus, Talon and Alex needed more help at this entrance, and Fifer was the only other flying option small enough to fit into the cave.

Simber would stay behind in the forest—feeling helpless, Fifer supposed. At least she didn't have to do that. Alex hadn't even suggested leaving her behind. It was a relief to really and truly be doing this without him always telling her no. She finally had a chance to show him what she could do. She hoped she wouldn't mess up.

When Talon and the birds rounded the hill, the quiet crater lake came into view. There was no volcano in sight, not that this team was expecting to see one. They circled above the lake as they waited for sunrise, barely able to see anything but the outline of the shore and a stream that rushed to meet the lake. When the sky began to lighten, they finally spotted the cave-like entrance to the catacombs. They moved toward it, trying to get a look inside at what they faced, while also being careful to stay out of sight of anyone who might be looking out.

"Do you hear that?" asked Crow when they got close to the cliff side. "That river? It's coming from inside the hill."

"That's strange." Fifer strained to listen, and she could hear it faintly. "Maybe it runs through the hill and somehow becomes that stream we saw." When they pulled up alongside Talon, Fifer told him and Alex about it. They waited for the signal to go in, all the while fidgeting and worrying.

Alex looked back at Fifer. "Are you ready?"

Fifer nodded. "Are you?"

Alex gave her a broad smile. "I've never been readier."

Crow nodded at Alex and said with respect, "It's really good to have you here, Alex."

"Thanks," said Alex. "It's good to be back." He hesitated, then added, "Once we have Thisbe, we're going to find Sky. I know everyone thinks she dead, but I don't. If Queen Eagala could survive the plunging volcano, Sky certainly must be able to. I . . . I can feel her still. Somewhere."

His face was filled with such conviction, it made Fifer believe it too.

But Crow smiled sadly. "If you say so, I'll take heart in that. Though I fear I'll never see my sister again."

At last Seth's seek spell came flying toward Fifer. It stopped and exploded into a little dance diagram that Fifer had sketched and given to him.

"Okay," said Fifer, feeling her nervousness ramping up. But she sat up quickly to remind everyone of the plan. "That's it. Let's go in. Talon, you and Alex first. We'll be right behind you. Go as fast as you can so we can get to Thisbe."

"Yes, ma'am," said Talon very seriously, and Alex nodded.

Fifer smiled to see them treating her as a valuable team member, and the nervousness washed out of her. "Let's do it."

Talon, carrying Alex, flew toward the cave opening, hovered for a moment, and disappeared inside. Fifer waited a beat, then directed Shimmer and the other birds. "Forward!" she cried. "Into the cave!"

LISA McMANN

The falcons turned sharply. Crow and Fifer sat up so they could see over the edge of the hammock. Crow held his sling-shot ready, though he hoped he wouldn't have to use it. Fifer fingered the spell components in her vest pockets, knowing by heart where each kind was placed. She was ready to take down anybody in her way.

Back in the city square, Samheed, Lani, Kaylee, Carina, Seth, and Thatcher waited, trying to guess exactly where the elevator would come up based on where Seth's seek spell to Kitten had gone down. It seemed to be taking her some time to figure out how to make the elevator move, and for a little while Seth worried that he'd sent Talon, Alex, Crow, and Fifer into the cave prematurely. Then he worried that something had happened to Kitten, and he began imagining all the disasters that could occur if he and his part of the rescue team couldn't get in.

But his fears were assuaged when the cylinder began to rise. The team ran over to surround the spot, armed with components in case soldiers were coming up with it, but the contraption appeared empty.

"Inside! Quickly!" whispered Lani. They flooded over and squeezed inside.

"Mewmewmew!" came a muffled sound from the top of the lever on the control panel. Kitten jumped up and down on the lever until it switched and the elevator began making a whirring sound.

"Kitten!" Seth cried, reaching out to her. "You did it. Great job! Come here and have a rest."

Kitten climbed into Seth's hand as the elevator began dropping again. "Mewmewmew?"

No one knew what she was asking, and Simber, the only Kitten interpreter, was hiding back at the edge of the forest waiting for a sign from them. Now that they were descending, everyone focused on what they would face at the bottom.

As their eye level dropped below the ground, they were horrified to see dozens of soldiers watching the elevator and waiting for them—no doubt they'd noticed it going up a moment before.

The rescue team was poised to fire spells from their cramped positions through the opening. As soon as they could cast an accurate spell, Samheed and Lani fired clay shackle components at the nearest two soldiers. The elevator stopped, and they shoved the shackled ones out of the way. Then they exited and, while each firing off a round of scatterclips, moved aside so their teammates could get out too. Some of the spells hit just right, sending multiple soldiers stacked and pinned to the wall. The soldiers, unaccustomed to fighting against magic, were so surprised they hardly tried to retaliate at first—they'd never seen nor expected anything like this before.

Behind the soldiers stretched a long hallway with several huge doors, and thanks to Dev, the Artiméans knew that Thisbe resided in one of these crypts. But was she in it now? She could be anywhere in the maze. And, unfortunately, more soldiers were arriving to keep them from finding out.

Kaylee swung out expertly with her sword, driving the soldiers back so her magical friends had room to take proper aim. She winced now and then as a spell whizzed by her ear, but she had faith that they wouldn't accidently hit her after all the training they'd done. Besides, she had other things to worry about. The soldiers had regained their senses and were fighting back hard.

The rescue team pressed forward a few steps, but another rank of soldiers came running from a side passage, pushing the Artiméans back against the elevator again. Despite making no forward progress, the mages leaned in and continued pelting the soldiers, setting off several dizzying backward bobbly heads just in time to stop from being skewered. At the moment, that was what counted the most. If they could stop the army from getting too close and capturing them, they might be able to knock some of them out of commission permanently. And hopefully Talon, Alex, Fifer, and Crow would be coming to help after a while. It was probably a good thing that they'd ended up having a head start.

As the first few soldiers' spells began to wear off and even more soldiers appeared, it became clear that the rescue team was far outnumbered, and their opponents were well trained. Samheed took a sharp hit to the side, knocking him down. Kaylee fought on, but the soldiers' swords connected with her and left her battered and bloodied.

While Seth and Thatcher covered the others, pelting the soldiers with spells, Carina dragged Samheed to safety and

LISA McMANN

called out to Kaylee, who was still struggling to fight. Kaylee gratefully dropped back behind the others and took Carina's medical kit so she could apply Henry's magical ointments to herself and to Samheed's wounds. Carina rejoined the fight.

Kitten was alarmed to see that two strong Artiméans had already fallen. Having overheard that somehow Crow and Fifer had arrived while she'd been gone and were now with Alex and Talon, she slipped out of Seth's pocket unnoticed to find them. She ran along the passageway, sniffing the air wildly in search of Crow, who, other than Fox, was her favorite. She could tell he was down here, but where? She paused at a hallway, noticing the symbols on the wall that she'd been studying all along on her underground journey, and darted down it. She galloped at full Kitten speed, which was quite impressive, determined to find the others and lead them to help as quickly as possible.

Every now and then Kitten slowed and sniffed the air again, then charged up a different hallway, always seeming to follow the same red arrows. But would she find her beloved Crow before he was struck down too? She raced, veering close to the wall when more and more blue-uniformed soldiers ran past her. Sometimes she had to dart between their feet. Magically she avoided being crushed, but how long would that luck last? Despite knowing she had seven lives left, she didn't want to lose even one of them to these smelly keepers of the bones. She had to get to Crow, and fast—or there wouldn't be a rescue team left.

In Pursuit

Fifer and Crow soared into the mouth of the cave, blinking hard as their eyes began adjusting to the firelit passageway. The hammock skimmed the floor and dipped precariously into the rushing river as they crossed it. The birds rose to the ceiling to lift the cargo a little higher as they continued into the catacombs.

"Wooo!" cried Fifer, thrown backward in the hammock as the birds screamed forward. "We are cruising!"

She regained her balance and planted herself on her knees, holding on to the edge of the hammock. Crow did too, and they could finally see where they were going again. Talon and Alex were a short distance in front of them, Talon taking care not to scrape his big bronze wings or body in the narrow passageways. He held Alex around the chest, and the head mage's robe flapped in the breeze. There was no one around.

"This seems too easy," Alex called out warily to Fifer and Crow. "Something feels off. Don't let your guard down."

"Okay, Alex!" said Fifer. She grabbed a handful of scatter-clips in one hand and a clay shackle component in the other. She glanced at Crow, whose jaw was set in a hard line. He held his slingshot and a sharp stone.

They flew through the hallways, Alex and Talon making split-second decisions as they tried to decipher the symbols on the walls, choosing the paths that went downhill. They saw no one for many minutes. And then they came to an intersection.

A group of soldiers heard and saw them coming, and they lined up across the hallway to stop them, swords raised. "Everyone hold on!" shouted Talon. He turned his body to shield Alex, made a fist with his free hand, and put his head down. Without slowing, Talon slammed head- and fist-first into the center of the lineup, sending several soldiers flying and skidding left and right. Alex fired off a series of backward

LISA McMANN

bobbly heads, blinding highlighters, and shackles, which cleared a wide enough path for the birds to advance without being struck down. Fifer cast her components at the remaining soldiers, hitting two and missing one, leaving him to help his fellow soldiers back to their feet.

They kept going. The soldiers charged after them but couldn't keep up.

When Talon and Alex reached another intersection, they did the same as before, and the results were just as predictable. Behind them Fifer nailed all three of her opponents this time. They pressed forward, seeing no one again for a long distance.

"I hope the others are all right," shouted Alex. He was deeply worried about them, imagining that the majority of the soldiers would be stationed near the elevator entrance since that one seemed the most vulnerable of the three.

When they neared a third intersection, spotting more soldiers on the run toward them, they heard a familiar cry. "Mewmewmew!"

"It's Kitten!" cried Fifer, looking around. "Where is she? Does anyone see her?"

Talon reversed his wings and stopped suddenly, forgetting to warn the birds. The falcons screeched and veered around him, trying and failing to stop in time. Some of them hit Alex and others crashed into the wall, causing chaos in the narrow hallway. Crow and Fifer were thrown from the hammock and found themselves rolling and scrambling among the birds to get to their feet.

Alex leaped out of Talon's grasp and ran to help them. But just as Alex, Crow, and Fifer were upright and reaching for their weapons, the soldiers from the intersection reached them and began swinging their swords, knocking them down again. More birds squawked, others lost hold of their ropes, and several scattered to save their own lives. Feathers flew everywhere. From the ground, Alex began pelting spells expertly at the enemy like he was a teenager again. Fifer grabbed a handful of components as she rolled and dodged the swords and cast freeze spells and scatterclips, trying to protect Crow, who was scrambling to get away.

Alex got up, sending a steady stream of spells at the soldiers as Talon plowed into a line of them. Then Talon chased after a few who were trying to make a run for it. With him far down

LISA McMANN

the passageway, one sneaky soldier who'd been faking injury jumped to his feet. He slid behind Alex and grabbed him, holding his arms down and pressing a dagger into his back.

Alex struggled but couldn't free himself from the soldier's grasp. "Fifer!" he yelled, trying again to get loose.

The soldier jabbed the dagger harder into Alex's back, making him yelp.

Fifer turned to see what had happened. Her eyes widened. "Alex!" She took a step toward him, but the soldier jabbed him again.

"Argh!" Alex cried, then tried to wrestle free. "Stay back!"

"Fifer," said Crow urgently. "Here!"

Fifer stopped and turned to Crow.

Crow, who'd been fumbling in his pockets, pulled out the heart attack components that Scarlet had given him. He shoved them at Fifer. "Take these!" he cried. "I don't trust myself to do it right. Just say 'heart attack' when you throw one."

Fifer took them as Alex called out for help again. He had a wild, frightened look on his face that Fifer had never seen before. It scared her. But she didn't dare get closer, worried that the soldier would stab Alex again. She looked at the heart attack components, then up at her brother. The soldier was using him as a shield. Could she risk trying to hit the soldier without hitting Alex by mistake?

Alex had seen the exchange and heard what Crow had said. He stared at what Fifer held in her hand. Then he flinched and cried out in pain again as the soldier brought the dagger to his throat. "If the girl makes a move, you die," snarled the soldier in Alex's ear.

But Alex had been threatened before, many times. And he wasn't about to let this soldier kill any of them. "Fifer!" he yelled. "Do it! Use three!"

Fifer froze. She'd never even used one of these before, much less the lethal dose of three. But the soldier was threatening her brother's life. Cringing, she picked three of the heart attack components and shoved the rest in her pocket. Taking aim and praying to miss her brother, she wound up and, focusing on the soldier, let them fly. "Heart attack!"

The components sailed through the air. Alex closed his eyes and swallowed hard, holding himself deathly still. All three of the little red hearts missed Alex. But they didn't miss the soldier. They struck him right where Fifer had aimed.

LISA McMANN

The soldier's face paled, and an instant later his dagger slipped from his grasp and clattered to the ground. His body dropped next.

Alex blew out a breath and stepped away from the soldier. A moment later Talon came flying back. Fifer ran to her brother.

Shaking, Alex grabbed Fifer and hugged her hard, not letting go. She could feel his heart pounding. "That," Alex said quietly near her ear, "was brilliant work. Brave and precise and true, just as I knew you would do it. Thank you, Fifer. You've saved me."

Fifer's eyes shone. She'd saved Alex's life. And he'd trusted her to do it. He'd instructed her to use a lethal dose of a spell, knowing he was putting his own life in danger but not hesitating, believing in her to get it right. She didn't have any words to say back, but her heart soared. They released their embrace, and smiled, and Fifer nodded. "You're welcome," she managed to whisper. Alex rested his hand on her shoulder and gave it an extra-brotherly squeeze. And then they turned to see some of the other soldiers getting up to fight, and the moment was over. But Fifer knew she would never forget it.

Kitten mewed again, and Talon located her and swept her

out of the fray. Then he plowed into the soldiers who were getting up.

"Let's keep moving!" Alex shouted, running over to Talon.

Fifer signaled to the birds to regroup.

In the larger space of the intersection, Shimmer and the birds flocked together again and straightened out the hammock, then took their ropes in beak and waited. Fifer laid down one last struggling soldier with a backward bobbly head, then grabbed Crow's sleeve, and the two ran and dove into the hammock before the soldiers could revive and come after them again.

Talon swung around with Alex and tossed Kitten to Crow, who caught her and set her on his shoulder. Then Talon and Alex continued forward. The birds took off right behind.

Seeing that the hallway before them was clear, Alex turned his head to look back at Fifer. "Are you okay, Fig? That was a big spell you did."

Fifer smiled. She'd known it was a major one, and she'd thought briefly before about what it would be like to use a lethal spell like that. But in the moment she hadn't really had time to dwell on it. She knew she could do it, and she needed to do it, so she did. But it dawned on her as they traveled through the passageway that over her lifetime, being as powerful as she was, and reading about the adventures in Artimé and knowing the stakes her brother and the others had faced in the past, this hadn't been a difficult decision at all. She hadn't hesitated, and she didn't have any regrets. She would do anything to save and protect her friends and family. And she wouldn't blink before using another lethal spell on the next enemy who threatened her brother. "I'm okay. Are you?"

"I've never felt better in my life," said Alex. "You're an excellent partner, and I'm so glad to be fighting alongside you."

"I think the same about you, Alex," said Fifer, imagining them fighting many battles together and wondering with pride what Lani would write about *her* in future books.

They exchanged a look of mutual respect and admiration. Fifer could tell by the expression on Alex's face that this adventure, plus the near-death experience, had truly made him come alive again in every way. Here was Alex the hero from Lani's books, right in front of her. Fifer's heart soared—seeing him in battle for the first time that she could remember, his spirits so high. She loved every part of this.

And he'd trusted her with his life. She was feeling just as euphoric as he most certainly was.

"Mewmewmew!" cried Kitten from Crow's shoulder, pointing. "Mewmewmew!"

"That way?" guessed Crow. "She's leading us to the others!"

"Mewmewmew!"

"Are we nearly there?" asked Fifer.

Kitten nodded.

"We're nearly there!" Fifer called to Alex. She looked down at Kitten. "Are there any more intersections with soldiers first?"

Kitten nodded wildly. She held up her paw and extended a single tiny claw.

"One more intersection?" Crow asked.

Kitten smiled and nodded again. Then, her duties complete, she yawned and curled up in the folds of Crow's shirt.

"One more intersection, and then we'll be there," Fifer called to Alex and Talon.

Crow set down his slingshot, took Kitten off his shoulder and slid her into his pocket so she could sleep. "Well done, Kitten," he said, and she began to purr.

As they neared the next intersection, they couldn't see any soldiers.

"Perhaps they've gone to the elevator area to fight," Talon said, sounding worried. He went forward into the large space, and suddenly a group of men and women jumped into view. Swords slammed into the bronze man, clanging like a thousand ancient bells, sending him hurtling off course. Startled and spinning, Talon shielded Alex the best he could and tried to take the brunt of the swings.

Behind them the falcons put on their air brakes, but they didn't have enough time. The hammock swung wildly, which messed up Fifer's aim, and she accidentally sent a clay shackles component into Alex. It pinned his arms to Talon so he couldn't throw.

"Whoops, sorry!" said Fifer, starting to panic. "Release!" she called out, freeing him. Then she pelted the soldiers with scatterclips and blinding highlighters. She was starting to run out of components. As she fumbled with the bag to reload her pockets, a sword went flying through the air straight at them, knocking two falcons to the ground and continuing toward the hammock. Crow, who'd turned to fire off his slingshot at a soldier, didn't see it coming. The sword hilt barely missed Fifer and smashed into Crow's head. He slumped against Fifer, unconscious.

Fifer shrieked his name, then kept flinging components until they were out of immediate danger. When she had a moment, she looked at Crow again and gasped. He had a lump on his head the size of a platyprot egg. "Oh no!" She checked him over and was relieved to see he was breathing, just knocked out.

"Let's push through this mess!" Talon called out.

"Right behind you!" Fifer said, signaling to Shimmer. The birds regrouped, leaving their two fallen ones behind, and diligently followed Talon.

When they finally neared the elevator passageway, they were relieved to hear sounds of battle—which meant the Artiméans were still alive and fighting. But then they saw that their team members were either wounded or doggedly fighting the mass of soldiers, looking like they were about to collapse.

Talon landed and set Alex on the ground. Fifer jumped out of the hammock, leaving Crow, still unconscious, for the birds to protect. Talon began punching soldiers left and right, and Alex and Fifer worked as partners, flinging spells at the rest of them, giving the others a chance to recover and take a breath.

They fell into a routine, as if knowing instinctively what the other was about to cast and working to enhance the effects.

With Talon's great help, finally all the soldiers in the elevator area were down and unmoving, and the Artiméans had a chance to fix up their wounds.

Alex and Fifer exchanged a satisfied look. "Good work," Alex said, giving her a quick side hug.

"You too," said Fifer, squeezing him around the waist and peering at the thin cut on his neck where the threatening soldier's dagger had left its mark. The blood had dried by now, and the wound looked like it would heal fine on its own.

"Let's go help the others," said Alex. "And check on Crow. He's going to have quite a headache when he wakes up."

Fifer nodded. The faster the others were back on their feet, the sooner they could start their search for Thisbe. They tracked down Carina's medical bag and helped to administer the healing salves to whoever still needed them.

After a while Crow regained consciousness and left the hammock to help Fifer and Alex. Fifer gave him some medicine for the huge lump on his forehead, and soon everyone had recovered enough to continue with the quest.

"Let's find Thisbe," said Alex. He quickly assigned duties pertaining to the new job of breaking down crypt doors. Talon led the way with Alex and Fifer right behind. Lani and Samheed followed.

"We'll take care of these goons in the hallway so they don't wake up," said Carina. She and Thatcher showed Seth how to do a permanent freeze spell, and the three began to freeze the many soldiers in place.

Talon went to the first crypt and knocked tentatively on the door to see what it was made of. "Clear the area!" he called, in case there was a person behind the door. Then he smashed his shoulder into it, breaking the lock and ripping the door off its hinges. He stumbled inside the crypt. A frightened girl with black eyes screamed and cowered behind some bones, but it wasn't Thisbe.

"Come out, come out," Fifer said, running inside and waving the girl toward the door. "It's okay. Do you know where Thisbe is?"

The girl looked puzzled and shook her head, then said something in another language.

Fifer shrugged helplessly. "Sorry," she said. "I don't

understand. *Thiz-bee*," Fifer repeated, slower this time, in case the girl would at least recognize her sister's name. But the girl shook her head again.

"Let's keep going," said Alex, glancing around uneasily. "I don't want to spend any more time down here than we have to. There may be more soldiers. And I'd like to get out before the Revinir learns we're here."

Talon led them to the next crypt. He smashed in the door like he'd done before, and this time Samheed ushered out a bewildered black-eyed boy. He and the girl they'd freed began talking fearfully together when they saw each other. They pointed to Talon, who was clearly unlike anything they'd ever seen before, and then at the soldiers being frozen on the floor. They started sneaking away.

Lani stopped the black-eyed children and tried to convince them that they were safe as Talon freed another boy and two more girls. But with the frightening happenings and scary bronze-winged man breaking down doors, combined with not being able to speak their language, it was impossible. The five of them pushed past the Artiméans and ran through the catacombs, out of sight. Lani and Samheed gave up trying and let them go.

Talon continued to the last crypt in the hallway.

"This has got to be hers," said Fifer, "unless Dev lied. I wouldn't put it past him." She stood on one side of the door, watching anxiously as Talon stepped back and prepared to break in. From the other side Alex strained to see. With extra exuberance, Talon smashed against the door and pushed it aside, then got out of the way so Alex and Fifer could be the first to enter.

"Thisbe!" Alex called out, going a few steps inside the dark room. "Are you in here?"

Fifer moved in behind him, trying to look around him and over his shoulder. "Thisbe!" she said. There was no reply.

At first Alex didn't see anyone at all—there was only a stub of a lighted candle near the door, its fire being drowned by wax. Imagining how scared Thisbe must be, he called out again. "Thisbe, it's me, Alex. We've come to take you home."

He thought he saw movement off to one side, and he stepped toward it. "Thisbe?" he said softly.

From out of the shadows came a horribly familiar face—it was the face that had plagued his nightmares for a decade. "Thisbe isn't here anymore," said a familiar voice. "But I'm glad we finally meet again."

Alex sucked in a sharp breath. He fumbled for a spell component.

From behind him Fifer had heard the woman's voice, and then, looking around him to see who it was, she witnessed the Revinir's scales beginning to glow. She screamed, "Alex, look out!" and reached for her vest pockets.

But they had no time to react. A long, thin spear of dragon fire shot out of the Revinir's mouth, striking Alex in the center of his chest. It threw him violently backward, limbs flying, knocking Fifer into the hallway. Then he hit the floor with a crack and skidded to the doorway, the lightning-like spear sticking with him. Skewering his chest.

Alex's body came to a stop. The dragon-fire bolt faded, and the Revinir stared as if she couldn't believe what she'd done.

From the hallway Fifer shot off her last two heart attack components into the dark crypt, but forget to yell the verbal component. She couldn't tell if they hit their mark. "Help!" she called out. Blind with fear for her brother, she abandoned further attack and scrambled to her hands and knees over to him.

"Alex!" Fifer shouted as Talon leaped over them, charging

into the crypt. The Revinir slammed a dragon-fire bolt at him, too, sending him back out the doorway and crashing against the wall of the passageway, stunned.

Several of the others had all grabbed spell components by now and took cover, peering into the crypt.

Still stunned by what she'd done, the Revinir's eyes widened to see so many of her former enemies. She took another dragon-fire shot, narrowly missing Lani's forehead.

"Fire!" Lani cried, retaliating with a spell Fifer had never seen before. But Lani's wheels seemed to catch and she lost her balance and missed.

The Revinir ducked and took a few steps back, like she was worried she couldn't take all of them on.

"Heart attack!" cried Carina, and she and several others sent a round of heart attack spells at the woman.

The Revinir turned and tried to dodge the components by scrambling up the bone mountain. But there were too many to avoid. The components slammed into her, and she cringed. But then they bounced off her, causing no harm. They hit the ground and rolled around.

"Carina, help!" Fifer called out. "Alex isn't breathing!"

The Revinir looked surprised to be still standing, and took the distraction as her cue to get away. As the Artiméans let go another round of heart attack spells, the Revinir turned and deftly climbed the pile of bones, again unaffected by the components. She slipped into the tunnel and disappeared.

Lani struggled with her wheeled vehicle to get back up, but it wasn't working right. Carina and the others rushed over to Fifer and the head mage. His face was ashen. His robe had a burned spot the size of a fist on his chest. Carina tried to revive him. Samheed ran for the medical kit and brought it back.

"Alex," Fifer pleaded. "Please wake up."

"Everyone stay back," said Carina, sounding frantic. Finally Lani was able to pull herself upright, and she gently pulled Fifer next to her in the hallway so Carina and Samheed could work. And that's when Lani saw what else was happening. The permanently frozen soldiers who lined the area were beginning to move.

"Oh my," Lani whispered. She quickly looked down at her wheels and noticed her contraption no longer had the magical shine it normally had. "No. This can't be."

"What's happening?" cried Fifer, straining to see Alex's face.

Lani let go of her and pulled a heart attack spell out of her pocket. She aimed it at one of the soldiers and flung it. "Heart attack!" she cried. The component bounced off him, and he kept moving. Lani gasped. "Oh no!" One hand rose to her throat, and the other rested on the belt around her hips. She turned sharply and nearly fell again. "Alex! No!"

The others of the rescue team looked up. Kaylee rushed over when she heard Lani gasp. Talon, who'd regained his senses after being speared with dragon fire, slowly got up.

"What is it?" Samheed asked, eyes wild and fearful.

"My wheels won't move magically anymore." Then Lani pointed at the soldiers. "And look."

"What's happening?" Fifer asked again, her voice breaking. Seth came to stand by her, trying to figure out what was going on too.

"Why didn't the spells work?" demanded Talon.

There was a noise at the crypt door as Carina stopped working on Alex. Her face was drawn.

"There can only be one reason," Lani told them, voice

LISA McMANN

trembling. She started to cry. Seeing Carina's face, she pulled herself over to Fifer and took the girl's hand. "And it's only happened once before."

"No," said Samheed, as the truth came to him. "No! That's not what this is. It can't be."

But Lani continued, trying to steady her voice. "When the head mage of Artimé dies, the magical world disappears. All the magic in it, too."

"What are you saying?" cried Kaylee. "Quick, Carina— give him some more medicine! Why are you stopping?"

"It's too late," said Lani, tears streaming. "It's too late. Don't you see? The soldiers are moving. The heart attack spells don't work. My wheels won't move according to my thoughts anymore. The magic—it's already gone! See?" Blindly she took out an origami dragon. "To the elevator!" she commanded it, and sent it flying. It dropped to the floor.

Carina nodded. "Lani's right. I can't do anything for him. It's too late. He's . . . he's gone."

Thatcher stared. He tried a spell too, which failed.

Fifer was numb. Her head spun as she tried to comprehend

what had happened. All she could do was stand and watch. Lani and Carina were telling the truth. It was too late.

Fifer's brother was gone. Alex Stowe, head mage of Artimé, was dead.

"We have to go immediately," said Carina in a low voice. "Before they realize we're weaponless. Talon? Will you . . . ?" She pointed at Alex's body inside the room, closed her eyes, and lowered her head. She couldn't finish.

"Yes, of course." Talon went in and picked up the mage as gently as he could.

The soldiers soon began to stagger to their feet. Kaylee kept them back with her sword so that they couldn't regroup. The people of Artimé slipped down the passageway, Samheed helping Lani move quickly. The first group of mages got into the elevator and rose out of the catacombs. They spilled into the square, where a few surprised townspeople traveled on foot. There was no market today. In the next elevator ride, Kaylee followed with Talon, who carried Alex's body.

With Fifer too distraught to instruct the birds, Shimmer ordered them to retrace their flight path to the cave exit, carrying the empty hammock. Even with Artimé's magic gone, Fifer's birds seemed to be unaffected.

In the square, Talon ignored the townspeople who gaped at his strange bronze presence and the lifeless body in his arms, and he and Kaylee hurried off after the others to their meeting spot in the forest. There they found Simber's body frozen in place where they'd left him, all the magic gone from him, too. Crow reached into his pocket and pulled Kitten out, placing her on Simber's back. She didn't move either.

"Oh, Simber," said Lani, shaking her head. "How will we ever tell you this dreadful news?" Silently she imagined Artimé in chaos, but they were helpless to do anything without a ride across the gorge.

"Arabis's wings won't work," Samheed said, beginning to calculate all the devastation and complications that Alex's death had brought. "We're stuck here."

"There are other head mage robes," Lani said quietly. "And instructions. Alex made sure of it years ago. Claire Morning has one somewhere."

"And Aaron," said Carina. "Though he might not realize right away what happened."

LISA McMANN

"Oh, dear Aaron," muttered Kaylee, shaking her head. "He'll be devastated. But he'll do anything he can—"

"He'll be stuck on the Island of Shipwrecks," Samheed pointed out grimly. "The tube won't work. So it'll have to be Claire who restores Artimé."

Fifer and Seth stared wide-eyed, trying to follow the strange conversation, unable to understand the depth of what had just happened. All Fifer knew was that her brother Alex, whom she was just coming to understand and really enjoy, was dead. Dead! How could it be? She'd saved his life once that day, but he had died anyway. It felt so wrong. It was completely bewildering. The word "dead" echoed in her mind. She was too stunned to cry, or maybe just too numb to feel the tears.

Crow blew out a breath, recollecting what the world had been like when the last head mage had died. It was just a short time after he and Sky had arrived in Artimé. He exchanged a devastated glance with Carina, who was the only other one of them who'd been present in Artimé when it had happened. "It can't possibly be as bad this time as it was back then," he said, wanting desperately to believe it. "Can it?"

Carina pursed her lips, not knowing the answer.

"How long do you think it'll take to get the magic back?" Seth asked nervously. "Days?"

"Not that long," said Samheed firmly, but his face was troubled. "A few hours, don't you think, Lani?"

"If all goes perfectly," said Lani. "If Claire has the robe."

"And the spell," added Crow.

"Yes. The spell," said Samheed.

"We will make it through this," said Carina firmly. "We always have."

"Let's hope for that," said Kaylee through silent tears. She rested her hand on Simber's frozen neck and stroked it. Then she petted Kitten's cold porcelain back with her fingertip. "Hope is all we have."

After a silent moment, a faint sound of trumpets came from far off.

Talon lay the head mage's body on the forest floor. Crow stood beside him, all of the memories of those early days in Artimé hitting him hard. He looked down at Alex's body and the burn hole in his robe, centered on his chest. In tribute Crow raised his fist to his own chest and tapped it, a symbol of solidarity that Alex had begun using in the darkest days. Then

Crow opened his lips to speak the line that went with it but couldn't get the words out. So he said them in his heart. *I am with you.*

Carina covered Alex's body with a blanket. And they all gathered around to mourn their beloved leader. Their friend and brother.

There was nothing else they could do.

What Hope Sounds Like

When Thisbe woke up to the distant bleat of trumpets, it was dark—she and Rohan had slept the day away. Her body ached, and her stomach twisted in pain. She'd dreamed she was back home eating something delicious that the chefs had prepared. It was such a real dream that she could almost smell the food. She poked Rohan awake.

He groaned and lay there a moment. Then he eased up to sitting. "Everything hurts."

"Yes. But we made it."

Rohan nodded. "We really did." The horns sounded again

from a long way away. His eyes widened, and he sat up. "Do you hear that?"

"Yes. What is it?"

"It's . . . it's the king's call to arms. Or at least that's how I've always imagined it would sound. If it continues all evening, we'll know for sure it is."

Thisbe gave him a solemn look. "What does it mean?"

"It means the king is calling the people of Grimere to join his army and fight for the kingdom. I knew it was inevitable, especially after the Revinir's soldiers killed the princess. She was his only heir, and he's got to be sick over her death. But even sicker worrying about the kingdom falling into the wrong hands once he's gone, now that there's no offspring to take the throne."

"So . . . this is the war?" said Thisbe, alarmed. "It's happening? Like, now?"

"Not yet. He's sounding the trumpets to see how many will come to his side to fight against the Revinir. He'll want to train them and organize first."

"Oh." Thisbe relaxed a little. The thought of being stuck in the middle of a war the day after their escape was not at all appealing. She looked at her fingertips, which were still red and blistered from yesterday's battle. She pointed her forefinger at a dead leaf and let out a spark, setting it on fire. She grimaced in pain. The magic made her finger hurt more. She'd want to wait a few days at least to heal before doing that again. Thisbe put out the tiny fire, then went to get some water from the lake.

Rohan wrapped his arms around his knees and remained in his spot, deep in thought and brooding with the trumpets. Eventually the call to arms ceased, and the silence was overtaken by crickets chirping.

Thisbe returned with a fresh green palm leaf that she'd rolled into a cone and scooped water into. She offered it to Rohan.

"Thanks." He took it gratefully and drank. "What's that smell?" he asked. He sniffed the air.

"Something cooking? I thought I was imagining it. Maybe it's coming from the catacombs." Thisbe pushed the brush aside and peered out. She could see a faint glow of candle-light coming from the circular opening to the catacombs high above them.

"We've never consumed anything in the crypts that smells this delicious," said Rohan. He slapped at a bug, then peered at it curiously, like he might be tempted to eat it. He sniffed again and looked around. "There's smoke over there along the shore. A fire. Someone's camping out."

Normally Thisbe wouldn't consider approaching anyone when trying to hide from everyone. But she was growing delirious with hunger. They had no fishing equipment, and she didn't trust the unfamiliar plants enough to try eating them—the grandfathers had taught her they could be poisonous. "Let's see if we can beg for some food."

Rohan looked skeptical, but he was starving too. "Do you think people are looking for us? What if this master chef vagabond notices our eyes? We're nowhere near safe, you know."

"You're right." Thisbe hadn't really thought much farther than escaping the catacombs and getting to the ground. Now they were faced with a whole new set of problems. "I'll pretend to be a beggar and see if I can get at least a little food until we can figure something out. Give me your shirt—I'll wear it like a scarf and cover my eyes and face a little."

Rohan was hungry enough to agree. He took off his shirt, and Thisbe folded it and wrapped it around her head. "Shall I come with you?" he asked.

"Are you an actor?" asked Thisbe.

"Me? No. Why?"

"I'm an actor," Thisbe said. "I know what I'm doing. I've had a lot of training. I can play the part of a beggar and nobody will ever recognize me again. Plus, in case people were alerted to the two of us having escaped, they won't suspect as much if it's just me."

Rohan thought about it and agreed. "Just hurry before they eat all the food without us." He grinned weakly. "Be careful. Sneak up and make sure it's not a bunch of soldiers first."

"I will." The call to arms sounded again, as Rohan had predicted, and Thisbe and Rohan looked at each other uneasily. Then Thisbe slipped as quietly as possible out of the brush and went toward the smoke and the smell.

She stayed along the lake near the steep rocky hillside, and eventually she saw where the smoke was coming from. There was a fire burning in a small cave. Over the fire was a makeshift spit made from sticks and thin, scorched vines, and on the spit was a big open-mouthed fish speared from throat to tail. Thisbe didn't see anyone there tending it. She crept closer. Maybe she could steal it without having to beg.

Staying in the shadows of the rock wall, Thisbe drew near to the opening, the delicious smell making her mouth water. Slowly she peered inside the cave. No one was there. Crazy with hunger, Thisbe crept forward. She glanced over her shoulder into the dark evening. Seeing no one, she went up to the fire and touch-tested the stick that speared the fish, trying to figure out how to pick it up without burning her already scorched fingers. Remembering Rohan's shirt, she quickly unwrapped it from her head and used it like a hot pad, lifting the stick from one end. It was heavy. She hoisted it up and turned carefully, feeling a huge rush of adrenaline. She had to get out of there.

She heard a crackle of footsteps, and her heart stopped. She moved away from the light, stumbling in her haste. Before she could disappear into the darkness, a woman's angry voice called out. "Stop! You thief! Bring that back here right now!"

Thisbe froze when she heard the footsteps coming swiftly toward her. Weak and carrying a huge fish, there was no way Thisbe could outrun anybody. She turned sharply to see someone coming at her, looking fierce. Thisbe didn't know what to do—if she tried to run, the woman could follow her, and she didn't want that. She and Rohan needed to stay hidden. And she didn't want to drop the precious food. Maybe if she begged, the woman would feel sorry for her.

The woman stopped in the shadows at the edge of the fire. "Come here this instant with my fish!"

Thisbe took a few steps toward her and hung her head to keep her eyes hidden. "I'm sorry," she whispered. "I'm—I'm just very hungry." She held out the stick with the fish and stepped to the fire to put it back in place. "I don't suppose you can spare a few bites for me and my . . . uh . . ." She thought quickly, trying to sound more pitiable. "My sick mother?"

Thisbe could feel the woman's stare nearly boring a hole through her head, but she didn't dare look up and risk capture. Finally the woman took a step closer.

Thisbe took a step backward and contemplated running for it.

"Wait," said the woman, less angry now. "Don't run." For an instant, Thisbe thought the voice sounded familiar. Was it one of the soldiers out of uniform? Someone else from the market or the prison? Or was Thisbe just out of her mind with hunger?

The woman knelt, trying to get a better look at the skinny, ragged thief in front of her, and then she sucked in a breath. "Thisbe?" she whispered. "Can it be?"

Thisbe's heart throttled. Despite her vow to keep her eyes hidden, she looked up. Her lips parted in shock, and her breath caught in her throat. She blinked and looked again, fearing a mistake due to her altered state of mind. But no—her eyes weren't playing tricks on her. A rush of hope surged inside her chest for the first time since her capture, and a gasp escaped. Someone from Artimé had come to rescue her after all.

"Sky," she whispered on a breath. "Oh, Sky. It's really you."

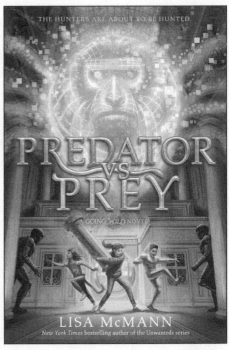